POST - CONTEMPORARY

INTERVENTIONS

Series Editors: Stanley Fish and Fredric Jameson

C L A S S

F I C T I O N S

Shame and Resistance in the British

Working-Class Novel,

1890–1945

P A M E L A   F O X

■

Duke University Press   *Durham & London 1994*

© 1994 Duke University Press All rights reserved
Printed in the United States of America on acid-free paper ∞
Typeset in New Baskerville by Tseng Information Systems.
Library of Congress Cataloging-in-Publication Data
appear on the last printed page of this book.

C O N T E N T S

ACKNOWLEDGMENTS

Like many books that began as dissertations, mine has benefitted from the seemingly inexhaustible generosity, guidance, and vision of graduate school mentors: sincere thanks to Susan Jeffords, Carolyn Allen, and Sydney Kaplan at the University of Washington. I am especially indebted to Evan Watkins, who believed in this project from its murky beginnings and served as an exceptional and compassionate director. I want to acknowledge here his assistance in matters large and small: from incisive analysis to painstaking sentence revision.

Numerous friends, colleagues, and scholars in the field have also made invaluable contributions to the evolution of the manuscript by offering rigorous readings of its chapters, practical advice, and, often, fabulous dinners!: Caren Kaplan, Eric Smoodin, Michael Ragussis, Leona Fisher, Rosemary Graham, Nancy Armstrong, and Cora Kaplan. Thank you, thank you, thank you.

Other friends, family, and students have encouraged my efforts and, best of all, proven to be good company: Norma Tilden, Kim Hall, Leslie Brown, Deb Kasman, Neil Fox, Barbara and Bob Fullone, the Bednar clan, Peggy Shaker, Holmes Brown, Barbara and Sam Dyer, Steve Stein, Kerri Flaherty, Vanessa Landegger, Brenda Carter, and Elizabeth Bleicher. Special thanks to Suzanne Sowinska—our countless conversations about class inform every page of this book.

Institutional support has been equally crucial. The University of Washington provided me with a travel grant in 1989 to conduct research in England. In addition, Georgetown University's Graduate

School has generously funded several summer grants and one junior faculty research fellowship on behalf of this project.

Ken Wissoker, of Duke University Press, has been a tremendously smart, kind, and capable editor. His enthusiasm and plain good sense have made the revision process a pleasure.

And finally, I must thank Mark Popovich for his tireless interest in my writing and teaching, his incomparable chicken curry, and his uncanny ability to make me laugh, day or night. Here's to us.

Portions of this book have appeared elsewhere in slightly different forms. Thanks to the University of North Carolina Press for permission to reprint a segment of chapter 4, which appeared as "Ethel Carnie Holdsworth's 'Revolt of the Gentle': Romance and the Politics of Resistance in Working-Class Women's Writing" in *Rediscovering Forgotten Radicals: British Women Writers, 1889–1939,* edited by Angela Ingram and Daphne Patai, copyright © 1993 by The University of North Carolina Press; to Oxford University Press for permission to reprint a segment of the Introduction in *Cultural Critique;* and to Brown University for permission to reprint a segment of Chapter 4 in *NOVEL: A Forum on Fiction,* vol. 3, no. 3, Spring 1994, copyright © NOVEL Corp.

CLASS FICTIONS

I N T R O D U C T I O N

Recovering the "Narrow Plot of Acquisitiveness
and Desire": A Methodology For Reading
Working-Class Narrative

■

In 1917, the Scoth coal miner-writer James Welsh published a poetry
collection entitled *Songs of A Miner*. Encouraged by George Bernard
Shaw to write his own introduction—"a bit of autobiography" (7)—
Welsh uneasily complied by furnishing the following statement:

> My songs are the expression of the moods I happened to be in
> when I wrote them. I do not ask the world to judge them be-
> cause a miner penned them—there is no credit in that—in fact,
> I rather dislike the fact that there is a tendency already in some
> quarters to dub one a "miner poet." Miner I am, poet I may
> be; but let the world not think there is virtue in the combina-
> tion. 'Ploughmen poets,' 'navvy poets,' 'miner poets,' appeal only
> to the superficialities of life. The poet aims at its elementals.
> These I have tried to touch, and let the world say whether I have
> succeeded or no; I want to 'stand on my own legs.' (12–13)

Though ostensibly concerned with poetics, the passage sets up a central problematic surrounding class and cultural production that I
believe has equal bearing on British working-class narrative of the
same period. Welsh's preoccupation with his own difference as a poet
from the mining class compels him to make two simultaneous claims:
he at once announces and resists membership in his "minor" culture. Much like other writers (past and present) of marginalized
groups, Welsh rebuffs the dominant literary world's categorization of
his work as "miner poetry." He declares the literary to be his rightful
territory, rejects their acknowledgment (and seeming legitimation) of
his outsider status. At the same time, the poems themselves are un-

deniably and often defiantly marked by his particular location within the social order. Inscribed with a range of anxious gestures, they proudly claim, and just as insistently deny, their own class specificity.

In my study I attempt to understand this conflict as a mode of resistance developed within the modern British working-class literary project. I focus on fictional narratives produced during a particularly charged period of working-class culture—1890 to 1945—which constitute a recognized, if long neglected, working-class literary canon. While such a "culture" can never be monolithic, the specific constellation of historical forces and events during this span of time did provide certain situations and mechanisms that fostered the development of an identifiable class outlook: the rise of the Labour party and trade union activism, including the General Strike of 1926; numerous depressions and the implementation of the welfare state; and the flourishing of "Independent Working-Class Education" through the Labour College movement. All of these contributed to a specific class sensibility.[1] And, as I will discuss below, that culture gradually promoted a master narrative of class pride and rebellion in the literary efforts of its largely nonprofessional writers—mill workers, seamstresses, housepainters, miners, and union organizers—whose work has been overshadowed by socialist and protest fiction produced by middle-class authors.[2]

Novels such as Robert Tressell's *The Ragged Trousered Philanthropists* (1914), Ellen Wilkinson's *Clash* (1929), and Walter Greenwood's *Love on the Dole* (1933) have been read as either straightforward political tracts or, more recently, as examples of a marginalized, radical discourse suppressed by dominant culture, but I am interested in making sense of another, equally important, dynamic at work: the encoding of dominant desires and gestures in narratives governed by a restrictive model of class-conscious politics and writing. While often directly challenging dominant ideology through theme (and occasionally through form), the novels contain contradictions that ultimately evoke highly complicated and conflicting forms of protest. Class shame, it seems to me, emerges as a strikingly powerful counterforce in this body of writing as a whole, competing with a more militant discourse to shape the presentation of working-class experience. Shame occasionally becomes an explicit focus of the narrative drama when it is depicted as a barrier to class consciousness, but it frequently remains an undercurrent, eluding safe containment within the surface plot. The following pages will situate my reading of these texts in relation to a particular stance of resistance theory— what I call the *reproduction-resistance circuit*—in order to suggest ways in which shame might function as a resource (as well as more obvious liability) in working-class culture and literary practice.

I. De/Re-fusing the Reproduction-Resistance Circuit: Cultural Studies Scholarship and Beyond

Seeking to understand resistance as a refusal of dominated, along with dominant, culture, I propose that any theorizing about oppositional strategies needs to begin by attending to the variety of ways in which members of marginal or subordinate groups redefine for themselves what is at stake as they mediate cultural and economic forces. Though usually well-intentioned, theories which categorically condemn the reproduction of dominant values and celebrate "counter-hegemonic" acts run the danger of obscuring or devaluing the desires of those who belong to such subcultures.

This danger is perhaps most pronounced in cultural studies work developed during the 1970s and 1980s addressing issues of class formation, hegemony, and opposition. The late capitalist transformation and incorporation of western working-class cultures, long a source of anxiety among Marxist intellectuals, had rendered the very term "working class" a problematic category in critical theory, posing dilemmas not only of definition, but of value. In response to this "crisis," cultural theorists have attempted to challenge the conservative stamp that had until recently stigmatized contemporary working-class culture by demonstrating its diversity and, most importantly, reclaiming its potential for agency. Contesting theories of social and cultural reproduction developed by Louis Althusser, Pierre Bourdieu, Samuel Bowles, and others,[3] this body of work argues for the existence of a dynamic and relatively autonomous working-class culture which always retains the capacity to resist dominant ideologies. It respects the aims of reproduction theory: to understand domination by delineating the exact material and ideological conditions which must be replicated to allow the maintenance and accumulation of capital. But it questions the astonishingly pervasive (and omniscient) power attributed to dominant culture. Charting the ways in which working-class boys "learn to labor," for instance, Paul Willis in his early ethnographic studies certainly recognizes the importance of analyzing forces of reproduction. However, he parts company with a theorist such as Althusser in his efforts to document, through fieldwork, actual instances of resistance which manifest themselves alongside instances of accommodation.[4]

As Willis made clear in his pointedly titled essay "Cultural Production is Different from Cultural Reproduction is Different from Social Reproduction is Different from Reproduction," reproduction theory makes the mistake of denying or simplifying the presence of subordinate cultures in part because it often conflates different arenas of production and reproduction. Whether targeting the education system (Althusser, Bowles and Gintis, Bourdieu) or the family (Bowles, Bourdieu) as ideological "apparatuses" imposing the needs of capitalism, the theory fails to allow for the possibility of momentary awareness and opposition among students, children, and workers. In the process, biological, cultural, and ideological practices become blurred, all endlessly replicating cultural norms. The resultant theory posits a hopelessly abstract, static model of social relations which cannot, in Willis's words, account for specific, lived "struggle and contestation," "the field of a creative collective self-making in the subordinate class" (49). He wryly notes, "Capital cannot really 'know' what are the fundamental social and cultural conditions of its dominance, partly because these are always changing—with the help of categories, meanings, and substances supplied, often through struggle, from below" (50).

The Birmingham-based Centre for Contemporary Cultural Studies (cccs) has been at the forefront of resistance theory. Though hardly a single school of thought, as Stuart Hall has recently reminded us,[5] its members (such as Willis) have accomplished some of the most influential and promising work in the area of subcultural resistance. And since it has more or less determined the future course of studies specifically centered on British working-class culture, I am concerned primarily with the model of opposition which it devised and which we have subsequently inherited. Drawing on the insights of Gramscian social theory and 1950s and 1960s British cultural theory (the work of Richard Hoggart, Raymond Williams, and E. P. Thompson), as well as basic formulations of structuralist Marxisms, the cccs has produced a highly flexible, rich model of class culture(s) which always preserves the efficacy (as well as contradictions and heterogeneity) of material, lived experience. In this model, "culture" broadly encompasses a "system of material practices and interlocking symbolic systems having, according to the region, their own practices and objectives which constitute the ordinary milieu of social life through which, amongst other things, social agents come to a collective, mediated, lived awareness of their condition of existence and relationship to other classes" (Willis, "Cultural Production" 58). This includes "oppositional forms and cultural penetrations at particular concrete sites or regions" (59). Through its combined ethnographic and semiotic approaches, the cccs has produced enormously useful, sensitive readings of "profane" working-class cultural forms and fields, be they studies of industrial shop floor practices, television spectatorship, female students' classroom behavior, or subcultural "style."[6] Its work complements and significantly expands the scope of other studies from the 1970s such as Huw Beynon's *Working For Ford* (1973), which similarly seek to verify vestiges of British class resistance in the public sphere, and has given impetus to a range of investigations into worker education and popular culture.[7]

I want to stress the value of the cccs approach to working-class experience and underscore its centrality to my own thinking about class culture. Though its mission has obviously evolved and expanded, cutting across (sometimes competing) disciplines and methodologies such as media studies, psychoanalysis, ethnography, and "English," it has to my mind been most effective at illustrating the drawbacks, as well as uses, of poststructuralist theory. The cccs recognizes that poststructuralism's politicizing of the cultural terrain at large has opened up the category "resistance" to entirely new possibilities, but it has strenuously argued for the necessity of re-rooting that cultural field in the material without collapsing back into a reductive economic model. As with strict reproduction theory, this approach makes the mistake, cccs members suggest, of assuming an entirely passive discursive positioning of the working-class subject, as well as glossing over essential material influences in its insistence upon perceiving discourse as an entirely autonomous arena.[8] The cccs's intent to preserve the integrity of working-class subjectivity demonstrates the wisdom of refashioning, rather than discarding entirely, the Williams/Thompson legacy. I am particularly indebted to the pioneering work of feminists affiliated with cccs, who have broadened the resistance theory agenda even further by studying the role of gender difference within British working-class culture.[9]

However, in its haste to recognize and value the "creative collective" powers of subaltern groups, resistance theory Birmingham-style often errs too far in the other direction: while it hardly underestimates the seductiveness of dominant ideology, it can underestimate the costs of exclusion from the controlling culture. Specifically, the complexity of the cccs's aims can get lost or stripped down in the process of theorizing/investigating when "reproductive" or "recuperative" tendencies of a particular subculture become somewhat simplistically marked out and separated from "resistance" gestures. Even an astute cultural critic like Willis, who is usually careful to avoid such tendencies, encourages this approach in his theoretical program surrounding working-class cultural production:

> What is specifically missing and should be our positive task is some notion of the 'counter-hegemonic' cultural principle that might link forms of Cultural Production into their own connected ideology against forms of oppression—and so to know more exactly what are, and how to hold and develop, the counter-hegemonic moments and practices which occasionally just flood over and are gone. It is that hegemonic principle, or principles of the articulation of differences of opposition and cultural forms, which is vital to develop if resistance is to be finally more than a formal moment in the dialectical domination of capital and other structures. ("Cultural Production" 65)

And all too often, theoretical texts following the cccs's lead have engaged in a kind of mad scramble to uncover "counter-hegemonic" or "emancipatory" practices which absolutely, categorically contest dominant cultural directives.

Henry Giroux's influential work in radical and "border" peda-gogy, grounded early on in the CCCS framework, affords one concrete example. I single it out here not to challenge its genuine commit-ment to liberatory intellectual praxis but to make that praxis more viable. His model of "dialectical knowledge," for instance, capturing both "ideological and utopian moments" (*Theory* 36), seeks to give the "traditionally voiceless" a way to speak, and hence discover, their difference: "working-class students, women, Blacks, and others need to affirm their own histories through the use of a language, a set of social relations, and body of knowledge that critically reconstructs and dignifies the cultural experiences that make up the tissue, tex-ture, and history of their daily lives" (37). But those experiences are only "dignified," it seems, *through* their reconstruction into a "pro-gressive" tradition. For the argument continues, "[I]t is important that students come to grips with what a society has made of them, how it has incorporated them ideologically and materially into its rules and logic, and *what it is that they need to affirm and reject in their own histories* in order to begin the process of struggling for the conditions that will give them opportunities to lead a self-managed existence" (38; my emphasis).

The basis of their choice—what to affirm and what to reject—ap-pears clear cut. But perhaps only for those not directly immersed in the process. Giroux's scheme appears to allow little legitimate room for survival, getting by—the state in between momentary de-mystification and cataclysmic transformation. Whether determining the criteria of "authentic" working-class student resistance or laying the foundation for a postmodern educational curriculum, he formu-lates what is finally a prescriptive mode of class agency. His most recent work, making much more visible use of feminist theory, places greater emphasis upon the value of "difference" and cites the risks of "reduc[ing] the issues of power, justice, struggle, and inequality to a single script" (*Postmodernism* 49). Still, I remain troubled by the evaluative distinctions of his evolving approach. Who finally decides upon the identities which students are allowed to "reclaim"?[10] As Willis recognized in his 1990 study of working-class youths' "sym-bolic creativity," "the ordinary people of common culture have not been queuing up to join the left intellectuals" because "the critical or counter-hegemonic impulse" can "seem dismissive of those very cultural materials which hold the prospect of advance and [another kind of] emancipation" (*Common Culture* 158–159). He advises those who practice "armchair semiotics" (6) and other modes of postmodernism to legitimate, rather than bemoan, the "contradictory empowerment" (159) of consumerist culture.

If we fail to do so, we endorse, it seems to me, a critical stance with a limited notion of "resistance" as a class tool and survival strategy. *Contestation, disruption, opposition, transgression, subversion—* all have become keywords in our profession for describing practices by which a range of marginalized groups can suggest some sense of both action and refusal. But refusal of what? Despite their attentiveness to (and frequently direct experience with) class-based cultural differences, resistance theorists tend to answer that question by proceeding from what are essentially dominant assumptions and values. Experiencing as well as sacrificing privilege, they can afford to accept the premise that incorporation is equivalent to defeat or regression. The Left stamp of approval thus falls on those behaviors, tendencies, and gestures which not only resist domination, but do so for decidedly progressive aims. The necessity of such a perspective on the one hand seems patently, even absurdly, obvious for all of us working to accomplish social change; yet it also risks misreading or dismissing the needs of those who occupy "minor" cultures. The very notion of a reproduction-resistance "circuit," the two practices logistically linked but conceptually operating in opposition to one another, can fail to accommodate the class culture we are attempting to reveal or represent.[11] They cannot be split so decisively: opposition can be at once the expression of "repressive moments inscribed by the dominant culture" *and* "a message of protest against their existence" (Giroux, *Theory* 103).

II. Toward a New Vision of Resistance:
Rethinking Shame

I take my cue from an alternate current in cultural criticism which insists that working-class culture carries with it a tradition of lack or loss, as well as revolt. Jacques Ranciere's studies of nineteenth-century French workers offer one model. His investigation of a small band of intellectuals who produced the journal *L'Atelier* during the 1830s, for example, deliberately listens to the voices of those who "dream only of fleeing" their existence (xi).[12] But Carolyn Steedman's recent version of working-class autobiography, *Landscape for A Good Woman* (1987), has been my particular inspiration. Her intimate connection to pre- and postwar British working-class life, pointed emphasis on gender, and unusual foregrounding of shame in the imbricated stories of her own and her mother's lives are of special relevance to my study as a whole.

Beginning with the awareness that contemporary studies of culture "cannot deal with everything there is to say about my mother's life" (6), Steedman "subversively" announces that her autobiographical narrative "is a book about *things* (objects, entities, relationships, people). . . . Above all, it is about people wanting those things, and the structures of political thought that have labelled this wanting as wrong" (23). Although her mother was a member of what is now nostalgically deemed "the old working class" (9) of 1920s Lancashire, steeped in "the articulated politics of class-consciousness" (7), she longed for certain material goods and signs of status: "a New Look skirt, a timbered country cottage, to marry a prince" (9). Much of Steedman's project involves documenting, validating, and above all, understanding such desires as they confound both Marxist and feminist accounts of authentic resistance.

As she herself notes, it is enormously revealing that her mother finally embraced Conservative, rather than Labour, politics. Her choice, the daughter claims, "did not express deference, nor traditionalism" (115); it did express "a proper envy of those who possess what once has been denied" (123). In sketching out the implications of this decision, she proceeds to articulate what I would consider another mode of working-class resistance: "[B]y allowing this envy entry into political understanding, the proper struggles of people in a state of dispossession to gain their inheritance might be seen not as sordid and mindless greed for the things of the marketplace, but attempts to alter a world that had produced in them states of unfulfilled desire" (123).

While Steedman finally grounds such struggles in the "legitimate"

mode of formal political activity (late nineteenth-century radicalism), they are, I would stress, inherently political and oppositional
in themselves. Much like the search for "dignity" and the suffering of "hidden injuries" in U.S. working-class culture documented
by Richard Sennett and Jonathan Cobb in the early 1970s,[13] or the
"yearning" among working-class African-Americans more recently
explored by bell hooks,[14] the "unfulfilled desire" that propels the
mother and daughter's lived class experience reflects an attempt to
achieve some measure of control, to perform some kind of operation
on the delimiting borders of their own lives. (Among other recurring
images and concerns, Steedman's intertwined narratives are overrun with allusions to "exclusion" and "exile.") Endeavoring to start
from a position within, rather than outside of, those vexed borders, I
am similarly interested in identifying alternate forms of oppositional
strategies by attending to working-class fiction's other tensions and
silences.

Shame Theory

To accomplish this task, I must reclaim the term "shame" for cultural
studies of class and gender, establishing it as a viable component in
theories of working-class subjectivity. Notoriously out of favor, the
concept of shame has a long and difficult history in the fields of
psychology and anthropology. Pressed to serve suspect (and often
conflicting) agendas, it has offered little to contemporary scholars
searching for nuanced, respectful approaches to class cultural forms.
And in its traditional guises, it has little to offer me here. To define
a particular moment of working-class experience, shame needs to
be dislocated from its exclusively psychoanalytic or anthropological
frames of reference.

Contemporary psychoanalytic theory, though marked by debate
about causes and effects, casts shame as a purely individualistic drama
of the psyche, a confrontation between the "self" and socialization
which remains paradoxically free of historical or material forces.
Associated with feelings of embarrassment, humiliation, or disgrace
—what several psychologists deem a "family of emotions"—shame
is generally perceived as a nearly universal experience involving the
loss of self-esteem (Lewis, *Shame;* Nathanson). To summarize a rather

vast area of study, two schools of thought predominate in the discussion. The first, influenced by Freud's early work on childhood sexuality and narcissism, subscribes to a theory of shame based in exhibitionist and voyeuristic libidinal drives; it thus essentially views shame as an intrapsychic battle between the id, ego, and superego. The second relies upon object-relations psychoanalytic theory to explain shame, accentuating instead interpersonal dynamics between individuals and others. Still, both focus upon a singular and homogenous psyche which appears to be free-floating, enduring occasional collisions with a singular "other" connoting loss of love or attention.[15]

Psychoanalysis can thus only offer limited insights into the workings of shame. Francis Broucek, for instance, insists that we view shame as an experience "about the self and its social context" (21), going so far as to recognize the important role played by objectification. Yet his theory of objective self-awareness, which even begins to acknowledge basic gender concerns, lacks an understanding of such processes as reification which potentially address class dynamics.[16] Similarly, Helen B. Lewis's highly regarded clinical studies have the potential to demonstrate how shame can function specifically "as a protection against the loss of self boundaries" (36) in working-class people's lives, rather than proposing a general theory of affectional bonds; her approach *could* be opened up to accommodate a class-determined subjectivity.[17] However, historical specificity and cultural and material differences typically remain absent even in the most promising recent work.

Anthropology, on the other hand, employs more collective as well as diverse classification schemas. Its explicit studies of shame, however, have failed to progress much beyond the problematic designation of "shame" and "guilt" cultures popularized by Ruth Benedict in the 1940s: "primitive" cultures—Asiatic, Oceanic, African, and Native American—value honor and enforce cultural mores through public exposure of shame, whereas "modern" cultures—American and Western European—are governed by a concern with sin and rely upon an internal sense of "conscience" (Piers and Singer 59–60).[18] (Interestingly, orthodox psychoanalytic theory has tended to affirm this differentiation, identifying shame as a "primitive" or "regressive" emotion.[19]) As Clifford Geertz summarizes, "Shame is the feeling of disgrace and humiliation which follows upon a transgression found out; guilt is the feeling of secret badness attendant upon one not, or not yet, found out" (401).[20]

Helen Merrell Lynd: Shame Theorist and Cultural Studies Pioneer

Although designation of the British working class as a "shame culture" would in some ways turn the above ethnocentric approach on its head, it would also codify notions of the primitive and contribute to the very stereotype of the "lower orders" most feared by the writers I am studying. I therefore want to investigate another method of theorizing about shame, one which utilizes both psychology and anthropology as well as history and sociology: the work of Helen Merrell Lynd. Lynd's 1958 monograph, *On Shame and the Search For Identity*, merits serious reappraisal as a tool for cultural theorists, particularly when read alongside her more explicitly politicized works, the now classic Middletown studies co-authored with her husband, Robert S. Lynd (1929 and 1937), and her own *England in the Eighteen-Eighties: Toward A Social Basis for Freedom* (1945). *On Shame* is recognized by contemporary psychologists as a respected contribution to the field of shame studies, yet its materialist framework and socially progressive subtext tend to be ignored or downplayed.[21] The following capsule discussion of Lynd's work will attempt to recover both, outlining her book's usefulness to the cultural construction of class.

Rejecting a strict division between shame and guilt, Lynd nevertheless delineates characteristics specific to the "shame experience" in various cultures. Her initial linguistic examination of the term itself leads to one of her most crucial suppositions. Noting that its Old English root derivation means "to cover up, to envelop" (23), she argues that shame typically involves some measure of "exposure"— exposure of "peculiarly sensitive, intimate, vulnerable aspects of the self" (27). While such a focus would seem to validate psychology and anthropology's emphasis on the "external sanction" threat of shame cultures—in other words, the fear of one's reputation being publically sullied or defamed—Lynd stresses the significance of "self" exposure, of revelation to "one's own eyes" (28). She explores the wounding that occurs when people come to recognize their own presumed shortcoming or lack, whether or not other spectators share in the recognition. It is most acute, however, when "unexpected": when we "are taken by surprise, caught off guard, or off base, caught unawares. . . . It is as if we were suddenly invaded from the rear where we cannot see, are unprotected, and can be overpowered" (32). Unlike guilt, which is typically experienced in reference to a specific act one has *chosen* to commit, shame involves the surprise revelation of one's very identity, the unprepared-for "astonishment at seeing different parts of ourselves, conscious and unconscious, suddenly coming together, and coming together with aspects of the world we have not recognized" (34).

It is these seemingly foreign material and cultural factors which intrigue me the most in Lynd's thesis. Though she distances herself somewhat from rigid Marxist "laws" of history and social change, she insists upon the importance of historical context and of transcultural analysis within single social formations (particularly Western). Her theory of shame finally hinges upon the clashing of different social or moral "values" in specific locations at specific moments, highlighting the trauma experienced by members of communities marginal to dominant culture: those most likely to feel shame are those made to feel "inappropriate" by dominant cultural norms. Examples are often (though not exclusively) class-based, ranging from table manners (42) to dress (53) to a school child's meager lunch (58).

Acknowledging that these incidents may appear trivial to those who have never felt themselves to be outside the bounds of the culture at large, Lynd seeks to prove that they are in fact profoundly significant, producing far more than a momentary "loss of face" (50). They expose the devaluing of one's very "self," which cannot be righted or expiated simply through admission of guilt. To borrow more contemporary terminology, they expose one's lack of cultural capital.

Lynd's approach to shame represents a radical departure on several counts. More obviously, she is challenging the "timeless objectivity" (112) claimed by her contemporaries working in psychology and the social sciences.[22] All too aware of the potentially catastrophic crises of her own historical moment (the atom bomb is a recurring trope), Lynd defiantly calls for attention to historicity. She does so, however, in order to identify the "concrete realities" which are at stake in shame experiences, from racially segregated communities in both the U.S. South and North, to the internment of Japanese-Americans during World War II, to the disappointment in a child's eyes. (220–223; 60–62). And this is where her commitment to social change is most clearly revealed. For Lynd wants to end oppressive social dynamics like shame, not merely describe them. *On Shame* makes a brief conceptual case for the necessity of understanding the logic of "historical development" (111). Her earlier scholarship more concretely undertakes and illustrates her concern with charting similarities between the past and present, as well as distinguishing unique differences between them.

Both *Middletown* and *England in the Eighteen-Eighties* aim to expose linkages between late nineteenth-century and contemporary cultural practices in order to shed light on current social problems within the United States. *Middletown,* the Lynds' exhaustive field study of Muncie, Indiana, compares the institutions and modes of behavior within a single American community between 1890 and 1925 in order to investigate the potential need for changes in child rearing, work, and educational practices. *England in the Eighteen-Eighties* looks backward to the radicalizing 1880s in Britain to "read the fears and hopes" (5) of America in the 1930s and 1940s. Focusing on the "discrepancy between material abundance and satisfaction of human wants" in both countries during these periods, it hopes to lend "some insight into possible directions of change in this country—their opportunities and hazards" (5). *Middletown* has been deemed a landmark exercise in "the social anthropology of contemporary life"[23]; *England in the Eighteen-Eighties* in effect replicates its methodology, though this time focusing upon a cultural history of the recent past and engaging in a more explicit class analysis. Together, these studies demonstrate a remarkable understanding of the relationship between social formations and structures of feeling. And shame is central to the cultural fabric under investigation.

Of the two, *England in the Eighteen-Eighties* is the more noteworthy precursor to *On Shame* (and obviously of particular relevance to the novels I am studying). Here, Lynd makes her own ideological agenda quite clear: she wants to pinpoint the twin failures of economic liberalism and of labor radicalism in late nineteenth-century

England to make possible a truly liberating society in America. Attempting to lay the philosophical foundations of what she terms "positive freedom," she simultaneously views the 1880s as "the beginning of a strong people's movement which is gradually bringing England nearer to the building of a better world for men" and the "'bourgeoisification' of labor and the abortion of a genuine working-class movement" (412).[24]

For Lynd, the attainment of "positive freedom" is unquestionably linked to the achievement of class consciousness. But how does she define such consciousness, and what role is played by class shame? On the one hand, Lynd points to a decisive break with middle-class allegiances. Working-class people by the 1880s, she argues, were no longer willing to be "impotent applauders" (296) of a political and economic system which ignored or destroyed them. To arrive at this new understanding, however, class shame needed to be acknowledged, analyzed, and overcome. This portion of her study in fact focuses upon dominant culture's transmutation of working-class shame into classless, individual "guilt." In the mid-nineteenth century, she writes, liberal ideology left "the individual's destiny strictly up to himself. . . . Workers accepted the code of 'each tub on its own bottom,' with all the moral guilt entailed by such boundless assumption of individual responsibility in a frustrating industrial world" (242). Working-class feelings of inferiority were thereby assessed to be "real" yet attributed to a lack of initiative rather than a lack of social power.

This crucial insight positions her work squarely in the camp of radical working-class writers like Robert Tressell, who similarly identified shame as one "step" in the process of class consciousness. Yet Lynd rejects what she perceives as a rigid "collectivism" as much as she rejects the isolating, oppressive ethos of individualism. Often a euphemism for socialism, collectivism is cast in this study as a potentially emancipatory philosophy which nevertheless sought to limit, rather than rethink, the notion of power and which promoted "false dichotomies between the individual and society" (429). She alternatively wants to stake out a middle ground between the two which would allow the "mutually enhancing and enriching . . . [of] each other" (*England in the Eighteen-Eighties* 430). The labor movement ultimately failed England's workers, she argues, by foisting upon them its own brand of "negative" freedom and a policy based in fear and avoidance ("freedom *from* want, from poverty, from anxiety, from ignorance" [427]). And significantly, it, too, perpetuated the notion of guilt, merely shifting the blame to "the wicked landlord or to the grasping capitalist" (427). According to Lynd, both dominant and oppositional ideologies in this period "neglected the question of the *kind* of social organization which might further positive individual freedom" (428): the freedom *to* act, *to* desire.

On Shame continues this concern with human agency. Its final chapter in effect seeks a new theory of resistance, envisioning the "kind of individualism that can be realized only through recognition of intermeshing social relationships and an adequate twentieth-century interpretation of Marxian theory" (195). While Lynd leaves this latter interpretive task to future scholars, her notion of oppositional shame begins to lay the groundwork.

How can shame be emancipatory? The dual experiences of exposure and vulnerability, which are part and parcel of the shame dynamic, not only wound; they aid in the production of self-knowledge, community, and social critique. After suffering involuntary exposure, one can *choose* to expose that exposure, as it were, to another: "If . . . one can sufficiently risk uncovering oneself and sufficiently trust another person, to seek means of communicating shame, the risking of exposure can be in itself an experience of release, expansion, self-revelation, a coming forward of belief in oneself" (249). Self-awareness and confidence become possible because in the process of revealing the shame of being shamed, often one is exposing oppressive societal norms and values as well. As Lynd notes, "[W]ays of life that one has accepted without question may appear in this new light to be cruel, hypocritical, destructive" (215). Essentially serving a demystifying role, shame can thus function as a key to, rather than accomplice of, dominant ideology. To quote Lynd once more, "Shame, while touched off by a specific, often outwardly trivial, occurrence initially felt as revealing one's own inadequacies, may also confront one with unrecognized desires of one's own and the inadequacy of society in giving expression to these desires" (231).

My study of working-class texts both confirms and contests this dialectical shame model. Early twentieth-century narratives typically strive to tell an authentic story of class existence, countering popular images and/or explanations of class divisions. Yet the very strategy they rely on—the process of demystification—results in an over-determined act of "exposure" that not only claims to reveal the "truth" about class power but also finally unveils the self-contempt that can underlie working-class subjectivity. The stripping of illusions about the English class system necessitates both a celebration and denial of class-based differences: the texts document their collective, oppositional identity while at the same time establishing their generic humanity ("we're just like you/them"). Despite their determination to "commit the sin of pride" (*On Shame* 250), as Lynd finally urges, these writers find it extraordinarily difficult to free themselves of both dominant and subcultural expectations in order to discover respect for their "own" identity. At times, they desperately want to meet the former and reject the latter in the hope of fashioning a separate "self." I therefore want to propose an alternate, narrative model of class shame which utilizes a number of Lynd's concepts—exposure, desire, resistance to both bourgeois individualism and class collectivism—but which accommodates or allows for "hegemonic" aspirations.

Shame, History, and Narrative

As Carolyn Steedman's autobiographical project attests, and as the impetus behind much cultural studies work suggests, the period between roughly the turn of the century and the end of World War II has traditionally functioned as the emblem of a distinctly modern and militant working class (which has since, so the reasoning goes, been eclipsed) whose texts afford us lasting examples.[25] Yet the period has also increasingly become a *contested* emblem among Left historians and cultural theorists as they continue to uncover the diversity within that culture itself and apply new methodologies. In addition to the claims for working-class agency in the post–World War II era, older, monolithic models of class and of resistance have been set against newer, postmodern models in a distinctly gendered battle over the source of later working-class "embourgeoisement." Conventional masculinist historicism tends to conceive of the prewar working class as a homogenous, public, organized unit of opposition which casts women as the central agent of recuperation, while feminist-directed cultural criticism emphasizes heterogeneity within the culture and focuses on women's distinct forms of class rebellion. Others have argued against *any* claims to militancy in this earlier period.[26] Questions surrounding its radical status thus seem especially pertinent to my concerns, allowing me to investigate a moment in working-class culture when the development of "class consciousness" had exceptional significance.

That consciousness may have found its most urgent expression in the period's fictional texts. Such narratives hardly stand as transparent reflections of the cultures that both generate and permit marginalized cultural production. They are, however, notable, if mediated, representations of the working-class communities which helped to shape their conditions and which struggled so dramatically to gain a voice at this time. Serving various kinds of "propagandistic" functions, literary practice came to join other, more direct forms of working-class political activism. Although the sanctioning of textual intervention developed gradually, scarcely encompassing all the writing produced between the turn of the century and the forties, the narratives do operate with certain shared assumptions, formulas, and aims that originate in a preoccupation with working-class experience and with a desire to portray its "difference" with integrity.[27]

As Peter Hitchcock notes, we must be cautious about constructing a "tradition" for working-class fiction, especially one which claims a simple correlation between working-class history and working-class literature (9, 17). Yet I do intend to chart here certain buried as well as evident connections between texts containing profoundly complicated responses to working-class identity and class struggle. Whether depicting factory lock-outs, days in the lives of pitworkers, or romantic entanglements, all can be read as oppositional texts which contend with the increasing expectations and pressures of their own class culture. Like Steedman's autobiography, these narratives refuse in the end to make clear distinctions between reproduction and resistance, revealing a conflicted investment in the dominant order. They enact what Patrick Joyce has called the "dialectic of poverty," in which "power and powerlessness, hope and fatalism, aspiration and accommodation," emerge as "different sides of the same coin" (228). By examining how the texts themselves construct, embody, and contain various forms of transgression/rebellion/defiance, we can begin to mark out a more expansive conceptualization of class resistance. For in their effort to articulate class consciousness, they inadvertently demonstrate that what we identify as a "conformist" attitude or position may be rooted in another kind of transgressive logic that is equally (if not more) compelling than the need to challenge capitalist or patriarchal ideologies directly. They illustrate, perhaps, another form of (self)-consciousness about working-class subjectivity.

Working-class narratives perform the additional, and equally important, service of nudging us into a new awareness of middle-class subjectivity. As Fredric Jameson has persuasively argued, all textual "objects of study" can be shown to embody and reveal "the essentially antagonistic collective discourses of social classes" (*Political Unconscious* 76). Through what he has variously termed the "logic of content" and the "content of form," he has demonstrated that "the production of aesthetic or narrative form is to be seen as an ideological act in its own right . . . inventing imaginary or formal 'solutions' to unresolvable social contradictions" (*Political Unconscious* 79).[28] Attempting to offer their own master narrative of conflict and resolution, these novels move dialectically between the rejection of and longing for a more conventional narrative of identity and progress. And in doing so, they challenge the presumed clean divide between working-class and bourgeois cultural forms, destabilizing certain traditional and revisionist literary histories.

This means that "we," as readers and scholars of this material, need to rethink our relationship to "them." Their fiction not only exposes those master narratives of the culture to be explicitly battled against, it also reveals to us our own need to create counter-narratives or formulas of working-class life. Whether claiming working-class origins, like myself, or lifetime membership in middle- or upper-class culture, we must guard against transforming "them" into our ideal Other.[29] Jameson himself illustrates this tendency when he articulates his notion of a political hermeneutics: the critic's task is to unveil the text's historical/ideological "subtext," which is seen to give voice to an ever subversive, ever vigilant cry of class warfare. The culture's dominant narratives must be questioned, thwarted, and rewritten, if not erased altogether (*Political Unconscious* 80–81; 84–86). Nothing else will do.

III. Theoretical Readings of Working-Class Fiction: "Deconstructive Guerrilla Warfare"?

Contemporary criticism which specifically addresses British working-class literature at times adopts a similar posture. I have chosen to concentrate on narratives from the earlier part of the century precisely because they have come to take on a particularly symbolic meaning for theorists operating within the cultural studies paradigm. On the one hand, novels from the teens through the thirties continue to be associated with a once cohesive, self-conscious, and radical working-class literary tradition which has only recently been revived through local worker-autobiography projects.[30] Their arguably militant content, however, is nearly cancelled out by their "conservative" realist form. Though realism's subject matter and style was viewed during the inter-war years as a direct affront to the reactionary politics of high modernism, it has been transformed into a problem for contemporary critics who view realism as an inescapably hegemonic form. The novels' reinscription of individualism through a more or less conventional narrative pattern, not to mention their often outdated and masculinist notions of class consciousness, seriously compromise their status as texts of resistance. The need to defend realism as an appropriate mode for oppositional writing has thus loomed large in recent critical discourse, to the point where the poststructuralist renewal of interest in working-class narratives began by assuming that it had to justify the validity of studying these texts at all. The novels have thereby become the most dramatic locus of what will later be explored as an ambitious "rehabilitation project" conducted by theorists and critics, since they function as a convenient site of both the most, and the least, opposition within a particular moment of working-class culture. Poststructuralist readers can identify "reproductive" elements within any given narrative's structure and, at the same time, unravel that structure to demonstrate the narrative's subtextual subversion of capitalist cultural forms.

At its best, this approach has proven invaluable in rethinking the actual construction of meaning in written forms of working-class discourse. At its worst, however, it can become reduced to a slick marketing maneuver, repackaging an old, hopelessly unhip product for enthusiastic reception and consumption. A very smart collection of essays such as *The British Working-Class Novel in the Twentieth Century*, edited by Jeremy Hawthorn, to some degree encompasses both ends of the spectrum. Tony Davies's illuminating essay, "Unfinished Business: Realism and Working-Class Writing," injects a much-needed dose of common sense into the debate over content and form by arguing that realism manifests itself in a number of ways and has many agendas—it "is not really a literary form or genre or movement or tradition at all but a contested space, the scene of an unfinished argument" (135).

Yet other Machereyan and Bakhtinian readings of individual novels relentlessly search out instances of resistance by pointing to the *de*familiarization actually at work in proletarian fiction. "Realist" texts become defiantly "non-real," interrogating the very premise and bounds of bourgeois aesthetics. Graham Holderness's piece on mining novels, for instance, along with Roger Webster's essay on *Love on the Dole,* isolate estrangement devices that disrupt the ostensibly naturalistic narratives of the working-class authors under discussion. Though they arrive at different conclusions, both make claims of a progressive goal achieved through a seemingly conventional genre.[31] Peter Hitchcock similarly works to locate resistance in unorthodox uses of realism, reading Alan Sillitoe's post-war novels through a dialogic lens.[32] In their attention to veiled, encoded oppositional maneuvers, the above critics usefully demonstrate that writing is an overdetermined practice for working- and middle-class novelists alike, unable to function as a singular class emblem, vision, or form. At the same time, in order to be considered a viable means of cultural intervention, working-class fiction with disturbingly conformist dimensions is in fact forced into a highly rigid model of cultural production.

The application of "theory" to working-class writing poses no problem in itself. My point is that this approach encourages a critical scavenging of neglected or marginal texts to promote (or exploit) as the next new example of what one enthusiastic commentator calls "deconstructive guerrilla warfare."[33] The temptation to draft working-class narratives for this purpose is powerful indeed, considering the arsenal it finally provides to Marxist literary critics anxious to prove the existence of working-class agency. (I also succumbed when I began this project.) Yet, as with the most general cultural-studies approach to working-class culture, it is an especially problematic temptation, since it, too, begins by assuming a certain middle-class terrain. Preserving avant-gardism as the privileged term and conceiving of resistance as a primarily discursive activity, poststructuralist theory can misidentify the cultural resources available to working-class writers and misread the very issues in question.

As I will demonstrate, growing encouragement of working-class writing by the 1930s suggests a recognition within the culture itself that language, specifically literary discourse, can function as an alternate class tool. But that recognition never presumes the same respect for the discursive realm—never grants it the same authority—as does this particular critical perspective. I would like to propose that working-class writers have a different relationship to that realm, unable to separate neatly the act of *recording* their experience "truthfully" through language from the act of *contesting* dominant culture through language.[34] A method of reading which privileges anti-individualism, anti-privatism, and dialogism can begin at the wrong place for analysis of this body of texts, since it typically fails to question the wholesale applicability of its values to a class cultural form operating with a different set of resources *and* exclusions. Such criticism may finally be less successful in understanding these texts on their own terms than in rescuing their reputation within a postmodern academy.

And while implicitly expanding the category of resistance to allow recognition of women's narrative strategies and trends, it has thus far shown little commitment to exploring the impact of gender difference within this class cultural context.[35] (Guerilla warfare indeed!) Several feminist literary critics working with tangential material have made more promising inroads in thinking through the connections between classed and gendered forms of opposition. Regenia Gagnier's study of subjectivity and value in nineteenth-century British working-class autobiography, and Donna Landry's overview of eighteenth-century British poetry produced by women of the "laboring class," both devise rich theoretical frameworks for their reading practices which are certainly influenced by poststructuralism but which hesitate to embrace it entirely as an approach. Each is attentive to the complexity of categories, definitions, and practices, especially those concerning working-class women. As Landry writes of her subjects, they call upon "the 'muses of resistance,' but it is never entirely clear where the resistance is coming from" (3). Similarly, Nancy Armstrong's recent "political history of the novel," *Desire and Domestic Fiction* (1987), takes up the Bakhtinian figure of "carnival" as a useful alternate concept of subcultural resistance, yet perceptively notes that "we need to create other ways of talking about resistance . . . for literary criticism too easily translates carnival— and all the material practices of the body that are tolerated within its framework—into the simple absence or inversion of normative structures" (23).

Still, these three exemplary works continue to employ a notion of resistance which assumes, as its foundation, the rejection of mainstream cultural practices. Whether cast in the form of "social participation" versus "antagonism" (Gagnier), or "subjection" versus "social critique" (Landry), their positions do more to endorse than dismantle the "circuit" model of resistance.[36] We need a more flexible set of concepts to address the contradictory pressures of class and gender in working-class literary production.

In this book I strive for such flexibility in both thought and design. Rather than engaging in distinct, expansive readings of individual works, I will employ examples from the same group of texts in different discussions that adopt varying conceptual approaches to the material. All will build, however, toward an examination of its distinctly gendered parameters. Robert Tressell's *The Ragged Trousered Philanthropists* (1914) and Arthur Morrison's *A Child of the Jago* (1896) function as two anchoring texts in the study, the former a definitive model of the "revolutionary" working-class novel, the latter a classic "assimilationist" tale highlighting the degeneracy of the East End slums. In chapters 2 and 3 I will review the status each has attained in the working-class canon and seek to challenge their roles in subsequent versions of literary history. Though seemingly opposed in aim, the two are linked, I shall argue, through their fear of and shame surrounding the exposure of their membership in a culture read as "Other." This fear evolves into another complex of resistance strategies that finally seek to erase the boundaries dividing classes; in their place, *intra*-class divisions are established which seemingly permit self-definition and conceal the stigmatized aspects of a working-class identity. The simultaneous suppression of, and desire for, such intra-class difference binds together protest narratives as diverse as C. Allen Clarke's *Lancashire Lasses and Lads* (1896), Patrick MacGill's *Children of the Dead End* (1914), Ethel Carnie Holdsworth's *Helen of Four Gates* (1917), Ellen Wilkinson's *Clash* (1929), and Walter Brierley's *Means-Test Man* (1935). In chapter 3 I will examine one specific strategy as it manifests itself in a variety of "exposure" scenes—episodes and representations of literal or figurative exposure (often of the body itself) which function as eruptions of anxiety about class location.

In chapter 4 I will examine another mode of opposition: romance. For importantly, class shame finally expresses itself in the desire for a specifically *gender*-marked difference. The "new" selves that are imagined or constructed in the above texts are conspicuously, excessively sexed. As both the third and fourth chapters will detail, conventional markers of femininity and masculinity become particularly coveted, as well as scorned, in this writing in response to the instability of gender codes in working-class culture. Perhaps ironically, in these texts' utopian moments, a fixed working-class identity becomes exchanged for a fixed gender identity, the absence of one making the other possible. The study therefore culminates in an exploration of romance, as both subject and narrative device, since as a genre it emerges as a particularly significant resource that allows the articulation of both (intra-) class and gender differentiation. The romance plot comes into play in these works to convey a longing for relations based in tenderness, rather than exploitation, yet also to represent a utopian private arena in which one is valued for one's gendered "self" alone. And when specifically utilized by working-class women writers, it further allows a strikingly different critique of gender relations. Exposing both the patriarchal and pleasurable dimensions of the private bonds between men and women, romance helps to redefine the scope of politics in working-class culture and of political narrative in working-class writing.

Class Fictions primarily aims to broaden the practices and values of resistance theories associated with working-class culture and literature. Its approach does not so much seek to discover completely new territory for working-class studies as to argue that the old territory— what is often dismissed as the "narrow plot of acquisitiveness and desire"—must be confronted anew and re-envisioned. I borrow that phrase from Virginia Woolf, remarking specifically (and somewhat sardonically) on the pedestrian concerns of working-class women.[37] Her introduction to the Women's Cooperative Guild collection of autobiographical writing, *Life As We Have Known It* (1931), has a certain resonance for contemporary approaches to working-class literature, capturing the tension between praise, fascination, and blame which continues to exist.

Despite her evident sympathy in the piece as a whole, she conveys considerable condescension toward the contributors' efforts to produce "literary" autobiography, convinced that their class position has a certain debilitating effect upon their writing.[38] From the outset, Woolf admits that she is more or less baffled by the "papers" which make up this volume; she laments that they fail to constitute a "book," and is at a loss to arrive at another definition of their status (xv). The women's writing signals "the extraordinary vitality of the human spirit" (xxxiii) yet "lacks detachment and imaginative breadth" (xxxvii). Obsessed with "baths and money" (xxv), she argues, they "never expressed the lighter and more detached emotions that come into play when the mind is perfectly at ease about the present" (xxii).

Sixty odd years later, as we have shifted from a modernist to a postmodern outlook, we are still troubled by that "narrow plot," threatened by its implications. The phrase remains remarkably useful, as a reminder of our own tendency to become "benevolent spectators" (xix) of this culture and as a starting point for our theorizing.

The "desire" which it names enacts a refusal of the boundaries circumscribing working-class existence and cultural production. Posed against more explicitly oppositional narrative formulas, it impels the writing of a secondary plot that tells another, equally pressing, class story.

C H A P T E R   1

Rehabilitating Working-Class Cultural and Literary History: The Critical Agenda

■

We may have serious doubts about the quality of working-class life today, and especially about the speed with which it may seem to deteriorate. But some of the more debilitating invitations have been successful only because they have been able to appeal to established attitudes which were not wholly admirable; and though the contemporary ills which particularly strike an observer from outside certainly exist, their effects are not always as considerable as a diagnosis from outside would suggest, if only because working-class people still possess some older and inner resistances.—Richard Hoggart, The Uses of Literacy *(1957)*

This chapter lays the groundwork for later discussions of individual literary texts by surveying the criteria by which a variety of cultural theorists classify oppositional strategies or activities employed by the British working class during its most striking, if erratic, ascendancy as a labor "movement." As suggested earlier, the CCCS model of resistance has been applied most zealously to *post*–World War II working-class culture in Britain in efforts to address the specter of the "affluent worker" popularized by Goldthorpe, Lockwood, and others in the mid-1960s.[1] Dismay over the perceived breakdown in working-class cultural values caused by changes in the economy, the workplace, and urban planning from the late 1950s onward created the sensationalized portrait of a gutted working class suffering from a "loss of function" and anesthetized by the pleasures of the market-place—a portrait which continued to influence analyses of class politics in the (very different) Thatcher era. But since the theory of a "new," "privatized" working class invokes the myth of an "old" working class, variations on that resistance model also inform the work of both labor historians and literary critics attempting to reconceptualize British working-class culture earlier in the century. They ask: did a single such class exist? How is resistance measured? Can we or should we link earlier political gains/defeats to earlier class cultural forms?[2] The dispute is intriguing in its own right, yet I am finally less interested here in its current outcome than in the terms of analysis used.[3]

The first part of this chapter addresses historical scholarship, which largely studies methods of resistance developed by workers in their daily cultural life. Part 2 addresses literary criticism, which studies methods of resistance manifested in workers' writing. Both segments span decades, combining earlier and more contemporary perspectives. In fact, the discussion of literary history primarily traces the antecedents of current Marxist criticism by detailing the literary standards originally devised for working-class writing through the confluences of working-class and middle-class interests. My intent is to demonstrate the ways in which a thematic of "decline" continues to be preserved within the commentary as a whole, despite some objections to the contrary, and results in the impulse to rehabilitate the status of working-class culture. Whether pinpointing women, music hall entertainment, or literary realism as potentially damning forces of cultural reproduction, these studies assume that susceptibility to dominant ideological norms signals an embarrassing defeat of working-class aims which requires remedying or rewriting.

Historians and contemporary literary critics, however, face different "data" and hence initially arrive at different conclusions: for historians, the years 1890 to 1945 tend to verify a tradition of militancy, tempered by conservative trends; for literary critics, they tend to verify a tradition of conservatism, tempered by a certain kind of militant content. In the end, it is the literary arena which proves the most advantageous to the documentation of working-class revolt. Historians clearly can cite more entrenched, institutional forms of resistance such as the General Strike and the growth of the Labour party (culminating in the 1945 election victory), along with the solidification of working-class culture itself. Yet these are ultimately imperiled examples—they have, according to one line of thinking, failed to create lasting structural change. They proved no match for the post-war transformation in the material conditions of existence which restructured both the public and private spheres of working-class lives. In contrast, novels like *Means-Test Man* and *Love on the Dole*, while seemingly conformist, can be marshalled as evidence of cultural intervention with demonstrable impact. Read against the grain, they can be shown to defy the strictures of the realist novel and can thus serve as examples of a distinct class cultural form. Both the historical and literary arenas, then, finally validate, as well as reject, a past of working-class agency.

I. Historicism

Despite E. P. Thompson's groundbreaking work in the field at large, much historical scholarship examining the first half of the twentieth century tends to separate the study of politics from the study of culture, measuring working-class radicalism by researching either the masses' relation to the array of Marxist and Labour parties—together with their collective forms of direct, public action—or their more localized community networks, activities, and household practices/relations. Since the argument surrounding Britain's "failed" working-class "tradition" typically hinges upon the checkered history of the Labour party, and all that history has come to signify, it is not surprising that such a separation has occurred, nor that historians have until recently accentuated the former. Studies of this bent attempt to determine Labour's ability to represent the working class authentically: Was it led by an elite or fueled by mass participation? And in the end, they aim to evaluate the impact of its reformist agenda: Has it (re)produced a passive, complacent class of workers?[4]

The most recent trend has moved away from such a monolithic approach and has attempted to recognize the variety of protest strategies and vehicles devised by various members of the working class during this period. Often, however, when failing to lead to explicit studies of working-class "culture(s)," the work continues to focus on mass political movements, and hence, mass forms of resistance. Thus, a project such as Stuart MacIntyre's *A Proletarian Science: Marxism in Britain, 1917–1933* (1980), which strives to be sensitive to the "untidiness" and "eclecticism" of working-class culture and ideology

(3), invariably centers on fluctuating membership rolls in Marxist organizations and a decline in working-class intellectual *leadership* in order to mark out his sense of a fledgling, "organic" militant strain within various working-class communities scattered throughout the north, the south, and Wales. MacIntyre's vision of resistance cannot accommodate more individual, momentary interactions with capitalist ideology. I will turn, therefore, to several examples of more culturally-oriented historical approaches which represent a range of contemporary opinion. Some, like Gareth Stedman Jones and James Cronin, operate in official capacity as historians; others, such as Robert Roberts and Richard Hoggart, are male intellectuals who are themselves a product of working-class culture and emphasize personal history in their writing. As "insiders" with varying degrees of historical perspective, they produce their own overdetermined readings of the past. But while they offer conflicting assessments, they share a common concern with working-class embourgeoisement.[5]

Working-Class Conservatism

Gareth Stedman Jones's provocative analysis of late Victorian class politics has established one classic mode of interpretation. In his 1974 essay, "Working-Class Culture and Working-Class Politics in London, 1870–1900: Notes on the Remaking of a Working Class," Jones tries to puzzle out what he perceives as the marked decline of class consciousness among urban working people by the Edwardian era. As his title suggests, he posits and traces the emergence of a working-class culture distinctly different from that laid out in E. P. Thompson's *Making of the English Working Class*. Following Thompson's lead, Jones operates with an assumed correlation between class politics and class culture. He argues, however, that a "new pattern" of working-class culture emerged in the latter part of the nineteenth century which focused on leisure and pleasure rather than radical trade union organization and political discussion. Because it was no longer a "work-centered" culture, he reasons, its revolutionary dimensions and political effectivity all but disappeared. It became "conservative and defensive," rather than "threatening or subversive" (215), overrun by the pub and the racetrack.

Though the essay in its original form did not contribute to the "affluent worker" debate, it does operate with similar assumptions (and as a reprint in his book *Languages of Class,* directly precedes the chapter entitled "Why is the Labour Party in a Mess?"). Jones clearly seeks to complicate the evolving history of the British working class and, in the process, rejects its simplistic symbolic function— what he calls the "social democratic mythology of Labour" in its "golden age" (*Languages of Class* 243; 239). But his analysis of class cultural "decline" validates the same restrictive vision of the political arena found in more orthodox historical accounts and employs a surprisingly familiar, conventional notion of resistance. Drawing upon Charles Booth's *Life and Labour* series of the 1890s, Jones concedes that this evolving class culture to a degree successfully resisted middle-class intervention and guidance. He describes at length the largely failed reform efforts conducted by Christian missionaries, temperance workers, and philanthropic societies to "civilize" and train the heathenish masses, arguing that any transformation in the culture primarily stemmed from "concern to demonstrate self-respect" (199) rather than religious "inspiration." Yet, in the end, these vestiges of revolt are robbed of stature: they illustrate a working class "impervious" to, but not "combative" with, dominant culture (215). It is his causal analysis that most successfully exposes the imposition of his own authentic terms of subversion: Jones first points to the erosion of an earlier artisan culture, which had provided political leadership and control over the work process, as the central problem; he next cites the growing importance of family life, resulting from reduced work hours and suburban migration, as a secondary marker of conservatism. Both are problematic examples. The first overestimates the power of that working-class sector and neglects its elitist relationship to others; the second, while accurately hinting at the fragmentation of social space that began to occur, too easily dismisses the appeal of a privatized existence and ignores the sexual, as well as class, politics pervading that sphere (for women, the home was hardly a "depoliticized haven" 220).

But Jones's greatest shortcoming, it seems to me, is his failure to comprehend the complexity of this new "culture of consolation" which did, unarguably, exist and which manifested itself most dramatically in leisure practices (though he detects its presence in the "new unionism"). Noting that working-class demands had shifted from "power to welfare" (238) in the post-1870 period, he dwells upon the weakness, rather than desperation, responsible for the growing acceptance of capitalism as an economic/social system. His discussion of late '80s/early '90s London music-hall culture encapsulates his overall attitude. Echoing Martha Vicinus's objections in *The Industrial Muse,* Jones asserts that music-hall entertainment was at once escapist and realistic: it often captured the unjustness of the workers' lot but shied away from radical solutions, thereby naturalizing class difference.[6] Music-hall symbolized both "the small pleasures of working-class life—a glass of 'glorious English beer', a hearty meal of 'boiled beef and carrots', a day by the seaside, Derby Day and the excitements and tribulations of betting" (225), and its lasting constrictions. As Jones summarizes one music-hall song, "Class is a life sentence, as final as any caste system" (228). But he simply identifies and critiques, rather than probes, this "fatalistic" view of class divisions, linking it solely with comic put-downs of socialism and a "mood of bombastic jingoism" (229). His reluctance to rethink the multiple motivations and effects of working-class popular culture—particularly its connection to the desire for pleasure—undermines the force of his entire decline thesis.[7]

Robert Roberts's *The Classic Slum: Salford Life in the First Quarter of the Century* (1971), which has itself achieved a quasi-"classic" status among cultural historians, works in tandem with Jones's perspective by offering a "realistic" account of working-class life in one particular community. His study picks up working-class culture where Jones's tapers off, centering on the Edwardian period through World War I. Looking back on his memories of this period, Roberts (like Carolyn Steedman) seeks to counter the faded blissful reminiscences found in autobiographical works spurred by the late 1960s explosion of radical labor history, as well as celebratory accounts of class agency found in historical studies proper, such as Thompson's. Contesting the image of one cohesive working class, he focuses not on its multiple identities and positions but on its inner divisions and own stratification—what he calls the "English proletarian caste system" (1).

Though Roberts touches on a range of issues and characteristics, his anthem is working-class passivity: "Ignorant, unorganized, schooled in humility, they had neither the wit nor the will to re-volt" (148). He gleefully recalls the failure of Marxist and socialist recruiting in his neighborhood which appealed, he surmises, to a nonexistent class "consciousness." According to Roberts, class divi-sion was perceived by his family and neighbors as a "natural law," a struggle against "life" rather than an oppressive employer; "fear," not rebellion, was the "leitmotif of their lives" (66). Excess energy was channeled into exiting, rather than preserving, their class commu-nity, be it through momentary escape at the cinema or an actual move to a different, better neighborhood. *The Classic Slum* especially targets this latter preoccupation, detailing a vast and intricate social "rating" network based almost entirely on appearance: house, clothes, head-ware, shoes, speech, pawn shop items. It returns again and again to the working-class obsession with objects, the drive for acquisition and importance of display. These outer signs reflect the skilled/unskilled labor divide and in turn suggest distinct moral codes which finally instigate what he terms a "chain reaction of shame" (30) running throughout the community.

Roberts largely offers disdain for, rather than analysis of, the social relations he describes. He is more concerned with working class people's comically crude notions of status—and their inability to ever reach a middle-class level—than with the complexity of their desires. And as with subsequent commentators, he identifies the accompany-ing "culture of consumption" specifically with women. While gos-sip and envy ("the besetting sin") mark men and women alike in Roberts's version of this class culture, both are seen as primarily femi-nine attributes. He specifically trivializes the elderly "matriarchs" of the neighborhood: they are "guardians, but not creators, of the group conscience" who form an "ultra conservative bloc," clinging to and upholding rigid material standards of "respectability" (26–27). It is only a transformation in the work sphere itself, he argues—the switch to mass production and increasing "dilution" of labor during World War I—that converts intra-class competition into solidarity, a nascent form of class-based consciousness. In this account, the cul-ture thus remains masculine only in its brutality and rawness; its conformist aspirations are feminized.

The Classic Slum, however, is most interesting when it is at its most sensational. On the one hand, Roberts is simply attempting to make working-class history more authentic by exposing its roots of shame and divisiveness. His unflattering portrait serves as a sobering reminder of the *internal* "drama of class." [8] However, unlike Steedman, a cultural critic with a similar intent, he never considers himself an actual member of the masses he describes. Roberts often reminds the reader that his family owned a small "corner shop" and was in a position to suffer the hostility of others (as well as to exercise its own notions of class superiority). That portrait thus has a different effect. Invested in distancing himself from the rest, his extreme resistance to the notion of working-class rebellion is fraught with tension. Emphasis on the lower strata's vulgarity and complicity with dominant culture provides him primarily with material for *their* critique, rather than for the historians who have "misread" working-class militancy. Roberts' denial of radical class consciousness, like others' denial of working-class passivity, seems suspiciously overzealous. As in the actual fiction produced within this amalgam of class cultures, it functions like an exposed nerve to which we must pay equal, if not more attention.

Working-Class Radicalism

T. A. Jackson's incomplete autobiographical manuscript, *Solo Trumpet: Some Memories of Socialist Agitation and Propaganda* (1953), acts for the most part as a revealing counterpoint to Roberts's reminiscences and establishes another conventional "story" of working-class consciousness. One of the most colorful (and apparently beloved) celebrities of the Labour College movement, Jackson emphasizes his early radicalizing experience as a worker at a print shop. His narrative is a tribute to traditional working-class militancy: first, sabotage, then organized opposition. In his youth, Jackson was "book hungry" and attempted to get through the one hundred "Best Books" recommended by a Working Men's College instructor as a "scholar aiming at all-round culture." In the autobiography, however, he warns against the ideological dangers of such a pursuit, which he believes accomplished assimilation rather than class awareness:

Insensibly, preoccupation with these 'classics' treated as a single category—the Best—caused a student to slip into regarding Culture as a fixed Mind-world in which one either ascended with the geniuses to supreme heights or sank with the dullards and the dunces to the uncultured slime . . . one acquired a complete detachment from—if not a downright contempt for—the 'uncultured' vulgarity and sordidness of everyday life. (21–22)

By contrast, his "true" education began in the work world, where he had looked forward to learning a craft. Devastated by the de-skilling of his trade, Jackson, along with his co-workers, became "mutinous": "We felt we were all the victims of a swindle and revenged ourselves by seizing every chance for a bout of 'devilment' " (27). He speaks of the "outstanding . . . solidarity" this brought to the group, lauding its "revolutionary" potential (31).

Jackson thus recognizes the importance of Culture as a measure of worth in working-class, as well as bourgeois, communities—in fact, puts his finger on one dilemma faced by the novels' worker-intellectual protagonists. But he dismisses the value it holds for those suffering the pain of exclusion from middle-class authority or status. In the same vein, he expresses little patience for those workers who could have hailed from Roberts's neighborhood. He describes his initial euphoria at discovering the "Great Idea" of socialism through Blatchford's *Merrie England,* but lingers over his subsequent disillusionment at converting the masses: "I had still to cope with the active or passive resistance of the dull, the unimaginative, the timorous, the greedy and the Philistine who wanted to know 'how it was going to be done' down to the last detail" (50). The inertia of these real-life "ragged trousered philanthropists" emerges as a less frustrating barrier, however, than the misguided romanticism of his mother, who appears to represent all of working-class womanhood in her conservatism. Jackson writes, "What both amazed and exasperated me was that—though she had a deal of sound common sense—she had contracted an irrational admiration for and belief in 'real gentle folks.' She thought of them as beings of a superior creation, and closed her ears and her brain against every argument to the contrary" (39). Though his father, a senior foreman, equally disapproved of Jackson's Marxist leanings and disruptive antics at work, he is clearly afforded a measure of class consciousness completely lacking in Mrs. Jackson (father teaches Tommy never to be a blackleg). The son manages to elude his mother's damning influence, yet she remains a (familiar) presence throughout the text—an embarrassing emblem of class shame. While Jackson does not operate with a "decline" thematic per se, his "memories" do uphold rigid categories of resistance and in the process relegate women to the most retrograde position of all.

Richard Hoggart's *The Uses of Literacy* (1957), recognized as a seminal (if also sentimental) work in British cultural studies, takes a somewhat middle ground between Roberts and Jackson in its perspective on resistance. He focuses on the exceptional culture of an "unexceptional" strata of the working class in his childhood Leeds and largely measures resistance by the degree to which this " 'older' order"—a "people's" urban culture—has been able to hold its own while being engulfed by a newer "mass" culture. Hoggart consciously avoids working with more explicit, confrontational forms of opposition, concentrating on less quantifiable indices of power that assert class autonomy and project class pride. He identifies an outlook based in the rejection of imposed, alien meanings and values: "living intuitively, habitually, verbally, drawing on myth, aphorism, and ritual" (20).

Hoggart constructs an archetypal "Landscape with Figures" to schematize this stubborn, resistant culture, which is above all rooted in "the personal, the concrete, the local" (20). He recognizes his inclinations to romanticize his past and takes pains to excise the excesses, rejecting a naive, "pastoral" working-class canvas. Yet it remains. Stasis, stability, and contentment form the foundation of Hoggart's memories. While these impose a balance, readjusting Roberts's picture, they also obviously exclude much beyond the frame. At the center of his landscape lies the home, which provides solace, affection, and private ties. The family, together with the neighborhood, creates a culture characterized by a "peculiarly gripping wholeness" (50) through which its members sustain a collective identity ("us" vs. "them"). More specific sub-traits include: "self-respect"; "putting up with things"; "tolerance"; the "intimate" and the "sensory" (or: "their strong traditional urge to make life intensely human"); the "immediate, the present, the cheerful." While at times convulsed by unspeakable poverty and trauma, this culture offers a "full rich life" that has, Hoggart argues, carried into the present. Its persistence demonstrates its value. And interestingly, this time women are its primary caretakers, particularly mothers. Hardly the assimilationist villain, the working-class mother in this scenario assumes heroine status as "Our Mam," sustaining the stronghold of working-class experience. She creates a "good and comely life" that is "elaborate and disorderly and sober"—and distinctly *not* "chintzy or kittenish or whimsical or 'feminised'" (37).

Despite the willful myopia of this portrait (and the nearly cartoonish proportions it has come to attain), Hoggart's perspective does contribute something important to discussions of class cultural forms of opposition often overlooked by even his most astute critics, such as Steedman: his very conception of resistance contains within it a recognition of working-class needs, working-class desires, that are in some senses distinct from any organized political agenda. The seeming passivity of the culture is in fact an active gesture, the exercising of choice: "The working classes have a strong natural ability to survive change by adapting or assimilating what they want in the new and ignoring the rest" (19). He notes their "ability not to permit themselves to be altered, but to take or not to take, as they will and in their own way; their energy in insisting on a place for, and in enjoying, their traditional kinds of amusement and recreation, even when circumstances seem unusually daunting" (114). Hoggart himself resists, however, the possibility of other dimensions to this "energy," longings and desires born of *dis*content and *dis*connection. Fascination with wealth and exoticism, momentarily satisfied by the "picture palace" and popular magazines, or imitations of upper-class finery are "less an expression of desire for a heavily material and possession-laden life than an elementary, allegorical, and brief statement of a better, a fuller life" (119). Preoccupation with self-respect has nothing to do with shame, or "an anxiety to go up," but with pride in one's position, "concern not to drop down" (58). He rarely considers (or admits) that such gestures can entail *both*.

The desire of working-class women becomes an especially anxious concern and example in Hoggart's study, something he cannot ignore but is quick to table. A story about his mother's generosity and self-sacrifice suddenly leads to memory of a "shocking" incident revolving around a "treat" she had reserved for herself, and her rage when asked to share it; when discussing her younger counterparts, single "girls" at work, he notes a certain "giddiness" and similar longing for pleasure. But both examples are finally dismissed as "temporary" lapses. "Most working-class girls do not much pine for their lost freedom," he concludes. Such suggestive evidence of lack threatens the formality and quiescence celebrated in *The Uses of Literacy,* yet is clearly connected to Hoggart's model of working-class resistance.

James Cronin's formal historical scholarship brings this perspective up-to-date, with a sophisticated theoretical twist. Like many others, he takes as his starting point the "decay" or "disintegration" (3) of Britain's contemporary working class, attempting to study its roots from the earlier part of the century in order to fathom "what went wrong."[9] In *Labour and Society in Britain, 1918–1979* (1984), he examines the relationship between the organization of Britain's working-class political structure and the complicated formation of its adjoining culture. But he proposes a different, Foucauldian analytic model based in "confusion and dissonance" rather than "synthesis." This model allows him to identify and underscore the actual *dis*junction between membership in a localized class culture, and endorsement of a national class-based politics, recognizing the semi-autonomous positions of the two. In turn, it also allows him to rehabilitate that culture. For while implicitly accepting Jones's verdict about turn-of-the century conservatism, Cronin rejects its finality. He takes a much richer view of social/familial relations as he works to uncover the brand of radicalism often associated with this earlier generation, arguing that it was the growing entrenchment of working-class culture (due to increasing class segregation of living areas) which was responsible for an intensified *oppositional* class sensibility directly after World War I. He writes, "[I]n becoming more solid and in coping with . . . changed external conditions, . . . [that culture] became far less defensive than it had been. It thus evolved from being a source of sustenance and protection into a basis of strength and, indeed, of actual organizing and resistance" (31).

Cronin's sense of "resistance" appears primarily to involve a transformed understanding of "class"—a developed "consciousness" of solidarity with one group and hostility towards another which replaces feelings of fatalism and powerlessness with "optimism" (22; 30). He makes use of interviews with workers and their families from sources such as Arthur Gleason's *What the Workers Want* (1920) and Whiting Williams's *Full Up and Fed Up: The Worker's Mind in Crowded Britain* (1921), as well as the intensive survey of Sheffield's working class, *The Equipment of the Workers* (1919), to document the existence of "an intense class awareness that encompassed an elementary critique of capitalism as a social system, a sense that reasonable alternatives existed, and a confidence that labour was solid and strong enough to bring about major change" (27). Cronin also devotes considerable attention to the translation of this new "awareness" into the subsequent flurry of trade union activity and other forms of collective opposition that carried into the early 1920s (including organized protests by women against food and hunger shortages).

But he refuses to reproduce, at least entirely, one traditional narrative of malaise and doom found in many historical accounts of the economic depression that followed and continued through the 1930s. In contrast, he suggests that mass unemployment only brought to the foreground and in fact boosted class cultural expression through the development of social networks, which subsequently ingrained a profound sense of pride in a distinct working-class identity. It is significant that working-class people themselves recognized that such an identity was rooted in an entire cultural apparatus rather than in income alone (70–73).[10] Cronin further points to family relations as an additional "source of strength and support" (78) in the midst of hard times, attempting to counter typical depictions of brutal working-class domestic life with images of warmth, love, and fierce loyalty. His conclusions here seem unusually strained, since he relies mostly on declining birth-rate statistics and testimony by working-class women which paints a seeming portrait of contentment and/or willing self-sacrifice. As with the other sources for working-class opinion, these are artfully selected: the Gleason and Williams collections, for instance, are both edited by sympathetic middle-class observers, while the Sheffield survey was sponsored by a local YMCA project with an explicit Christian Socialist program of "Reconstruction."[11] And, as I will suggest in later chapters, the material concerning gender and the family is particularly susceptible to misreading. Yet the spirit of Cronin's analysis is valuable, searching as it does beyond simple mass signs of "opposition" by tapping individual manifestations of class-based antagonism.

It is his ensuing scenario of British working-class recuperation that proves most disturbing. Though Cronin makes notable efforts to avoid falling into the affluent-worker analytic trap, his alternate explanation of contemporary "stagnation" seems closely aligned. He makes explicit what is implicit in Stedman Jones's indictment of the home as a sphere of leisure. From the beginning, he points to working-class women as the force that steered this burgeoning class culture from "the [active] sphere of production to that of [passive] consumption" (69). He minimizes the pejorative connotations of such a charge and attempts to understand why women were in fact much more ambivalent about their class identity, as well as necessarily more preoccupied with actual commodities, due to division of labor both at home and in the workplace. Nevertheless, he regretfully notes their reluctance (or inability) to participate dramatically in unionization drives and later cites Ferdynand Zweig's admittedly "rather superficial study" (153) from the early 1950s, *Women's Life and Labour,* to substantiate his claims without further elaboration or analysis. Cronin centers on a crucial aspect of working-class subjectivity which has been consistently devalued in part *through* its feminization: women, as argued by Zweig, "were less proud of being working class, more aware of its deprivations. The result was a different form of class awareness—less aggressive and self-satisfied, more bitter and, in a sense, more 'pecuniary.'" Cronin sums up, "As Zweig himself concluded, 'It is fair to say that class consciousness, *as we understand the term,* is primarily a masculine conception'" (153; my emphasis). Indeed. He himself fails to develop the alternate definition hinted at in this last passage, issuing in his concluding chapter only a challenge to understand how this "pecuniary" sensibility among the "new" working class has transformed "how class is lived and experienced . . . in contemporary British society" (208). His analysis withholds moralism but does, in fact, chart a fall that originates predictably enough with Woman.

Feminist Re-visions

Even from the distanced vantage point of male commentators, then, working-class women in these communities can be seen to have a distinctive relation to ideological reproduction and resistance. But that relation primarily serves as a convenient symbol—be it of a feminized working-class materialism or more authentic class cultural "tradition"—more than a recognized autonomous component of class experience requiring much further exploration.[12] As can be seen, women's own distinctive practices are at best treated superficially, if sympathetically, and at worst dismissed entirely.

Though much work remains to be done, feminist historians such as Ellen Ross and Elizabeth Roberts have made encouraging progress in revising this perspective through their studies of Cockney and Lancashire working-class women: they not only make patterns of gendered behavior and attitudes the center of their work, but also reconceptualize terms of resistance almost entirely according to women's activities in the "private" sphere (the family and the neighborhood). Much of the cultural studies scholarship focusing on working-class women between the turn of the century and the Second World War is careful to recognize that their multiple restrictions and exclusions produced a different (often ambivalent) view of class struggle.[13] Yet the trend, as in women's studies across the disciplines, has been to offset an emphasis on passivity and dejection with an investigation of oppositional strategies and an accent on active resistance.

Jane Lewis's broad historical survey, *Women in England, 1870–1950: Sexual Divisions and Social Change* (1984), follows this model by acknowledging the ignorance, fear, and caution that pervaded working-class women's lives (from sexual relations to work relations) while simultaneously attempting to understand the ways in which they exerted control, pushing against an oppressive system which they experienced as both capitalist and male. She calls attention to the economic strategies available to them as managers of the household

budget—rent strikes singled out as an "important and relatively neglected form of working-class direct action" (27)—as well as the less
dramatic construction of a neighborhood credit system revolving
around the pawnshop. Lewis also recounts women's activities in the
avowedly "public" arena, acknowledging that women workers organized fewer strikes than men, but nevertheless engaged in more
spontaneous, and equally disruptive, acts of protest (183).

Elizabeth Roberts's "oral history of working-class women" goes
even further to reveal the traditional, often conservative, attitudes
held by her respondents (via memories of the past), but she similarly
attempts to detail distinctive moments of class consciousness. Based
on interviews with elderly women in Lancashire about their experiences between the years 1890 and 1940, the study is divided into
thematic sections which correspond to typical phases of working-class
womanhood: growing up; youth, work, and leisure; marriage; house-
wivery; and families and neighborhoods. In each, emphasis on such
traits as obedience, conformity, and respectability, as well as a professed fondness for bourgeois feminine ideology, is posed against a
recognizably oppositional sensibility: valuing of the familial/commu-
nal over the individual; intrinsic (and long-lasting) sense of class identity linked not only to economic position but to common cultural ties;
mother as dominant family authority who wields "undoubted power"
(117); and finally, a markedly different formulation of "working-class
solidarity." Roberts, quoting historian Standish Meacham, notes that
"in the struggle to counter . . . unsettling conditions of . . . daily
life," they "looked to neighborhoods for stability and connectedness"
(186). In this scheme, working-class women occupy various and overlapping ideological positions, incapable of being pinned down to
either Cronin's or Hoggart's models.

One important form of working-class female resistance that has
yet to be mentioned, however, is direct opposition to working-class
male authority. Ellen Ross's work on cockney culture and gender
subjectivity fills in this gap. To begin, she argues that working-class
culture in London developed its own distinct gender arrangements
and codes during the Victorian and Edwardian periods, shaped by
the particularly precarious economic conditions of the East End.
The instability of male labor not only made it more ideologically ac-

ceptable for wives to work outside the home intermittently, thereby granting them more autonomy and authority; it also gave rise to a largely female neighborhood economy based in "sharing" and exchange ("Fierce" 576; 587). But most important for Ross, the culture was characterized by open "sexual antagonism" (576), so that it was specifically "unchallenged *male* power" (my emphasis) that proved "relatively rare in large parts of working-class London" during this time (576). She suggests that cockney women took control of family finances much like working-class women in other areas and exercised a similar, dominant position within the home, but seemingly more than others, countered their husbands' frequent violent outbursts with violence of their own. Refusing to be "obedient," many—who were typically larger and stronger than their husbands—literally fought for a different sort of power (as well as survival): "Couples did not decorously exchange punches, but wrestled, slapped, kicked, bit, and threw household objects. . . . [M]arriage created no sacred or separate space" ("Fierce" 592–593). Only sexual violence remained passively withstood, and this due to Cockney "silence" (public and private) about sexuality. Ross surmises that such silence prevented women from arriving at communal meanings about their own experiences in that arena and from developing "a collective sense of where their 'rights' lay" ("Fierce" 594).

The gender division of worlds in East End communities, however, spurred another, more cooperative, form of *class* resistance. Ross establishes that women were not only the "transmitters" of working-class culture, as in Hoggart's view, but held a "pivotal place" in the very structuring of that culture, which she broadens to include "a compound of household, marriage, and child-rearing practices; male and female workplace culture; a broader political culture; formal and informal adult male neighbourhood institutions . . . and the neighbourhood and female-centered institutions of domestic sharing" ("Survival" 5–6). Women facilitated "shared working-class values and identities" by "organizing ties between households" and by shaping the social and psychic selves of their children. Specifically through neighborhood "self-help networks," which were more acceptable in combatting poverty than either private philanthropy or the welfare-state apparatus, working-class women cultivated a distinctly anti-bourgeois ideology and a distinctly communal economy of exchange.

Ross's particular focus is pawn shop culture, the crucial link between household and neighborhood economies and an almost exclusively female sphere. But more than pawn tickets were "transferred and traded in complex patterns between groups of women" in the neighborhood. Also exchanged were household items—among them children, usually daughters. As Pam Taylor's work on domestic service in the inter-war years demonstrates, working-class mothers helped reproduce conservative attitudes in their daughters to train them for "exchanges" in other women's households (both working and middle class) and caused them considerable anguish.[14] Ross herself hastens to note that coldblooded "interest," as well as "compassion," incited this female culture of sharing ("Survival" 14). Yet the culture as a whole is presented in the context of more acceptable resistance strategies developed by women, such as "emergency aid" (a protest against demeaning Poor Relief laws and contributions), harrassment of representatives of state power or dominant culture who invaded East London (the police, rent collectors, bailiffs, school authorities, clerics), and finally, establishment of a separate female pub culture. Like Hoggart, Ross's conception of resistance is certainly marked by a recognition of the deprivation and fragmentation experienced by its agents, along with the power and collectivity. Her orientation, however, similarly remains "counter-hegemonic," even if not immediately "subversive," to the extent that *rejection* of dominant cultural values always operates as the baseline measure of worth.[15]

The bulk of Ross's work demonstrates that, despite their enormously useful recentering of the entire cultural "landscape," recent feminist readings of this earlier class formation can take us only so far. In the understandable temptation to challenge charges of working-class women's complacency, they, too, make resistance the focal point of their investigations. But their conclusions often appear forced. Though acknowledged as one facet of women's experience, assimilationist gestures can be converted too quickly into easy-to-read radicalism. Carolyn Steedman and Sally Alexander make much the same point in their examinations of clothing as a means of working-class women's "escape": detailing the sacrifices that were made to obtain a fashionable (or respectable) look, Steedman concludes that such a practice aided in the understanding of class identity, or more simply, in "trying to have a modestly good time," rather than in "subverting patriarchy, or expressing a series of stratagems that had been hidden from history" (89). It could be read that way, of course, but to do so would overlook its complexity. Alexander similarly asks us to interpret young working-class women's longings for finery or silk stockings as the desire to "refuse their mothers' lives" (263) on class, as well as gender, grounds.[16]

Later chapters will explore in greater depth other specific transgressive gestures that I believe are equally susceptible to misinterpretation, such as working-class women's longing for a public/private split (chapter 3), their fascination with romance ideology (chapter 4), and, what seems to be their ultimate goal, possession of femininity itself. The work here still essentially apologizes for women's recuperation. It only targets a different victim of traditional reproduction theory and proceeds to rescue her, rehabilitate her status, rather than recast the foundations of the theory itself. The source of trouble in more traditional conceptualizations of this period in working-class history thus lies not simply with their gendering of modes of resistance, which could then be "corrected" by an exposure of gender stereotypes within Marxist scholarship and alternate emphasis on women's forms of class opposition. It lies in the judgment of working-class desires which cannot be neatly categorized or justified.

II. Literary Criticism

Discussions of working-class literature reproduce (and reconfigure) this schema of resistance through debates over content and form. They perhaps have even more at stake, since working-class writing has been overwhelmingly neglected as an academic field. Until recently, the British working class has been presumed to provide fascinating material exclusively for historians. (Indeed, almost all who have asked me to describe the subject of my study and who understand that it concentrates on literature have still assumed, even insisted, that I must work in the field of history.) This is more than a matter of anachronistic disciplinary divisions. The relatively minute circle of critics associated with "proletarian" literature must contend with all sorts of assumptions from both the Left and Right about the connections between class and (high) "culture." And to a certain extent, they reproduce those assumptions even as they militate against them, sensitive to the "crude," "naive," as well as "reactionary," stamp of much of the material they study. They become caught between championing the challenge to hegemonic ideological values that these texts pose and cringing over their seeming distance from other kinds of counter-hegemonic literary values (namely, avant-gardism). They must equally, of course, contend with each other. Their work bears the strong mark of its own anxiety of influence in response to the crippling legacy of vulgar Marxist criticism, further determining their theories of resistance/assimilation.

Although the basis of a revolutionary working-class literary model is easiest to detect in contemporary critical discussions of these texts, it has its origins in criticism developed on the "inside" of British working-class culture. That earlier history can be pieced together from miscellaneous reviews, short-lived position statements, and writing competition guidelines found in working-class newspapers and journals of the 1920s and 1930s, as well as in literary magazines (such as *Left Review*) dominated by middle-class radicals. As the cccs Thirties study group has shown, working-class literary standards were primarily conceived of and debated in the context of adult education. Much greater initial emphasis was placed on literacy, which was considered a more viable cultural resource, than on literature. But by the early twenties, even a Marxist Left devoted to a strictly economic point of view turned its attention to both the reading and writing of literary texts as a strategic tool in the class war (Batsleer 43–46). Despite clear differences in aim and focus which quickly developed, the various publications from these years stressed the revolutionizing of content: substituting the introspection and elitism of modernist themes, as well as the romanticism of popular fiction, with a gritty realism meant to reflect the inherent radicalism of working-class experience.

Labor Journalism

Widely read newspapers such as the *Weekly Worker* and the *Sunday Worker* (the latter representing the "Left-Wing" of the labor movement) primarily covered trade union politics and world events but also ran sporadic fiction sections, as well as occasional book reviews of novels written by both middle-class socialists and working-class authors. Their literary preferences can be gauged by the satiric attack they launched on dominant culture as a whole: as the papers' fashion sections highlighted the gross extravagance of the middle and upper classes, fiction columns were titled "From Real Life" to point up the "un"-reality of bourgeois and aristocratic lifestyles. (The *Sunday Worker* went so far as to reserve a separate column for the middle- and upper-class arts scene—"The Books They Read," "The Plays They Play," "The Films They Screen"—ridiculing its concerns through wonderfully funny mock plot summaries.) Emphasis was placed primarily on the frivolity and waste of high culture. But writing contests sponsored by these publications in the mid-1920s underscored the value of proletarian realism through their suggested titles for solicited pieces: "A Day in A Miner's Life," "Life in our Village By a Miner's Wife." Realism was considered an oppositional strategy in itself, a deliberate choice of the working-class writer potentially leading to wide-ranging reform if not outright insurrection. Like the Victorian social novelists, they believed that documentation of their own horrendous living conditions would win certain important concessions from liberal quarters. Yet working-class realism was also intended to capture the kind of utopian spirit that the earlier reform writers sought to contain. The labor press relished the divide between "the revolutionary passions (latent or revealed) of the proletariat and the sexual passions of the Fat and Idle" (*Sunday Worker* 22 March 1925: 9). Those proletarian "passions" ensured that any expression of despair would be tempered by an inspired sense of mission that sought dramatic structural change.

But the contrast between working-class vision and middle-class decadence also created problematic categories of resistance and utopianism: sexuality and other forms of pleasure became equated with class betrayal. Turning the tables on popular images of class difference, unproductive excess was *always* associated in these publications with the bourgeoisie. (Wealthy women were a particular target of derision, their massive bodies, cleavage, and voracious appetites lampooned in cartoons and jokes.) Varieties of spectacle and desire became conflated, so that excess of any sort was forbidden. One female columnist for the *Sunday Worker,* Helen Crawfurd, voiced her objection to this condemnation of pleasure by defending workers' attraction to "lurid tabloids." She insists they are nothing more than *"pictures of life"* and concludes that her own paper "must try to provide for these very human needs." Her plea continues:

> Give us pictures of the men, women, and children of the future. Give us pictures of the romance and beauty of life, under the common ownership of the workers. Show the tired women how drudgery *can and will be abolished when sane communal methods of feeding the people are adopted.* . . . Let us talk less of the right to work, and more of the right to live, the right to leisure, the right to beauty, the right to think. Paint for us the picture of that wonder-world which some of us live for, pray and work for, and we will get in behind you a band of women whose righteous wrath will be more terrible than any army of banners; which will sweep out of the way everything which seeks to hinder the realisation of those dreams. (29 March 1925: 7)

Hers is a singular voice that echoes in Ethel Carnie Holdsworth's writing but is more-or-less refashioned in male texts into a masculine mastery of Culture itself.

The two prominent adult education journals of the inter-war period present similar difficulties in their more explicit treatment of literature. The Workers' Educational Association (WEA) publication, the *Highway,* offered a fairly conservative view of culture based in universal values and self-improvement. In retaliation, the *Plebs* magazine, organ of the Plebs League and later the National Council of Labour Colleges (NCLC), promoted an openly Marxist view, seeking to "provide a fighting culture for a fighting class" (14 [Feb. 1922]: 41). Yet both contain enough noteworthy variations and peculiarities to challenge the rhetoric which frequently fuels contemporary discussion of these two perspectives, wherein the WEA is cast as reformist enemy, and the Plebs League as revolutionary vanguard.[17]

The Workers' Educational Association

Founded in 1903 by Albert Mansbridge, the Workers' Educational Association sought to modify the adult education made available to working-class men and women through the late nineteenth-century University Extension Movement (Cambridge and Oxford extension classes, Toynbee Hall, etc.) by increasing the participation of trade unions and cooperative associations. Mansbridge envisioned the enterprise as a joint effort of labor and scholarship—two "streams" which form the "great and powerful river of education" flowing towards the "open sea of a free people" (this metaphor preceded the later "highway").[18] Though highly popular, the WEA came increasingly under attack for its nonconfrontational approach to education and assimiliationist goals. Mansbridge's own history of the organization makes its Arnoldian foundation very clear: he believed that education was linked to "the increasing determination on the part of men and women to realise a larger ideal of citizenship" (v) and claimed that a "conscious or unconscious *pursuit of the best* is the condition of ordinary human nature" (xvi).

But while the WEA indeed consistently argued for "neutral" education in general, and for nonideological literature specifically, this stance more than occasionally broke down in various *Highway* articles and literary pieces written by WEA students themselves. Miss E. Lanigan might celebrate "The Passing of the Propagandist," Mr. I. Drazin might argue that "group [rather than "class"] laws rarely interfere" with "self-expression in speech and writing" (17 [Spring 1925]), and WEA literature classes might have primarily taught the classics of the elite, but an article by Joan Beauchamp, addressing "Twentieth Century Poetry," cheers on the "spirit of revolt" conveyed by the "poets among our navvies, miners, tramps, railways porters and others" who "describe at first hand lives of toil and discomfort" (17:1 [Winter 1924]: 7–8). This WEA literature tutor rejects the notion of "'art for art's sake,'" preferring those poets who "sought to voice the indignation of the oppressed" and "to raise the banners of freedom" (7). Similarly, "The Cultivation of Taste" by A. A. Eaglestone, a pitman, establishes and defends the existence of a working-class readership which can offer a "corrective" to classical interpretation, arguing that its "independent judgment, cutting across even an established literary reputation, is the most important quality that we can preserve" (26 [April 1934]: 5). (One example: working women find *Forsyte Saga*'s Irene "something very different from the objective figure of beauty that Galsworthy sought to establish in their minds.") And most telling of all, the pieces of fiction published by the *Highway* are virtually indistinguishable from other short works by amateur working-class writers found in more radical collections. Sporting titles such as "Just Another Day" and "Northern Day," they combine exhaustive realistic detail with playful parodies of the "conventional society story."

The *Highway* thus arguably brought to the fore the value of working-class experience in its discussions of literature, even as its goal overall was to curb the subversive dimensions of that experience. If, as the *Rewriting English* authors claim, the "major aim of the association was to ensure that working-class women and men *read* literature, not that they should write it" (51), the WEA nevertheless often attempted through its local branches to recognize, rather than erase, the class identity of its students. It also attempted to satisfy their desire for learning. The WEA program attests to the lure of "civilized" status within working-class culture, signifying the tension between resentment of, and longing for, membership in a dominant order. And perhaps to its credit, its own growing anxiety about the association's purpose and audience becomes increasingly visible in the journal, as articles such as "How Do We Stand with the Workers?" (26 [Jan. 1934]: 18–19) and "Can We Sustain Our Non-Political Bias?" (26 [March 1934]: 28–29) debate the value of a nonpoliticized education program.

The Plebs League

The Plebs League mounted a ferocious campaign against the WEA, originating with the now infamous break with Ruskin College at Oxford in 1908. Dissatisfied with the college's traditional curriculum and subordination to the university at large, the League established the rival Central Labour College (first at Oxford, then in London) in an effort to promote "Independent Working-Class Education" (IWCE). A 1909 editorial in the *'Plebs' Magazine* describes its position on Oxbridge Culture this way: "So long as the uncultured lift up their eyes to it, admiringly, or shut their eyes to it, indifferently, all is for the best. . . . But it is different if . . . a considerable number outside the cultured zone open their eyes to the fact that this culture is the hall-mark of a system of caste inherited from the past" (I:2 [March 1909]: 21). The IWCE Movement declared that education could not help but be "propaganda." "The important question . . . for Labour to decide is: What sort of propaganda? Propaganda definitely designed to assist it in its ultimate aim, the abolition of slavery; or propaganda which at best is useless for . . . that aim?" [19]

With its motto "I can promise to be candid but not impartial," the *Plebs* undercut WEA aims by privileging tendentious literature: demanding not only barebones realism but radical writing that empowered and mobilized. Its book reviews tended to honor socialist writers who depicted militant "solutions" to working-class problems and dismissed those who painted a negative picture of working-class life (Batsleer 56). (The 1933 review of Walter Greenwood's *Love on the Dole* proves to be one major exception, lauding the novel largely for its authenticity and ignoring its despair: "It is a perfect . . . picture, as detailed as a Dutch painting, of life as it is lived by millions in the industrial North to-day," with characters "as real as life itself" [25 (Oct. 1933): 221–222].) Several philosophical pieces attempting to sound out the relationship between Marxism and literature promote the same message of radical intent. "The Workers' Culture," for instance, argues for the subordination of the arts and literature ("elegant" pursuits) to such "rudimentary" fields as economics and history, yet finally sees the importance of replacing the "individualist" strain in the bourgeois literary tradition with a "new creative cultural effort on collectivist lines" (*Plebs* [Feb. 1922]: 39–40). Another article, which outlines a model literature course syllabus for the Central Labour College, proposes that literature be used to illustrate "the principles of Historical Materialism" (*Plebs* [June 1922]: 169). Its author laments the absence of a definitive "*proletarian* standpoint" in contemporary literature, but recommends those works which are "decidedly anti-bourgeois" (Ibsen, Wells, Shaw).[20] Finally, a hand-ful of articles branch out to call for the development of indigenous working-class art forms in the cinema and the theatre. These are seen as "rendering an incalculable service to the cause of Labour": the worker's "dramatic potentialities, his experiences in the factory, field and mine, and his intense struggle for existence, have made him a fully trained actor requiring only a stage to put forth his point of view in his own language, the language of action, with which the machine, the sports ground and the gymnasium have made him familiar" (22 [Sept. 1930]: 207).

Such self-righteousness was, and is, appealing. But the strictures of the *Plebs* position left little room for the "fullness" of existence that the *Highway* acknowledged. Its formula for Marxist aesthetics, inspired by the newly developing Soviet *proletcult,* produced a highly rigid master narrative. W. H. Marwick's lengthy letter to the editor ("A W.E.A.er's Case Against the Labour Colleges") is not completely in error when it charges that "[t]he supermen of the Plebs League, modestly claiming to be the 'intelligent minority,' prescribe to the mere workers what they 'ought' to think, and the type of conscious-ness they 'ought' to have"; or when it suggests that "the ordinary man is sufficiently intelligent and fair-minded not to be 'confused' (as is sometimes suggested) by the impartial presentation of divergent opinions, but rather to be enabled to form his own judgment upon them" (June 1922: 175). As even one dissenting *Plebs* contributor complained, literature in the Labour Colleges had to be "disguised as supplementary social history, or as propaganda for beginners" to gain legitimacy (Oct. 1922: 367). A *Sunday Worker* reader who called himself the "Clydebank Riveter" expressed similar frustration in his letter to the editor:

> Every week there's a chunk in this page about Workers' Theatres, written by nice people, who deplore the fact that the ordinary Worker at any rate prefers to see Celtic and Rangers and Elky Clark to prancing across some imaginary stage yodelling Bread, Bread, BREAD, etc., etc., ad lib. Does anybody in the *Sunday Worker* imagine that this dope is taken seriously by anybody ex-

cept a few cranks who are endeavoring to act their way into Socialism. It gives me a pain to read it. (26 Sept. 1926: 6)

He concludes by asking for reviews of "good detective yarns." The *Plebs* and other radical journals thus risked alienating a fair portion of their audience as they worked to cultivate a working-class readership of class-conscious writing.

Left Review

Left Review demonstrated by far the greatest enthusiasm for "Left" literature written by working-class people and devoted the most care to carving out a manifesto for proletarian writing. Run by England's 1930s intelligentsia who were primarily members of the newly-founded Writers' International, *Left Review* often engaged in a transparent form of slumming, announcing an all-too-earnest wish to "proletarianize" themselves and the world. The journal played an important role, however, not only in its willingness to encourage and give exposure to working-class writers, but specifically in its desire (and ability) to mold the direction of such writing.

Like the earlier publications, *Left Review* concentrated on transforming literary content yet also attempted to mediate the type of realism adopted by untrained writers. It boasted a propagandistic purpose but disdained propagandistic form and jargon. The third issue, appearing in December 1934, includes a partial reprint of the "statement of aim" adopted by the British section of the organization, which at first glance seems to champion realism of the most jarring sort. The statement calls for working-class writers who "desire to express in their work, more effectively than in the past, the struggle of their class" to join with their middle-class allies in an "association of revolutionary writers." The Writers' International deplores "the decadence" of the modernist literary movement in Britain, seen to be "developing in technique while narrowing in content." It demands a rejection of the "present triviality" in order to engage with "the events and issues that matter: the death of an old world and the birth of a new" (1:3 [Dec. 1934]: 75). Other published responses to the statement concur: "[A]ll our writing has one end in view, the revolutionary end of establishing a socialist republic" (Alec Brown); "I believe that a writer should use his pen in support of the great struggle to emancipate the workers of the world from economic slavery" (Rev. T. E. Nicholas); Simon Blumenfield added that the proletarian writer "is the voice of the inarticulate. . . . He expresses in words the struggling, dark consciousness of the broad masses, the revolutionary thrust immanent in the daily struggle for bread" (76; 79–80).

However, *Left Review*'s book reviews and writing competition instructions/commentaries help to clarify the organization's position. Jack Conroy's American novel *The Disinherited*, for example, was praised for including "authentic" dialogue and sensory description of factory life while also moving beyond "local colour" to depict "that supreme and saving quality of the proletariat: the potentiality and the capacity for struggle, and for eventual victory" (1:3 [Dec. 1934]: 94–95). At the same time, the reviewer critiqued the novel's "didactic" section, accusing Conroy of performing "the propagandist['s] job," substituting "speech-making" for "the natural play of conversation." The competition criteria, used to judge submissions entitled "A Street Scene," "Shift at Work," "An Encounter," and "School Days," reinforced such standards by valuing—indeed, insisting upon—"concrete" writing which shows rather than tells. ("Every job has *smells, sounds* and sensations of *touch* besides heat and cold that will help to make it real to the reader. Remember that is the heart of this whole business to make the reader feel as if he or she were actually there." (1:3 [Dec. 1934]: 74). Sentimentality, cliches, and slogans were frowned upon, "pictorial effects" encouraged.

The discourse surrounding the writing competitions is in fact particularly revealing, since it directly targets workers' writing and exposes a set of literary standards clearly at odds with the solicited material. The competitions sought to foster and discover literary talent in the "silent" masses, rewarding winning entries with publication and small prizes (usually books). But they primarily provided the *Left Review* editors with a forum for cultivating working-class "taste," encouraging their readers and writers to pay equal attention to content and form. Alternately praising and berating the amateur writers in post-competition reports, they established nearly impossible criteria which demanded that entrants both follow and ignore directions: submissions were critiqued for either imitating the sample too closely or failing to imitate it enough; for being too wordy or too laconic.[21] The writers were anxious to please, as concerned as the judges about working-class cultural competence. One reprinted letter of praise from an early contributor succinctly captures the *Left Review* approach: it argues that the competition judge's advice "should go a long way to assist us to evolve a literature which, though revolutionary in content, does not make too big a break with the bourgeois forms of expression which, in this country, are the only standards" (71). The letter hints at the continued preoccupation with respectability that lies beneath this new emphasis on polish and sophistication, revealing *Left Review*'s tie to an ostensibly antithetical journal like the *Highway*.

Ralph Fox: *The Novel and the People*

Though the various forums of discussion inevitably took up the issue of literary form through their attempt to radicalize content, the latter tended to be highlighted. These journals fought not only for more prevalent represensions of the working class, but for more inspiring, empowering representations. As seen, they do debate amongst themselves the limits of "revolutionary" realism, but they do not quite yet address the lasting political implications of literary form. Ralph Fox's overriding concern in the late 1930s with the middle-class origins and tradition of the novel began to set Marxist criticism on a different path. A political as well as literary theorist, writer, and Communist Party activist, Fox was greatly admired by intellectuals such as John Lehmann for his "wide" knowledge of the British novel and his accompanying intolerance for vulgar Marxist criticism/literature. His work galvanized the attacks on modernist experimentation that served as a symbolic point of reference for the others, but also sought to resolve much more forcefully the bourgeois conventions governing realism itself.

In *The Novel and the People* (1937), he popularized what was essentially a Lukacsian position on realism. His study called for a "humanist" Marxism which gave allegiance to the "whole man" (with both a "personal" and "social" history) and attempted to reclaim the novel form specifically for the forthcoming socialist culture. Adopting the Trotskyist line that radicals must reclaim the cultural past, he argued that the novel is "the great folk art of our civilization, the successor to the epic" (7); though it had deteriorated into the degenerate epic of capitalist culture, it could be transformed through a "revolutionary" perspective (46) to offer a "steady vision of the whole" (25). Recentering proletarian literature around his version of the individual epic hero, Fox finally worked toward a combination of the "old naturalistic realism" and the new "novel of endless analysis and intuition" (106), balancing representation of the exterior and interior life, of external and internal contradictions. He critiqued modernism's infatuation with individualism, marginalization, and decenteredness (particularly its focus on the "mad" and the "sick") but not its potential for depicting the "fullness" of human experience. *The Novel and the People* thus equally opposed the strain of naturalism popular in proletarian literature, proposing a new realism based in imagination, rather than observation (132–133).

Literary Revolt: Masculine Scripts

Despite its challenge to *Plebs*-style tendentious writing, Fox's blueprint for Marxist fiction shares one critical common element with other "manifestos" produced through the twenties and thirties: assumption of distinct gender requirements for the revolutionary novelist. In some ways, it appears the most enlightened—Fox was at least aware that gender issues could be distinguishable from, as well as part of, class issues and recognized that "sex bias and sex antagonism" were specific "fetters" on the "growth of world literature" (45). But he proceeded to make statements which confidently proclaimed, "[T]he author must know his people, be as familiar with them as though the men were his constant tavern companions, the women his loving doxies and the children his own brats. . . . The author who cannot . . . is condemned from the start to impotence" (145). He seemingly speaks for all of the above editors, critics, and journalists, especially when he satirizes women readers' concerns in his discussion of model socialist drama: "The drama is too harsh, too masculine, objects the tender-hearted reader. Perhaps you want love?" (129)

Given the fact that "resistance" emerges in these texts as a visible, preferably collective, assault on a capitalist class and its portrayal of reality, it largely remains a male province. "Revolutionary" writing thus typically results in male-centered narratives. Recall the most frequently invoked symbols of proletarian writing: factory, field, mine; machine, sportsground, gymnasium. As Rebecca O'Rourke asks in her brief reflection on this genre, "[W]ere there no women?"[22] The very act of confrontation involved in being a working-class writer seemingly guarantees its masculinity. (That may also explain in part the much larger population of women students in the WEA, rather than National Council of Labour Colleges (NCLC) classes, despite the Plebs League's public support of feminist concerns: they perhaps felt less dramatically excluded by its "apolitical" curriculum.[23]) Even *Left Review*'s relatively open policy of publishing working-class women writers, made much of by the CCCS *Rewriting English* volume, does little to change the gendering of the model. Maintaining a prescriptive goal and realist form, as well as establishing the very occasion for writing (be it a strike, work, school, or "encounter" narrative), it limits women's options and tends to give preference to those pieces which simply transfer the same message of class outrage to domestic or "feminine" scenarios: at home with the children ("Day in the Life of a Working-Class Mother"), with other women factory workers, and so on. The working-class literary formula that evolves and stabilizes into a recognizable genre by the inter-war period thus places all writers, but especially women, in a compromised position. It allows a much-needed forum for working-class voices, yet restricts the range of their expression.

Post-War Criticism and Beyond

Contemporary criticism has picked up these various strands of argument surrounding working-class writing but has attempted to complicate the discussion in a number of ways by shifting the focus much more directly to form. While undergoing some significant convolutions as the field of (and politics surrounding) literary criticism has changed, the preoccupation with the ideological dimensions of narrative, typified by Fox, has persisted. As the introductory chapter's overview of current theoretical scholarship demonstrated, working-class writing continues to be considered one viable form of intervention into dominant culture, involving an active reworking of its most popular and accessible literary genre, yet the critical agenda has moved from an embracing of the "humanist" and the "real" to the anti-humanist and decidedly non-real. In this chapter's closing pages, I want to fill the remaining gaps in this brief review of working-class literary history by discussing criticism produced during the 1960s and 1970s.

Jack Mitchell's work serves as the most vivid example of a certain tendency in post-war criticism against which younger generations have defined themselves. His theory of the modern "proletarian-revolutionary novel," a la Fox, assumes a purely economist understanding of cultural production (superstructure reflects base). Using this model to dismiss earlier Chartist examples of working-class literature, he traces the origins of the authentic proletarian novel to the early twentieth century, a time which he believes first produced and witnessed "the general maturing of the international revolutionary proletariat in the age of imperialism" ("Aesthetic Problems" 250). Mitchell argues that this new class fostered a "proletarian humanism" that could grasp the permanence of the working class and its culture and most importantly, could portray the working-class person as a subject, as well as object. My discussion in chapter 2 of *The Ragged Trousered Philanthropists* will explore Mitchell's perspective in much more detail by focusing on Robert Tressell's feature role in his theory of the novel. It is sufficient to note here his assertion that self-recognition and confidence among workers gave rise to a new "aesthetic" that developed "artists" rather than "pamphleteers" who envisioned "the common people . . . as, even in their existing form, in the midst of their misery and degradation, humanly valid, in the last resort containing within themselves the only ultimate yardsticks of human value" ("Aesthetic Problems" 249).

This human "validity," however, is founded upon a curiously narrow version of class "struggle": the "total objective politico-cultural activity" with which it is equated consists of trade unions, political parties, campaigns and strikes, and international worker solidarity ("Early Harvest" 68). And at the same time, it is equally critical for Mitchell (as for Fox and the *Left Review* crowd) that the new proletarian writing achieve literary status, that it be able to compete with bourgeois classics as "art," rather than lag behind as propaganda. (In fact, his primary goal in *Robert Tressell and the Ragged Trousered Philanthropists* is to position Tressell in a tradition of great English novelists.) Along with announcing the need to *appropriate* dominant cultural codes for the production of subversive narrative, he belies a need for legitimacy within the traditional academy that necessitates a rehabilitation of working-class cultural forms.

Among Mitchell's colleagues, those who pose the most immediately visible, and equally extremist, backlash to his brand of Marxist criticism are Roy Johnson and Carole Snee. Johnson's deliberately rancorous, much-cited argument in "The Proletarian Novel" (1975) denies the very existence of a proletarian literary culture, citing as "evidence" the absence of an independent, greater working-class culture from which it would arise and the failure of working-class novelists to challenge the bourgeois values laden within the novel form. He uses Mitchell's same economic premise to come to the opposite (and more predictable) conclusion, asserting that "a *genuinely* proletarian point of view" cannot and will not materialize until the proletariat become the new ruling class—"only then will it have the time, energy, control, and confidence to develop a separate culture" (88) with its own literary form.

Johnson focuses on those values attributed to contemporary working-class culture which he believes reinscribe the worst of capitalist society at large: these include "a support for monogamy and the nuclear family, a puritan work-ethic, and a respect for private property and middle-class legality more intense than that of the middle class itself" (88). This orthodox ideology is reproduced by working-class writers, he maintains, through both subject matter and genre. From Johnson's perspective, they lack the "artistic skill" to transcend the dominant cultural trappings of the novel form, imitating—however poorly—middle-class language, style, and ultimately, beliefs (92–93). Yet, in what is by now a familiar critical response,

Johnson himself ironically endorses the same bourgeois standards. He winces at those crude efforts which are, at best, "no more than a documentary or a piece of propaganda" (290):

> Naturally one sympathises with a class which has traditionally been excluded from literary life in either a productive capacity or as a subject of interest. . . . But this does not mean that an account of workshop life or 'My Week Down The Pit' is intrinsically interesting, just as the deprivations caused by working-class poverty do not instantly become art of a high order because they are spelt out in remorseless detail. (90)

Recalling the condescension of the *Left Review* editors and the dogmatism of the *Plebs,* Johnson's point of view represents perhaps the apex of vulgar Marxist criticism in the mid-1970s.

This stance still echoes, however, in Carole Snee's "Working-Class Literature or Proletarian Writing?" (1979). Snee attempts to problematize the issue, cautioning early on against the notion that all writers using the novel form are doomed to reproduce dominant values: "I hope to show that the realist novel does not simply at best reveal and interrogate the dominant, unstated ideology, or exist uncritically within it, but can also incorporate a CONSCIOUS ideological or class perspective, which in itself undercuts the ideological parameters of the genre, without necessarily transforming its structural boundaries" (169).

Yet in the end, she reserves the term "oppositional" for those working-class novelists who directly challenge the realist form, as well as ideology, of canonical texts. Her discussions of Walter Greenwood's *Love on the Dole,* Walter Brierley's *Means-Test Man,* and Lewis Jones's *Cwmardy*—the bad, the marginal, and the model proletarian texts—ultimately object to any focus on individual experience and demand a very specific sort of class agency. Greenwood's novel is first dismissed as too "real" (mere surface description, flat reportage), then indicted for not being "real" enough (omissions of historical events), and finally critiqued for its pessimistic, individualistic vision. Jones's novel is alternately praised for its commitment to "the shared experience of the collective life" (182) and for its accompanying alteration of realist form. Snee thus begins her study on fruitful ground: she recognizes the multiplicity and contradictory character of any class group, even going so far as to admit that working-class culture "may have a different perception of the individual, and what constitutes individuality" (169). The essay collapses, however, into a reductive account of reproduction and resistance in working-class literary practice. Snee refuses or is unable to see that the "bourgeois" strains of these narratives are not a denial of or regression from working-class experience but another legitimate part of it.

Scholarship from the 1980s has adopted a more middle ground, either implicitly or directly interrogating the above positions and offering the most thoughtful commentary to date. Though still pondering and for the most part upholding distinctions between "working-class," "proletarian," "proto-socialist," and "socialist" texts, it has become more generous in its categorizations and more sensitive to the contradictory relations between oppositional and dominant literary practices. H. Gustav Klaus's collections of essays on British socialist and working-class fiction tend to engage in thematic, rather than structural, analyses, yet they usually recognize the complexity involved in any act of cultural production. Klaus's introductory essay to *The Socialist Novel in Britain* (1982), for example, challenges condemnation of the novel as an irredeemably bourgeois genre, pointing to the reader's ability to rework the text, as well as the writer's increasing ability to "functionally reorient" formalistic devices to serve working-class interests. The more theoretical camp of current criticism, represented by Jeremy Hawthorn's edited volume of essays (1984) and the *Literature and History* issue devoted to autobiography and working-class writing (1988), similarly attempts to isolate those dimensions of a working-class sensibility which contest capitalist ideology specifically through the activities of reading and writing. But, as argued earlier, that critical approach has thus far been limited, caught up in its own mission to salvage working-class texts. As with the historical scholarship, it exposes the need for a new reading of working-class cultural practices.

Working-class fictional narratives have several stories to tell, it seems to me, that finally speak to a much different "rehabilitation" of their own status. In the following chapters, the more celebrated narratives called upon by historians and literary critics alike will be complemented by lesser-known works that amplify the range of voices and perspectives. Together, they represent an anxious elaboration of a particular culture that can help us rethink the specific cultural practices and oppositional gestures of contemporary working-class communities.

The *Ragged Trousered Philanthropists*
and After: Epistemologies of Class,
Legacies of Resistance

■

*Those whose life has touched the misery recounted by Robert Tressell can get out of
it many things: a bolstering of class feeling; pure rage; reinforcement for their own
pity; a call to action; maybe a good and beneficial dose of all these things.—Alan
Sillitoe, introduction to* The Ragged Trousered Philanthropists *(1964 ed.)*

Any study intending to uncover the intricacies of class resistance in
working-class writing must contend with the spectacular presence
of Robert Tressell's *The Ragged Trousered Philanthropists* (1914; 1955)
within the working-class literary canon. Traditionally touted as the
first, and definitive, radical working-class text in modern Britain,
it serves as a fitting point of departure for discussion. Tracing the
effects of material exploitation and ideological domination on a circle
of Hastings housepainters, Tressell's novel is, as even its most avid
fan, Jack Mitchell, admits, a rather anomolous "classic" of proletarian
literature: its tumultuous publishing history, sprawling and quirky
form, "backwater" setting (here called "Mugsborough"), and tragi-
comic vision of working-class culture set it apart from most others
that have followed.[1] Yet *The Ragged Trousered Philanthropists* certainly
ranks as a highly compelling master narrative, establishing criteria for the representation and enactment of working-class agency
and achieving nearly mythic stature among generations of English
working-class readers.[2] Taking as its very focus the struggle between
"false" and "true" class consciousness, the novel's exhaustive narrative
(600-plus pages) becomes a rich source of assumptions and anxieties
about authentic class subjectivity and opposition. As I will outline
below, the text's bold interrogation of dominant ideology in both

theme and design would seem to codify a certain explicit and long-term mode of class resistance that dismisses less aggressive, more momentary gestures of dissatisfaction. But *The Philanthropists* is a novel that both castigates, and is itself steeped in, working-class shame: through the figure of Frank Owen, Tressell's own buried "assimiliationist" longings are in fact recast as the privileged, "revolutionary" route of resistance. This chapter will be most concerned with the novel's interdependent concepts of class knowledge and class agency, concluding with a look at how both are carried (with modification) into the ideological frames of succeeding works.

I. "The Likes of Us": Tressell's Redefinition of Class Consciousness

Claimed at various moments by Victorianists and avant-garde enthusiasts alike, *The Ragged Trousered Philanthropists* has a unique structure that can indeed seem all things to all critics:[3] multi-plot and disjointed; naturalistic and utopian; and always kept in check by an authorial narrator while chock full of jarring discourses/forms, including advertisements, jingles, lectures, business cards, timesheets, charts, and sales receipts. An unruly mixture of recognizable styles, it defies categorization. Mitchell asserts that Tressell's innovative form derives finally from a "new dialectical grasp of the relationship between working-class individuality and the collective," supplanting the "old plot-in-length" with a new "plot-in-breadth" ("Early Harvest" 71). The narrative operates spatially by shifting between work and recreational spheres and temporally according to the impermanent, always changing work season—as Mitchell correctly notes, the "slump-boom-slump" rhythm of (early) monopoly capitalism ("Early Harvest" 72). The middle-class bildungsroman format is not so much scuttled as reconfigured, parcelled out among various players in the narrative to discourage simplistic and singular identification. In Tressell's words, "[t]he action of the story covers a period of only a little over twelve months, but in order that the picture might be complete it was necessary to describe how the workers are circumstanced at all periods of their lives, from the cradle to the grave" (Preface 11). And as Mitchell especially relishes, the text disrupts narrative conventions merely by devoting so much attention to the activity of work itself. Its unprecedented focus (*Robinson Crusoe* excepted) on the daily labor process demonstrates that the "true" protagonist of any modern novel is an exploitative economic system, not individuals who seemingly create or suspend their own destinies (*Robert Tressell* 58–61).

The intricate narrative that surrounds the novel's own gradual production *as* narrative through its many bouts with editors, however, seems pertinent as well to its shaping and final emergence as a model working-class text. That story, originating with Tressell's biographer F. C. Ball and passed along by other critics, runs as follows. *Punch* editor Jessie Pope learned of the unpublished manuscript through Tressell's daughter, who happened to be a governess in her household (and who had been entrusted with the novel shortly before his death). She agreed to read its 1,600 handwritten pages, then offered to submit it to her friend, publisher Grant Richards, who found the novel "damnably subversive, but . . . extraordinarily real" (*Robert Tressell* 5). Pope proceeded to cut the manuscript considerably in length, creating a politically suspect abridged version that emphasized despair rather than optimism, eliminated transitions between episodes, and excised several domestic scenes that might offend a middle-class audience.[4] That version went through numerous editions (and became a best seller) until Ball and others bought the manuscript in the early 1950s to make it available in its original form, thereby recording and preserving Tressell's faith in a future socialist utopia. The novel's publishing history, while fascinating in its own right, is particularly interesting as a variation of a familiar gendered scenario of working-class resistance: male working-class scholar/writer rescues radical working-class text from bourgeois villainess. Pope clearly altered the message of Tressell's narrative, yet she becomes a problematic target of criticism in these accounts, a reductive emblem of Woman's hostility to working-class interests. (Curiously, Richards endorsed her editing decisions, but escapes most of the scathing commentary.) Her casting here helps to underscore the gendering of the text's "original" master narrative. The unabridged version, first published by Lawrence and Wishart in 1955, is invested with a strikingly "masculine" class pride that champions the restored text's active, rather than passive, stance and appeal to the more rough-and-ready tastes of male working-class readers. Despite the fact that several generations of the British working-class reading public had embraced the "feminine," expurgated version, the novel's structure is finally prized for its original, and lasting, virility.

But whatever the version, *The Ragged Trousered Philanthropists*'s revolutionary message is accomplished in part through its candid look at the *non*revolutionary character of Britain's turn-of-the-century working class. To some extent, it reflects the mood of certain despondent tales found in left-wing journals of the 1890s which highlighted, indeed often satirized, the lethargy and conservatism of the "B.W." (British Workman).[5] The novel is preoccupied with capitalist culture's grip on workers' minds. Though the narrative circulates between different figures, it tends to focus on or create a single protagonist, the worker-intellectual Frank Owen, who takes on the frustrating mission of winning over his fellow housepainters to socialism. The "hands," as they are called, continually resist learning the truth about their oppression, even as the very work they perform both mimics and preempts the process of demystification: at the beginning of every job, Linden, Harlow, Philpot, and the others strip away artificial, rotted exteriors, exposing the real condition of the building structure; but as dictated by the boss, they simultaneously "stop holes," fill gaps (in plaster), with the least care possible. Though Owen tries his best to educate them, they subject his lunch-time talks to merciless ridicule and disruption. Any momentary recognition of their exploitation is soon lulled away by spectacular popular attractions, such as horseracing, pub games and brew, daily tabloids (the *Obscurer* and the *Chronicles of Crime*), and religion. (All are mere manifestations of the greatest spectacle of all, capitalism itself: Owen's signature lecture "The Great Money Trick" brilliantly describes the swindle that takes place during the extraction of surplus value.) These "ragged trousered philanthropists," "willingly" giving up their freedom and dignity to their masters, internalize and reproduce bourgeois explanations for their class's deprivations:

"... 'an' thers plenty of 'em wot's too lazy to work when they can get it. Some of the b———s who go about pleading poverty 'ave never done a fair day's work in all their bloody lives. Then thers all this new fangled machinery," continued Crass. "That's wot's ruinin' everything. . . ."

"Another thing is women," said Harlow, "there's thousands of 'em doin' work wot oughter be done by men."

"In my opinion ther's too much of this 'ere eddication, nowadays," remarked old Linden. "Wot the 'ell's the good of eddication to the likes of us?"

"None whatever," said Crass, "it just puts foolish idears into people's 'eds and makes 'em too lazy to work."

Owen maintains his characteristic distance, "listening to this pitiable farrago with feelings of contempt and wonder. Were they all hopelessly stupid? Had their intelligence never been developed beyond the childhood stage? Or was he mad himself?" (25)

Exchanges like the above, combined with explicitly didactic sections, allow the text to operate as a piece of propaganda. (Peter Miles has called the novel a "self-contained kit for the dissemination of ideas" celebrating "the activity of persuasion itself."[6]) Tressell anticipates the reader's similar delusions, teaching his audience to decode their own ideological mindset by juxtaposing the socialist's "madness" against that of the hands. Mitchell's monograph study of *The Ragged Trousered Philanthropists* in fact goes to great lengths to argue that the text achieves a breakthrough—a "modern working-class sensibility"—precisely through its "realistic" portrait of working-class passivity and "mental dry-rot" (116). Tressell possesses, he maintains, what the housepainters lack: a "self-confident" vision of his class as multi-dimensional "Humanity," the "salt of the earth" with the *potential* for triumphant resistance (24–29). He concludes:

> It is this tremendous underlying confidence in his class which enables Tressell to penetrate naturally and fearlessly to the weaknesses and illusions blocking our path of advance. . . . From him alone we learn why there has been no socialist revolution in Britain—yet. . . . On the other hand, using his apparently unpromising materials and confining himself to the day-to-day existence of the workers' collective, he reveals, as if by magic, an elusive poetry in their lives, a kind of beauty which points into

the future because it has to do with the immortal, undefeatable creative vitality of the People. (28)

Indeed, though the heart of the narrative dwells on the painters' material and psychological misery—"the story of twelve months in Hell," the original title page announces, "told by one of the damned" —it incorporates a distinctly visionary perspective. The "Great Oration," never excised from the manuscript through its various editions though delivered by different speakers and shifted about within the narrative, distinguishes itself from other lectures by sketching out a program for socialism itself. Rather than attacking capitalism and thereby attempting to "explain" to the men their ignorance, the "Great Oration" spins a tale of seemingly outrageous promise (retitled by the rank-and-file audience, "The Great Secret, Or How To Live Without Work"). The speech attempts to denaturalize capitalism, as well as demonstrate how the system can be reconstructed for collective use rather than individual profit. As several commentators have pointed out, the oration actually advocates a quite tame form of revolution: public ownership of means of production, which can be accomplished through government intervention and a subsequent state monopoly.[7] It is a crucial observation, not so much to place Tressell on a political continuum (Fabian vs. Marxist) as to pinpoint the type of resistance valued in the novel: ideological, rather than bloody, upheaval.

Such a revolution may be more sophisticated than crude calls for mass revolt at factory and mine, but it operates with an equally crude notion of authentic class consciousness. While arguably operating within a tradition of comic caricature upheld by Swift, Fielding, and Dickens to reflect the damaging effects of the social system,[8] *The Philanthropists* privileges a specific class stance that fails to recognize the validity and complexity of the rank-and-file consciousness, Linden's "the likes of us." In the novel's scheme, the workers's "potential" is measured exclusively by their ability to create a new social order. The "balance of forces" at work in their consciousness, and the battle between Owen and the capitalist system for its control (Mitchell 16), has just one acceptable resolution. The text occasionally moves beyond caricature when it attempts to display momentary flashes of class pride and opposition among the rank-and-file. "Gettin' your own back" is their frequent rallying cry and most common gesture of defiance; it involves such small acts of subversion as resting instead of working and stealing time (or materials) from the boss. But the gesture is finally invalidated by serving as further evidence of false consciousness: the moment of agency it potentially represents is deflated by its associations with a bourgeois mentality. As Owen sneers, "Grin and bear it. . . . Get your own back whenever you have a chance" (47). From his perspective, the hands only participate in their own exploitation through such acts, maintaining the logic (and very existence) of the underlying system. Yet I view "gettin' your own back" as a viable, expansive resistance strategy, expressing protest on a number of levels.

The rank-and-file's discourse is one particularly embattled site of consciousness within the text. While Owen speaks standard, educated English, the "slaves" and masters alike speak the same uneducated class dialect. In a cleverly engineered reversal, Tressell has the oppressor speaking the language of the oppressed (and vice versa) to demonstrate their commonality and mutual ignorance. Malapropism is at once a primary source of comedy and index of character in the narrative. From the owner of the painting company, Rushton, down to the youngest of the hands, Bert White, all misuse language, continually choosing words ineffectually or incorrectly. Though many of their rhetorical mishaps are simply nonsensical, an equal number are suggestive: "pint of order" for "point of order," "dissolute" for "desolate," "fissical policy" for fiscal policy.[9] These are represented as unconscious slippages, and rather than score some (unintended) points on the speakers' behalf, have the effect of producing further laughter at their own expense. Significantly, the hands do demonstrate some initiative in the discursive arena by appropriating the power of naming. Like Tressell himself, who names a pair of low-level foremen Slyme and Crass, they nickname their general manager "Misery" and "Nimrod."[10] On the whole, however, they are judged by their embarrassing—and disingenuous—performance in the realm of public discourse:

> They never thought or spoke of them [Misery and Rushton] except with hatred and curses. But whenever either of them came to the 'job' the 'coddies' cringed and grovelled before them, greeting them with disgustingly servile salutations, plentifully interspersed with the word 'Sir' . . . it made one feel sick to hear them, because it was not courtesy: they were never courteous to each other, it was simply abject servility and self-contempt. (430)

Along with Owen, we finally gauge their ignorance, and hence enslavement to hegemonic culture, by their surface dialogue.

Yet their class-based "wrath" is not completely "voiceless" (523), as he charges. They indeed find language mystifying, forever complaining *to him,* "Why the 'ell don't yer talk plain English . . . ," and mistrust it as a tool that can be deployed simply and "naturally." (Unlike the narrator and protagonist, they place no faith in the reliability and transparency of language.) But they find means of expressing resistance that entail both nondiscursive and discursive practices. As Crass dilutes his paint to trick Misery (cheating the cheater), the hands "dilute" or penetrate their masters' version of reality. Such minor acts as the paint tampering itself challenge the capitalist's insistence that quality work can be accomplished with the shoddiest materials and most exploitative measures.

The painters also take up mimicry and drama. One of the most startling examples of the latter occurs in "The Reign of Terror" Chapter. During his "Money Trick" lecture, Owen attempts to dramatize the production and circulation of capital by enlisting the help of his rank-and-file audience. Harlow, Philpot, and Easton agree to represent the compliant Working Class, who "produce" commodities (in the simulacrum, slices of bread cut into square blocks) in exchange for wages. After receiving their instructions, "The Working Classes set to work, and the Capitalist class [Owen] sat down and watched them. As soon as they had finished, they passed the nine little blocks to Owen, who placed them on a piece of paper by his side and paid the workers their wages" (227). But when he informs them that they have to buy back the blocks (clothing, food) at a rate that exceeds their wages—and soon confiscates their very work tools, closing shop due to "Over Production"—they reject the script:

"Well, and wot the bloody 'ell are we to do now?" demanded Philpot.

"That's not my business," replied the kind-hearted capitalist. "I've paid you your wages, and provided you with Plenty of Work for a long time past. I have no more work for you to do at present. Come round again in a few months' time and I'll see what I can do for you."

"But what about the necessities of life?" demanded Harlow. "We must have something to eat."

"Of course you must," replied the capitalist, affably; "and I shall be very pleased to sell you some."

"But we ain't got no bloody money!"

When the Capitalist retorts that they should have been "thrifty" with their wages, "[t]he unemployed looked blankly at each other, but the rest of the crowd only laughed; and then the three unemployed began to abuse the kind-hearted Capitalist, demanding that he should give them some of the necessaries of life that he had piled up in his warehouses . . . and even threatened to take some of the things by force if he did not comply with their demands" (228–229). Upon the Capitalist's counterthreat of violence, however, the Working Class reverts to its expected role. They mimic their own "real" behavior, now exposed as a construct that benefits the master:

"The only thing as I can see for it," said Philpot mournfully, "is to have a unemployed procession."

"That's the idear," said Harlow, and the three began to march about the room in Indian file, singing:

'We've got no work to do-oo-oo!
We've got no work to do-oo-oo!
Just because we've been working a dam sight too hard,
Now we've got no work to do.'

As they marched round, the crowd jeered at them and made offensive remarks. Crass said that anyone could see that they were a lot of lazy, drunken loafers who had never done a fair day's work in their lives and never intended to. (229)

The hands similarly mimic the master discourse proper when they scornfully repeat to one another official management phrases such as "however trifling" ("Under no circumstances is any article or material, however trifling, to be taken away by workmen for their private use," 457), make puns on technical terms at their supervisors' expense, and actually write notes to one another imitating the boss.[11]

The rank-and-file consciousness, then, fails to be completely immersed in dominant ideology, despite Tressell's frequent undercutting of, and cynicism towards, episodes like the above. Rather, a model of dilution/saturation emerges, alternately demystifying and reproducing the bourgeois standpoint. Their own self-contempt, conveyed through laughter at the idea of deserving the benefits of socialism, becomes acted upon, and thus undermined. Other examples of resistance that similarly fall into the category of "gettin' your own back" include unauthorized (beer) breaks, destruction of tools or work materials, performance of arduous tasks with creative, less strenuous, and more time-consuming methods, as well as more directly confrontational acts of protest: defacing management correspondence with excrement, playing violent practical jokes on the supervisor. Much of this of course comprises poststructuralist territory: strategies for momentarily articulating or enacting opposition to dominant culture by appropriating areas of power (discursive, cultural, and otherwise). For the contemporary reader, however, these can all too easily reduce to a streamlined signifier that stands in for all types of resistance. Wim Neetens, for instance, seizes on representative examples of such opposition to claim *The Ragged Trousered Philanthropists* as an interrogative text, without either noting the immediate containment and delegitimation of such strategies by the authorial narrator (whom he champions) or perceiving that the hands' defiance is often instinctively performed out of necessity, rather than self-consciousness (and hence misreading the politics of its source).[12]

Perhaps most important, this form of poststructuralist critique supports Owen's refusal to recognize the authenticity of such practices when they are used by the hands to resist *socialist* ideology. The rank-and-file's frequent disruptions of Owen's lectures are not always the result of mindless allegiance to their oppressor. Occasionally, their challenges seem sensible and more than understandable as they question their fellow worker's "explanations" of reality. Owen attempts to communicate his critique of capitalist culture by balancing abstract language and definitions with drawings and charts, but in the end, his discourse is not all that distinguishable from the hollow slogans of Mugsborough's capitalist politicians. Given his painstakingly wordy analyses, we should do more than smile amusedly when Harlow complains, "'e takes sich a 'ell of a time to say wot 'e's got to say. Nobody else can't get a word in edgeways" (160), or when another unidentified listener quips, "'Wonder wot the bloddy 'ell 'e thinks 'e is? A sort of schoolmaster?" (160) Their observations pinpoint the significance of Owen's difference.

As registered in his very speech, Owen is marked by a highly distinctive subjectivity that becomes linked with the novel's perspective of valid class "knowledge." We are introduced to his character by the narrator, who immediately accentuates Owen's marginalization within the mass. Unlike the others engrossed in the day's racetrack drama,

> Frank Owen . . . was as usual absorbed in a newspaper. He was generally regarded as a bit of a crank: for it was felt that there must be something wrong about a man who took no interest in racing or football and was always talking a lot of rot about religion and politics. If it had not been for the fact that he was generally admitted to be an exceptionally good workman, they would have had but little hesitation about thinking that he was mad. . . . There was a suggestion of refinement in his clean-shaven face, but his complexion was ominously clear, and an unnatural colour flushed the thin cheeks. (16)

Reminiscent of past (but declassed) worker figures in the British novel such as Felix Holt and Gilbert Grail, and establishing a model for future radical working-class autodidact figures such as Larry Meath (*Love on the Dole*) and Ewan Tavandale (*A Scots Quair*), Owen's privileged consciousness is linked to his "refined" artisan-intellectual status. Much is made of his skilled craftsmanship, along with his love of learning. The "Hands and Brains" chapter, which details Owen's joy at receiving a rare commission to design and decorate a wealthy client's drawingroom, does more than merely establish Tressell's line of connection to William Morris's arts and crafts movement.¹³ In embracing Morris's vision, the chapter (along with the entire novel) reproduces one traditional, privileged conception of working-class culture that is as problematic as it is alluring. Signifying a respect for aesthetics and unadulterated, nonalienated labor, the artisan legacy certainly challenges dominant stereotypes of working-class savagery, laziness, and ignorance. It also legitimizes one form of working-class utopian "desire" which, as E. P. Thompson proposed in his study of Morris, expresses faith in a transformed system.¹⁴ Yet intermixed with the pride reflected in that legacy is class shame—the desire to flee a culture of the Other which appears to (and often does) degrade and corrupt its people. Here, working-class culture is the antithesis not of bourgeois culture per se, but of a utopian culture that, as it turns out, privileges hegemonic Culture.

Owen's political mission in the narrative can thus finally be viewed as an entirely different sort of "philanthropic" enterprise—a self-appointed cultural ambassadorship that brings the promise of "civilization" to the working-class "savages." Culture, rather than money, emerges as the key term in his socialist definition of "wealth" (and conversely "poverty"). Balking at the hands' fixation on wages, Owen explains early on, "What I call poverty is when people are not able to secure for themselves all the benefits of civilisation; the necessaries, comforts, pleasures and refinements of life, leisure, books, theatres, pictures, music, holidays, travel, good and beautiful homes, good clothes, good and pleasant food" (28). The right to desire and have such pleasures should, as he notes, belong to all; yet the "benefits of civilisation" here become conflated with a kind of cultural competency *imposed* on the others. He states, when a man "cannot enjoy the advantages of civilisation he might just as well be a savage: better, in fact, for a savage knows nothing of what he is deprived. What we call civilisation—the accumulation of knowledge which has come down to us from our forefathers—is the fruit of thousands of years of human thought and toil . . . by right the common heritage of all" (29). Owen desires for his class not mere access to knowledge, but equal access to a specific type of cultural knowledge. The hands' ignorance of their own "deprivation" in this regard is depicted as the root of their greater political ignorance, their false consciousness. Their refusal to perceive their condition *as* deprivation only functions as further proof. Linden's objection to Owen's analysis and terminology—" 'You can speak for yourself, but I can tell yer I don't put *myself* down as a slave' "—is supposed to be read as a tragic blindness to the reality of his class position, rather than as potentially valid resistance to Owen's particular value system. Far from neutral (our "common heritage"), that system reflects the text's own resistance to, or flight from, unsavory elements of working-class subjectivity. By associating class consciousness with a certain exclusive sensibility, the novel suggests that it is itself deeply embedded in class shame.

Much like the hands, then, who at once accept and reject grounds for their own self-contempt, Owen's refusal of the shameful dimensions of working-class existence is ultimately enacted through an equally complicated—and equally understandable—appropriation of middle-class models. His valorization of an outdated artisan culture, while meant to emblemize a worker-controlled mode of production, actually reinscribes a bourgeois aesthetic sensibility. And his very conception of class consciousness, which must be acquired or taught, rather than gained instinctively at an experiential level, ultimately makes use of a middle-class logic of rationality to explain working-class exploitation. As hinted at above, that concept is equated with an epistemology rooted above all in causal reasoning: the ability to pinpoint or trace the source of poverty objectively. After persistent efforts to educate the others, Owen grows

> weighed down by a growing conviction of the hopelessness of everything, of the folly of expecting that his fellow workmen would ever be willing to try to understand for themselves the causes that produced their sufferings. It was not that those causes were so obscure that it required exceptional intelligence to perceive them; the causes of all the misery were so apparent that a little child could easily be made to understand both the disease and the remedy; but it seemed to him that the majority of his fellow workmen had become so convinced of their own intellectual inferiority that they did not dare to rely on their own intelligence to guide them. . . . And if one explained those causes to them in such language and in such a manner that they were almost com-

pelled to understand, they were neither glad nor responsive, but
remained silent and were angry because they found themselves
unable to answer and disprove. (581–582)

While "obvious," his socialist demystification doesn't stand a chance
against the hands' "common sense"—the naturalizing vision of dominant ideology. Although they themselves term their outlook "'eart"
rather than "'ead" knowledge (153), the narrator invites us to adopt
another view: "They accepted the present system in the same way as
they accepted the alternating seasons" (218). And according to the
text, this outlook has an additional blindspot. It precludes imagination, the partner of rationality in the novel's schema. The rank-
and-file's nonfunctioning minds can only crudely demand "facts" to
support any challenges to their perspective. They want to know how
another system will function down to the last detail without the willingness to envision possibilities. Frank is not set apart as a suspicious,
alien figure in their circle merely because of his intellect and elevated discourse; he is branded more than once as a "conjurer," a
mad dreamer who is continually "supposin' wot ain't true." (Indeed,
their greatest contempt is reserved for those instances in which Owen
attempts to explain a point or envision the difference of socialism
through hypothesis or conjecture.)

It is significant, however, that Owen's approach to knowledge
proves problematic for those few who do attempt to achieve some sort
of consciousness. They experience difficulty in using rationality to
cope with a fundamentally *ir*rational system. Easton, the worker most
akin to Owen (appearing more "civilized" than the others), offers
one glimpse of this dilemma in the text when he attempts to master his finances. Overwhelmed by a never-ending mound of bills, he
proposes to his wife, Ruth, that they draw up an official household
budget, itemizing both income and monthly expenses in exhaustive
detail, in order to get to the bottom of the problem—to "know exactly
where we are" (54). But though they engage in frenzied calculations
and produce endless lists, they grow only more confused and despondent. The budget refuses to balance. The Eastons' methodology in
this scene ironically resembles Owen's in his "Oblong" lecture, which

makes use of charts and graphs to explain to his audience "where they stand" in the social formation.

The novel's privileged version of proletarian epistemology thus, to some extent, remains part and parcel of capitalist culture, reproducing its logic even as it operates from a production, rather than consumption, standpoint. *The Philanthropists* employs similarly rigid categories and definitions from the "other" side as it values strict patterns, boundaries, and teleological thought. (The Oblong lecture offers the most visual example: Owen's drawing of England's population, reprinted in the text, carves up a geometric space into neat blocks that resolutely divide groups of people according to their work function.) Its particular socialist analysis retains a fundamentally capitalist organization of production, merely shifting the terms of debate to the means of gaining control over that organization.[15]

The dominant cultural basis of Tressell's radical class consciousness is most evident and perhaps most damaging when the bounds of that production/consumption economy are examined from the vantage point of gender relations. As feminist challenges to Marxist theory have long argued, such a limited conceptualization of labor and exploitation excludes other arenas of power and retains (vestiges of) patriarchal privilege for working-class men.[16] Its own rigid categories and boundaries have the potential to reproduce inequities and oppressive strictures. The novel, then, one can argue, also constructs a masculinist model of consciousness in its traditional notions of "work"/"production" as well as in finally seeking to preserve gendered working-class spaces that benefit one sex over another. *The Philanthropists* concentrates on experiences of class encountered primarily at public work and leisure sites by groups of men. Women clearly remain outside such experiences and thus outside the bounds of class knowledge. It is simply wild misreading on Jack Mitchell's part to assert that women "[f]or the first time in the English working-class novel . . . make their presence felt on an equal footing with the men," though it is quite true that the "women folk" ("[l]ike the children") are given "an integral part to play in Tressell's scheme" (*Robert Tressell* 19). The few, and most notable, scenes in the novel involving working-class women suggestively threaten the ordered fictional world that the narrative constructs by moving between its distinctly divided spheres.

Ruth's surprising appearance at the pub (chapter 24), for instance, reveals not only the gendering of the working-class cultural institutions represented within the novel, but the gendering of its primary system of "knowing." Although the narrative ensures that she has an innocent enough purpose—to collect her husband—her presence operates as a severe transgression for which she pays later in the text. The tavern is one area where working-class men *can* theoretically exercise control through declaring ownership of space. To Ruth, the discourse and scene are distinctly unfamiliar, "novel and strange"; she is coerced into having several drinks, yet it is her crossing of the boundary into this public and masculine world, rather than the alcohol, that ultimately causes her disorientation: "Everything around her . . . seemed vague and shadowy and unreal" (264).

Her foray into unknown territory indeed proves unwise, for directly afterwards, she becomes a spectacle in the street and is subsequently "seduced" and "shamed" by Slyme, the Easton's lodger. It is significant that the episode is followed by Owen's "Oblong" lecture, which reinstates "order" through its model of rationality, and is preceded by the brief, but key, scene featuring Miss Wade, Rushton's "young lady clerk" who foreshadows Ruth's error (and punishment). Miss Wade enters another forbidden masculine sphere—the work place—and is immediately transformed into a sexualized spectacle. We watch her being fondled in the boss's office through the eyes of three male workers "peeping through . . . [a] crack in the partition" (254). Failing to enter the secretary's consciousness, as we do Ruth's, we are left only with this lasting image, which hints as much of collusion *with* exploitative forces as victimization by them. The male workers may need to be instructed in class consciousness, yet their appearance in legitimized realms of experience within the narrative at least seems "natural," throwing into relief women's alien relationship to the novel's recognized mode of agency.

II. Post-Tressell: Plotting the Revolution in Knowledge

While I hesitate to propose a definitive line of influence between *The Ragged Trousered Philanthropists* and subsequent working-class novels—and bristle at Mitchell's ranking of Tressell as the "father" of modern working-class writing—this text does establish one powerful norm for the representation of working-class subjectivity and radical consciousness. I have tried to unpack the assumptions and anxieties which pervade that norm and render it an enormously complex model of resistance. My isolation of the shame invested in Tressell's conception of "true," as well as "false," consciousness is meant to function predominantly as description rather than critique: in demonstrating Owen's own flight from working-class subjectivity, highlighting the links to dominant cultural values and methodology that underlie his socialist vision, I have intended to show that he is, in fact, an "authentic" working-class figure. Like the hands, Owen displays a class "consciousness" (though expressed in different terms) whose pride and defiance are intermixed with self-doubt and self-contempt; their seemingly conflicting mindsets and practices share a similar source in the experience of shame and in the desire for self-production. As I suggest, however, in the attempt to mask or reconceptualize that shared source, the novel offers an ideal of class consciousness that proves to be highly prescriptive and gendered, limited to working-class men's positioning in the social formation. This chapter's closing section will briefly survey a group of representative texts from the 1920s and 1930s which reproduce, as well as rework, aspects of *The Philanthropists'* master ideological (if not structural) scheme. Paired according to gender focus, they help to accentuate the ties to dominant culture that characterize even the most "radical" proletarian epistemology.

Male Autodidacts

Walter Greenwood's *Love on the Dole* (1933) and Harold Heslop's *The Gate of a Strange Field* (1929) are equally concerned with the "problem" of class consciousness in modern working-class communities, and both adopt versions of the worker-intellectual figure to function as an emblem of class agency. Greenwood's novel seems most akin to

Tressell's in this respect, advocating the same route to class knowledge. The narrative ends on a much more grim note, succumbing (as its critics are fond of citing) to the despair that pervaded some working-class communities during the early 1930s: its panorama of a Manchester neighborhood assailed by economic depression offers little hope of lasting reprieve or change in its (non)closure.[17] Yet the narrative does make available to the dulled masses who inhabit Hanky Park a blueprint for revolution via socialist organizer Larry Meath, who attempts to train his fellow workers in the art of demystification. Although Meath remains somewhat of a background presence throughout much of the text, he serves as a purposeful point of contrast—like Owen, a man of high principles, high discourse, and high culture. Larry is even introduced to the reader with nearly the exact same set of crucial signifiers:

> Nearer the gates Harry glimpsed Larry reading a newspaper and leaning against the wall. Larry Meath! Harry's heart leapt and his eyes glowed with eagerness. . . . His quality of studiousness and reserve elevated him to a plane beyond that of ordinary folk; he seemed out of place in his lodgings in North Street. He wasn't for drinking, gambling, swearing or brawling. Though if you went to the library to look at the illustrated papers or to watch the old geysers playing dominoes, you sometimes saw Larry at one of the tables absorbed in some book or other that looked as dry as the desert. And argue! . . . he could talk fifty to the dozen. . . . [H]is face attracted you, too; lean, a gentle expression and a soft kindliness, a frank steadfastness in his eyes that invited confidence. (22–23)

Harry Hardcastle's reverential attitude here certainly differs from the hands' derision of Owen in Tressell's text, but it is an exception to the rule within Greenwood's narrative and quickly has its limits. The other workers at the local engineering plant regard Meath's difference with a mixture of scorn, curiosity, and fear, which Harry adopts as well when he attempts to become a member of their enclave. Their mindset is most dramatically evoked by the character Blind Joe, whose daily job consists of waking his neighbors at dawn to get them to work (he wields a long pole used to rattle bedroom windows).

Considered somewhat "daft," he emerges as a pathetic and rather mysterious figure whose very "blindness" is at issue: "His back was bent, beard stained and untrimmed, his rusty back bowler hat was tipped over his eyes. Blind Joe he was called, though he never gave wrong change out of a shilling nor had need to ask his way about. Whether or no he actually was blind none could say; he was Blind Joe Riley, that was all" (13). Maintaining the system that exploits his world without revealing any awareness of its costs or the part he plays, Joe enacts the blurred line between false and true consciousness. It is "difficult to say" whether he in fact perceives the "real" workings of capitalist relations (as well as his own complicity with them). Those he wakes on his early morning routine are only less extreme versions, appearing in their own ways to be equally "barmy" and blind. They are awakened but refuse to see. Like the earlier "ragged trousered philanthropists," their minds are marked (and marred) by distortion and alienation, a "riot of confusion" (205).

Even more so than Tressell, Greenwood emphasizes the reification of the working-class "brain" as it suffers the humiliating conditions of both work and unemployment. His characters increasingly imagine the mind as a distinct and separate component—Harry's father goes so far as to experience "an urgent desire to be able to take out his brains and plunge them in cold water" (94). Their "inward spiritual discontent" remains unarticulated, unexplained. As Larry perceives the problem, they are

> [d]iscontented and wondering why they were discontented; each keeping his discontent in his own bosom as though it were a guilty secret; each putting on a mask of unconcern, accepting his neighbour's mask as his true expression, and, often, expressing inarticulate revolt in drunkenness, in making desperate, futile efforts to relieve their poverty in gambling hazards they could ill afford. (24)

And even when they momentarily attempt to "reason it all out," they fail, stymied by their own persistent "mystified silence" (160). Mrs. Jikes and the others in the neighborhood take comfort in "consulting the oracle" to understand their past lot and future fate.

Although they are depicted sympathetically, these stunted figures at times barely escape the narrator's open contempt. Their lack of consciousness and accompanying vulgarity are a source of embarrassment, even as they are balanced by other vestiges of dignity and struggle. As in Tressell's novel, working-class discourse becomes one particularly vulnerable area of critique. The inhabitants of Hanky Park rival the Mugsborough hands in slovenly, uneducated dialect. Here, their language is not so much comic as ugly. Speakers curl their lips, snarl, and swear ("Aaach! Y'brazen bitch"). Harry's sister Sally, who admires Larry's intelligence and "class," immediately becomes conscious of her own family's "loose way" of speaking when she notices the difference in his speech. (She scolds Harry, "And don't say 'mek,' it's 'make.' Oh, I've no time to muck about—I mean, mend collars for nobody," [89].) Their "uncivilized" behavior comes in for an unusually blunt attack, however, in the "Tangle" chapter, which targets their "disgusting" sexuality and spoiling of a pristine, natural space on romps outside the town: the countryside is violated by "crude" drawings ("the ribald handiwork of obscene boys and youths") and "raucous screams of counterfeit shocked laughter from groups of mill and factory girls parading the banks who have been surprised by louts from the slums lying in the grass peeping at lovers" (138). The narrator attempts to contextualize and explain this behavior by deeming it "the activit[y] of unpleasant people whose qualities, perhaps, are sad reflections of sadder environments" (139). Yet their mannerisms are still represented as a simplistic mirror of their conditions, with a lasting sense of debasement.

Larry's polite manners and standard dialect are in turn a "reflection" of his enlightened class perspective. Like Owen, he perceives the value of Culture and employs a Marxist analysis rooted in causal reasoning. His first streetcorner speech outlines the "cost" of the capitalist system: "Labour never ending, constant struggles to pay the rent and to buy sufficient food and clothing; no time for anything that is bright and beautiful. . . . That is the price we will continue to pay until you people awaken to the fact that Society has the means, the skill, and the knowledge to afford us the opportunity to become Men and Women in the fullest sense of those terms" (86). A later lecture on the definition of poverty appears straight out of Tressell's text (or, by this time, a Plebs League pamphlet). His revo-

lution in knowledge—controlled, dignified, and thorough—is juxtaposed not only with his neighbor's apathy and confusion, but with
other, more volatile forms of class resistance. When another "Red"
at the plant becomes frustrated in efforts to stir up opposition and
explodes in anger, Larry attacks both his ignorance and his behavior ("If you'd learn your subject properly, nothing would make you
get your hair off"). And during the climactic Means Test protest, he
counters an "inflammatory" call to revolt with a plea for more dis-
ciplined, thoughtful opposition—he "reminded the crowd that the
cause of their protest was of their own making; recalled the scares
and the people's response at the general election" (198). His attention
to ideological domination—backed up by a seemingly contradictory,
but distinctly middle-class code of behavior—emerges as the most
authentic model of class consciousness in the novel.

The Gate of A Strange Field is much more openly conflicted about
the authenticity of working-class epistemology taught from "above."
Its distrust of the Marxist education movement, the principal influence on (and often source of) worker-intellectuals like Owen and
Meath, calls into question the forms of agency and consciousness
privileged by the above novels, yet the force of Heslop's critique appears driven by equally troubling notions of resistance and similar
feelings of shame about working-class culture.

The novel, set in a Welsh mining community during the 1920s,
adopts a classic bildungsroman form to capture the political tensions
of that decade, highlighted by the General Strike. From the beginning, protagonist Joe Tarrant is set apart by his "sensitivity" and
"imagination." His eagerness at the age of 14 to enter the colliery is
first inspired, then dampened, by his free-ranging mind. The antici-
pated "adventure" of work soon fades into the reality of "slavery," the
"shackles of industry" imprisoning him. The narrator accentuates
the revolutionary potential of Joe's intelligence: "[H]e was unaware
that he was developing into a potential rebel. His imagination, re-
volted by this filthy machinery, compelled him to strain at the leash
which held him fast" (14). When he is a youth, this imagination gives
rise to fanciful means of escape—running away to sea, becoming a
great football champion. But as Joe settles in for a life-time term as a
miner, he yearns to understand, rather than flee, his plight. His ini-

tiation into trade union leadership only fuels his determination when he learns of the union bosses' "ignorance" of their own class history and lack of analytic skills. His search leads him first to the labor press, where he becomes acquainted with a formalized critique of capitalism, then to the "vortex" of institutionalized worker education (111). The novel's critique of Joe's experience there offers somewhat conflicting assessments: scorn at both his mindless search for "facts" and his inability to ever actually comprehend them. Heslop appears particularly offended by the Plebs League's pretense to authentic, radical knowledge, sniping "Karl Marx is its lord and king, not Marx in the spirit, not the theoretical head, but the figure head, the bogeyman to frighten the others" (111).

Joe's subsequent education emerges as little but a "masquerade." Attempting to gain "a correct understanding of economics,"

> [h]e read seduously and collected a few books. With the knowledge thus gleaned he was soon able to lord it over the rest of his workmates. He began a stern tussle with the Law of Value according to Marx, before he entered upon the task of understanding the Law of Surplus Value. It is doubtful whether he ever mastered these laws, but he always made it appear that he had mastered them. So successful was his masquerade that he became a tutor himself. The Labor Party compiled a list of available propagandists and he put his name down. The halls of knowledge are full of fools who wear strange motley. (112)

His ignorance is placed on the same plane as that of the "average miner," who "cannot reason beyond his paynote" (113). Here, the "enlightened" and the unawakened worker are equally guilty of false consciousness, each "willingly giving his fate into the hands of those who seem to shine more brilliantly than the rest" (113). Joe is, in the end, an "imposter" not simply because he fails to reason effectively, but because he fails to care about his superficial grasp of the material: "He was confident that if he was made to sit down and put into writing all that he knew of the political world he would not fill many pages of a notebook. But he also knew that it was not the knowing of things that counted, it was the successful harlequinade in the halls of knowledge. . . . He had but to glitter before them" (113).

The Gate of A Strange Field thus seems to indict the spectacular nature and function of institutionalized proletarian knowledge rather than the pursuit of such knowledge itself. However, it also reflects an uneasy suspicion that the working class might be unable to imitate "real" scholars, to perform true mental labor. Perhaps to compensate for this perceived deficiency, the narrative gradually shifts to a valorization of "instinctive" and direct resistance among the rank and file, while still making attempts to establish the qualitative difference of Joe's mind. In a sense, Heslop's novel finally encourages a demystification of the ostensibly "true" class consciousness endorsed by Tressell and Greenwood. But wanting it both ways, it is an overdetermined act of exposure which in the end acknowledges the validity of the other novelists' values.

The gendering of epistemological models in *Love on the Dole* and *The Gate of A Strange Field* were only hinted at in the above capsule discussions. Though both novels employ men as privileged figures of resistance, their assumption of masculine codes is complicated and varied. Their resemblance to the gendered dynamic of *The Ragged Trousered Philanthropists* only becomes clearer when we shift focus to substantial sub-narratives in both texts that feature women. The "private" sphere where they reside emerges, it seems to me, as the site of Greenwood and Heslop's most urgent messages about class agency. That is, while the novelists present somewhat different views of authentic class knowledge and resistance, they each finally find their narrative vehicle for those views in the "opposite" arena of gender relations—specifically, in romance plots. As with the following texts which emphasize women's experiences in class culture, *Love on the Dole* and *The Gate of A Strange Field* demonstrate the necessity of an expansive look at the incorporation of a feminized genre in order to understand how representations of class resistance, knowledge, and agency get played out within these texts, and how these representations are *always* refracted through the lens of gender.

Female Rivals

Ellen Wilkinson's *Clash* (1929) and Lewis Grassic Gibbon's *A Scot's Quair* trilogy (1932–34) offer more straightforward alternatives to Tressell's model of working-class epistemology, even as they both retain his fundamental utopian vision and evince varying degrees of distrust toward intermittent oppositional gestures. As narratives that focus on working-class female figures, they have a different, but equally anxious, relationship to the worker-intellectual tradition and its accompanying definition of radical class knowledge. In the arguable need for authenticity, they are at once freed from and bound to its strictures.

Wilkinson is placed in a particularly difficult position as a woman writer seeking at least some degree of legitimacy within a working-class literary genre. *Clash* tells its version of the 1926 General Strike in part through its charting of Joan Craig's seduction by left-wing intellectualism and struggle to recapture her "instinctive" class consciousness. The parallels to Heslop's novel are obvious, yet slight, since *Clash* explicitly critiques the bourgeois orientation of formalized worker knowledge and idolizes the mindset of the rank and file. Rather than representing "average" workers as dupes of dominant culture lacking both "logic" and "imagination," this text marvels at their inherent wisdom; though often kept to the margins of the narrative, they function here as symbolic bearers of true class consciousness.

To make the point, Wilkinson situates the left-wing intellectual arena in Bloomsbury. Most of the mouthpieces for quasi-Marxist theory and socialism in the narrative are privileged Fabians, rather than self-taught workers or Labour College students (Harry Browne being the exception). The artists, writers, and labor sympathizers of this circle are clearly of a different breed than Owen, Meath, and Tarrant. But only in degree. They come to be aligned with the bureaucratic laborism of William Royd, Joan's mentor and supervisor, and other trade union officials who claim to know what is "best" for the workers. Both camps are associated with a "civilized" and rational outlook which initially proves appealing to the protagonist. Joan begins the narrative as a beleaguered union organizer disappointed by the short-sightedness of the workers she attempts to reach. Soon, she is drawn to the comforts afforded by a literal as well as ideological separation. But she sees through the others' rhetoric as often as she succumbs: Joan becomes incensed when they claim cultural superiority—"really, one might think they were Hottentots, the way your crowd talk about the miners, instead of decent, ordinary, respectable people" (73). From the start, she detects the simplistic, formulaic base of their "higher" consciousness.

Throughout the novel, she expresses particular impatience with the intellectuals' logic of causality, arguing that it is inordinately difficult to discover singular causes of oppression. Early on, she chides one of the Bloomsbury crowd, "The most difficult thing to find in modern industry is the place where the power is. Everyone blames every one else" (24). She continues this thought again late in the narrative after having experienced much contact and conflict with various "players" in the Strike. While in the company of the nascent *Wednesday Weekly* staff, a labor paper founded by both middle and working-class Left intellectuals, she notes, "What a complicated business English social life is. . . . There must be a line between capitalist and worker somewhere, but whenever you think you've got it, it's always somewhere else. There's an obvious gulf between Harry Browne and the Duke of Northumberland, or Mr. Gordon Selfridge, or his own immediate boss, but where does the line shade off?" She concludes, "It was a difficult conundrum, but, meanwhile, the talk was good" (297). Their "talk" is also echoed in the perspective of the Communist leader Tom Openshaw, of whom Joan equally disapproves. One of his admirers (a writer and prominent member of the London group) claims, "[h]e's the only man I've met so far who has got the strike into proper perspective. He doesn't see it as a bolt from the blue. After he had put the case, one saw the whole thing as an inevitable part of a new phase of capitalism"; but Joan retorts, "It's easy enough to be logical if you don't worry how far ahead of your followers you go, or even whether you have any followers" (125). The novel conveys distrust of any epistemology that appears divorced from, imposed on, the masses.

In contrast, Wilkinson's "ordinary, decent" miners from the North possess the most crucial and authentic knowledge of working-class reality. (The London writer's growing recognition of that fact— "They know such a lot about life, Joan"—signals one turning-point in his character.) "Unself-conscious," they are positioned as the privileged source of "first-hand contacts with life" (262), rather than as pathetic savages of a somnambulant class culture. Joan simultaneously displays her membership in and distance from that group through her "shy worship" of one "matter-of-fact miner, smoking stolidly at her side" (61) during the climactic moment of the strike vote. It is only when she spends a significant amount of time back in the North with "her" people that she becomes reacquainted with the more sobering, as well as inspiring, elements of their consciousness. After reading from a selection of verse sent by the writer, Tony Dacre,

> [s]he warmed to the simple beauty of the poem, and then her thoughts went back to Carey's Main. Carey's Main didn't read poetry. Some of the miners were well read in economics and history, but poetry would have seemed too grim a mockery in the mining towns. The young souls who might be thrilled by it had to keep this a dark secret like some fearful vice, unless they could stand endless chaff. . . . Carey's Main was up against life in the raw. (249)

It is significant that the stories Joan is eventually asked to write for the *Wednesday Weekly* are meant to capture this "raw," realistic vision, with a feminine twist (" 'Simple Stories from a Woman's Heart' "—"no propaganda, no moral, just the plain yarn," 258–259). What would seem to be another patronizing appropriation of working-class culture by this educated group is ultimately taken quite seriously in the narrative, a demonstration of their changed, sincere interest in the "simple" voice of the worker (though obviously transmuted through Joan, who appears both inside and outside that circle). Their editorial preferences finally encapsulate the novel's attitude as a whole toward working-class epistemology: the very instinctiveness and "plainness" of the Northern worker's perspective is valued over the more calculated and "propagandistic" efforts of the intellectual strata.

In some ways, then, *Clash* ironically outdoes *The Ragged Trousered Philanthropists* as a classic narrative of working-class resistance. While it suggests that Marxist theory mistakenly simplifies power relations and class "knowledge," the battle between false and true consciousness in the narrative itself is ultimately quite streamlined, easy to recognize and decipher. Joan's own fight to regain her class identity demonstrates its complications, of course, but the novel overall locates radical knowledge squarely in the rank-and-file arena. As in

Tressell's text, momentary acts of resistance are equated with compromise, recuperation, though here they are the ploys of intellectualism itself; they have no place in "average" working-class culture. *Clash* laments the leadership's 1926 sellout of the workers who were, the narrative suggests, willing to fight against all odds—they embody the "true" triumphant proletarian spirit. The novel champions the most traditional form of masculinized resistance—sheer tenacity and force—which increasingly becomes exemplified by Joan herself. At the same time, Wilkinson reveals her own persistent, if often masked, longings to escape that culture. As my forthcoming discussion of the text will argue, its intertwined cross-class romance plot permits a (suppressed) softening of Joan's masculine orientation and reaffirms the attractions of a "civilized" identity.

In Gibbon's trilogy, which traces the transformation of the Scottish peasant class into an industrialized proletariat, the challenge to the false versus true consciousness debate is inscribed in the titles to the individual volumes themselves: *Sunset Song, Cloud Howe, Grey Granite.* The female protagonist, Chris Guthrie, expresses similar skepticism toward formalized theories of class knowledge, though here they are subdivided more clearly between socialism, represented as the "clouds" of delusionary imagination, and Marxism, the hard "granite" of facts. The former approach is embodied by Chris's second husband, Robert, a dreamy socialist minister who lives a middle-class lifestyle and grows increasingly alienated from his congregation. Chris calls him the "Hunter of Clouds" (301), of ideals that "darken men's minds—loyalty and fealty, patriotism, love, the mumbling chants of the dead old gods that once were worshipped in the circles of stones, christianity, socialism, nationalism—all—Clouds that swept through the Howe of the world, with men that took them for gods" (300). She appreciates the intentions of his plan for change, but considers it too abstract and visionary. However, she also disapproves of her son Ewan's equally limited Marxist path. The anthropological knowledge of his people that he sought as a child when he studied flints (and the history of their makers) is, in the adult, transformed into a consuming passion to gain a "scientific" understanding of class conflict. His "specimens" of Bronze Age stones, fastidiously "labelled" and "catalogued," (284) are later replaced by (Owen-like) rigid diagrams illustrating class difference. Chris chides him in his youth, "Oh Ewan, you're hard and cool as—grey granite! When you too grow up you'll find facts over much—you'll need something to follow that's far from the facts" (283). Her warning indeed predicts his demise, set in motion by his lack of imagination and flexibility.

Throughout the string of narratives, Chris strives to grasp and name an alternate vision reflecting her own peasant orientation: "The men of the earth that had been, that she'd known, who kept to the earth and their eyes upon it—the hunters of the clouds that were such as was Robert: how much was each wrong and how much each right, and was there maybe a third way to Life, unguessed, unhailed, never dreamed of yet?" (301) "[W]as there," she later asks herself, "nothing between the Clouds and the Howe?" (332) The trilogy fails to resolve her question. For it is suggested that her different, instinctive, consciousness both is and is not enough. Chris's "sunset song" is appropriately named, alluding to the obsolescence of her social positioning (and accompanying epistemology). But since she is also a gendered figure in the narrative representing an arguably feminized version of class knowledge, we must again turn to the novel's romance plotting to understand Gibbon's overall conceptualization of class agency. The trilogy is in fact structured around Chris's relationships with men; and as I will suggest in chapter 4, its unusual focus on the private sphere enacts an exhilarating departure from the proletarian novel formula with intriguing, if problematic, implications for both male and female working-class writers.

As the above readings demonstrate, a "master narrative" or "formula" of working-class resistance in some senses always remains a construct, never fully realizable within working-class texts. Be it Tressell and Greenwood's revolution in ideology, or Heslop and Wilkinson's professed allegiance to rank-and-file activism, the desire to record class rage and depict class dignity (in their many forms) creates a narrative that perhaps inevitably buckles under its own weight. *The Ragged Trousered Philanthropists* begins by plotting shame and pride as opposite conditions or types of class consciousness because it seeks to represent working-class solidarity as an active choice, a recognition of one's (collective) worth in defiance of an exploitative dominant order. But as with the later works, it is ultimately incapable of preventing their convergence. Though it attempts to structure the two so that they result in a "positive" resolution (the valorization, and eventual triumph, of socialism), their intermingling cannot be suppressed. Shame emerges in these texts as *another kind* of defiance that rages against the dehumanizing dimensions of working-class culture. As the next two chapters will illustrate, the privileging of rigid categories and epistemological boundaries eventually evidenced by all the novels (with the possible exception of *A Scots Quair*) is ultimately a manifestation of both the "master" model of authentic consciousness, which seeks to fix the contours of radical class knowledge, and an alternate mode of resistance, which expresses a (seemingly) "narrow plot" of dominant desires and escape routes. Though they appear to accomplish contradictory ends, both convey a desire for difference within class and across gender lines to demarcate "self"-controlled spaces.

CHAPTER 3

On the "Borderland of Tears": Reputation, Exposure,
and the Public/Private Dynamic
of Working-Class Culture

■

She cried, because tears are cheap; and then she stopped, and got by, because no
one gives you anything in this world. What was given to her, passed on to all of
us, was a powerful and terrible endurance, the self-destructive defiance of those
doing the best they can with what life hands out to them.—Carolyn Steedman,
Landscape for a Good Woman

From *The Ragged Trousered Philanthropists* to *A Scots Quair*, the "difference" of working-class texts can be located in their challenging
representations of reality. Novelists such as Robert Tressell, Ellen
Wilkinson, and Lewis Grassic Gibbon make affirmative use of their
marginality, rewriting versions of history and conflict to insist upon
their own integrity. But as I suggested in chapter 2, difference is both
an effect and preoccupation of this literature. Its claims of authenticity, realism, and demystification set in motion a dialectic of "exposure" which reveals not only the fabrications of the master class but
the shameful dimensions of working-class cultural and material life.

Here, I want to examine that dialectic more closely, in effect charting the development of class shame over a forty-year span of time
within the study's chosen set of narratives. My readings are framed
by the public/private compound of relations that developed with
particular urgency in working-class communities from the 1890s
through the 1930s due to the logistics surrounding social, domestic, and leisure practices. The chapter begins, then, by studying the
dynamic surrounding public and private space in working-class culture generally, focusing on its increasing concern with reputation.
Part 1 ends with a brief look at public and private discourses as they

appear in the narratives to aid in the construction of public and private selves. In Parts 2 and 3, I turn to a series of scenes and themes found in a number of late nineteenth and twentieth-century texts revolving around the literal or figurative exposure of working-class identity. Informed by the sense of vulgarity or unworthiness which working-class characters strive to conceal from each other, the scenes ultimately convey the desire to establish *intra*-class "difference" or division. Beginning with Arthur Morrison's *A Child of the Jago* (1896) and ending with Walter Brierley's *Means-Test Man* (1935), they construct an alternate history of modern working-class narrative.

I. Reputation and Working-Class Cultural Space

As we know, it has usually been in the best interests of dominant culture to mystify the nexus between private and public spheres. Creating an illusory, neat division between the two, it conceals the classed and gendered power relations underlying (and benefitting from) their ostensible separation. But while the working-class writers I study often make it part of their demystification project to expose and explore the connections between social and domestic worlds, they also betray their own fascination with the myth. In fact, this literature reflects a strong desire to *separate* the public and the private, at a time when their actual conflation was especially visible —and painful—in working-class lives. The convergence of domestic and social arenas reinforced an emphasis on communal experience and values, but at the same time placed a high premium on private space—both material and psychological.

Within working-class culture, the attempt to invent a public/private construct can thus mean much more than simply succumbing to dominant cultural directives. Permitting control over class borders, that construct protects against exposure of a stigmatized class identity, meeting a very real need to seal off from view one's own lived, seemingly "dirty," working-class experience. Even as they often understand the distorting practices of capitalist ideology that are responsible for their shame, these writers seek seemingly self-created and self-contained parameters in order to flee their association with an "outlaw" or alien culture, as well as to protect themselves from violation (of all sorts). But perhaps most importantly, the alternately public and private selves that are desired or actually produced are also notably gendered. The subtextual agenda of this writing necessitates, in the words of *Love on the Dole*'s socialist, "becoming Men and Women in the fullest sense of those terms."

An array of cultural historians has attempted to grapple with the public/private dynamic as it pressed on working-class culture between the turn of the century and 1945. The blurring of boundaries between home, community, and work place was accomplished through a variety of means: the frequent sharing of actual household living space between neighborhood families; women working both within and outside the home (though much more erratically after marriage); and the more global implementation of the "welfare state," whose official representatives literally and symbolically crossed the line dividing individual households from public territory.

In theory, state assistance challenged bourgeois precepts of self-improvement, recognizing inequities structured into the class system itself. But in practice, it more often than not succeeded in antagonizing those "lacking" in self-sufficiency. The government's agents were perceived as but another manifestation of state power seeking to exercise control through the offering of aid. And certainly, the founding pieces of welfare reform centering on health care introduced during the 1906 to 1911 Liberal government originated in twin concerns over Britain's "declining" imperialistic prowess and economic superiority: alarm over the unfit state of soldiers during the Boer War (and soon World War I) and of an increasingly beleaguered work force led to legislation which would restore the commonwealth's competitive edge.[1]

The Family Wage

Working-class women were at the forefront of opposition to state assistance at this time, and generally supported a separation of private and public spheres. That stance should not in the least discount their participation in struggles for social reform and governmental responsibility which sought to gain power for women within the public sphere, such as the suffrage battle and the Women's Cooperative Guild's Maternity Campaign.[2] But women in working-class commu-

nities were, as a rule, wary of such struggles. Their work on behalf of
a fundamentally conservative social structure has posed a challenge
for feminist scholars, who have been prompted to investigate the
oppositional possibilities that underlie such seemingly reactionary
interests.

Studies of the family wage are representative of such work and
critical to my overall project, since they attempt to fathom working-
class women's compliance with a specific dominant cultural institution. The family wage's male breadwinner model was both bourgeois
and patriarchal, investing working-class men with at least a modicum
of economic and ideological power and subordinating working-class
women through the subsequent division of labor.[3] As might be expected, it was encouraged by state officials (along with independent
philanthropists) as they began to institute reform in working-class
areas. As Jane Lewis notes, "A breadwinning husband and dependent
wife and children were . . . believed to secure male work incentives
and hence national stability" ("Working-Class Wife" 100), renewing
in turn a "strong ideology of maternalism" in the early twentieth
century (*Women in England* 32).

Distilled into the notion of a "family wage," however, this model
became a "shared ideal" among women and men in both the working
and middle classes (Lewis, "Working-Class Wife" 103). It was endorsed most vociferously by the trade union movement, whose male
members resented competition from women workers and looked
forward to benefitting from their absence.[4] Yet the idea of an expanded, "living" wage won support from other quarters as well.
It was considered one method of maximizing and protecting the
family's interests, increasing the man's potential to provide material
sustenance and the woman's potential to provide moral guidance to
their children by keeping watch over the home.[5] It was also seen as
a way to ease women's "double burden," limiting their labor to the
domestic arena. According to Lewis, few women looked forward to
additional grueling work outside the home, and those who did paid
work typically insisted on receiving a "woman's," rather than "man's,"
rate ("Working-Class Wife" 105). It should be acknowledged that the
working-class women's groups cited as family wage supporters, such
as the Women's Cooperative Guild and Women's Labour League,

were among the more affluent within the culture—both claimed to represent the "thrifty" and "respectable" segment of the working class. And as Caroline Rowan's research on the family wage suggests, concensus within those groups was not easily won.[6] But the Women's Trade Union League, which did speak to the needs and interests of the average working-class woman worker, approved of the "withdrawal" of women's labor to foster child welfare ("Working-Class Wife" 105). It thus seems safe to say that the family wage enjoyed general support within working-class communities.

Though it rarely materialized into an actual practice for most working-class families, the family wage ironically promised freedom from state intervention even as it imposed a middle-class domestic arrangement and regulated the distribution of funds. A stable, sufficient income could ensure against the need for government assistance, which many working-class women found intolerable. The Mother's Defence League, for instance, was organized in the 1920s to protest state intervention by a host of "visitors" inspecting the fitness of their home and children. Lewis points out that welfare programs such as the 1906 and 1914 Provision of Meals Acts were perceived as an insult to the husband's masculinity (or a threat to his obligation as provider), as well as to the woman's maternal and domestic capabilities (*Women in England* 39).

London settlement worker Anna Martin's report on the "Married Working Woman" offers vivid documentation of such objections. Martin's study, published in 1911 by the National Union of Women's Suffrage Societies, seeks to provide a "truer view" of this "voiceless and voteless class" (5, 4) by showing that the working mother is anything but a "creature of limited intelligence and capacity" (3). In a much-quoted passage that refutes theories of working-class female passivity, Martin explains why the subjects of her study rejected free school meals for their children. They were not only sensitive to their husband's pride, resisting "anything which weakens the link between the breadwinner and his home," they were well aware of their own:

> The women have a vague dread of being superseded and dethroned. Each of them knows perfectly well that the strength of her position in the home lies in the physical dependence of hus-

band and children upon her, and she is suspicious of anything that would tend to undermine this. The feeling that she is the indispensable centre of her small world is, indeed, the joy and consolation of her life. (30)

According to Martin, state assistance posed a "perpetual struggle between their consciences and their pockets" (31). Resolution of that struggle on the side of "conscience" reflected a "nobler" value system, rejecting those bourgeois "maxims" which encouraged "giving . . . over to a sordid materialism" (24). The family wage appeared to free women from such moral dilemmas by having the money earned "rightfully."

Gossip and Working-Class Respectability

The pride that informed working-class women's resistance to state relief is easy enough to discern in passages like the one above. But its complexity should not be overlooked. Reputation was a prime concern in working-class culture, across regions and borders, and proved burdensome, as well as empowering. In the converging public and private spheres of individual neighborhoods, the need to represent one's self and family as decent, self-sufficient members of the community derived as much from other working-class spectators as from condescending middle-class investigators. Ellen Ross's work on women's neighborhood sharing networks in pre–World War I London argues that reputation functioned as one of many communal strategies that, as examined earlier, facilitated both class and gender resistance against the state. "Neighbours shared hallways, sculleries, and toilets, and might have to walk through each others' rooms routinely to reach the shared facilities," she writes; "Collingwood Place . . . had only one pump and tub for 23 households. . . . On Diss Street near Hackney Road, ten families shared a single toilet" (10). While creating difficult living conditions, this "public character of domestic life" subsequently fostered, Ross surmises, a positive "sharing" and "intimacy" between members of families (9).

It also contributed to an obsession with respectability. Ross notes that women were chiefly responsible for both the family and the neighborhood's status: "Wives' dress, their sexual, drinking, and socializing habits, their housekeeping and supervision of children —all contributed to the establishment of their family's (and often their street's) reputation on the continuum between 'tough' and 'respectable'" (4–5). And that reputation was maintained or destroyed through the primary form of female discourse to emerge from this overlapping of public and private space—gossip. Gossip became the central currency of the culture's communal economy, "the channel through which flowed the goods and help neighbours needed from one another" (10) to maintain honor, as well as survival. Circulated information included details about rent collectors, child rearing, and money management, which allowed neighborhoods to circumvent, and often retaliate against, the welfare apparatus and in the process to maintain their integrity.

Yet gossip could be as treacherous as it was comforting. In order to establish the grounds of a "good" reputation, contrast was frequently necessary—another's status had to be diminished. Ross provides the example of local women moneylenders who exploited gossip as a way to "threaten their debtors with public exposure" (10), but essentially all neighborhood inhabitants feared exposure of their private lack, their cultural "debts." Local talk took on a policing function, regulating conformity to certain expectations which safeguarded the community's reputation. Those who carried on illicit activities and relationships, those who could not keep up with their neighborhood's exacting housekeeping standards (which stressed exterior rather than interior cleanliness), those who could only afford pauper burials, were shunned, their decline useful to the rest wishing to demonstrate their own respectability (Ross 10, 14). (Robert Roberts's reference to a self-devised working-class "caste system" is not far off the mark.)

The Women's Cooperative Guild volume *Working Women and Divorce* (1911) underscores the tensions surrounding gossip and reputation. Gathering testimony by guild members on their attitudes toward marriage and divorce laws, the report relays a sense of helplessness and isolation among the respondents: the "Dread of Publicity" merits an entire section, documenting the stigma attached not only to divorced women in general, but to the (presumably) degenerate character of the husband which typically incited the divorce or separation in the first place. One woman writes, "A mother feels it a duty to suffer and bear unkindness in silence for her children's sake. She will suffer much to prevent the finger of scorn being pointed at her children, or that they should have the knowledge of a drunken and brutal father" (40). Another, discussing her reasons for remaining with an abusive spouse, states emphatically, "I *could not* wash our dirty linen in public" (69). It is no wonder that women frequently quarreled over the very boundaries they shared. Although Ross concedes disputes over literal household dividing lines, such as fences, walls, and porches (15), other kinds of borders were also delineated and protected in the attempt to preserve one's inviolability. The need to construct an appropriate public self could thus function as both help and hazard in day-to-day existence, depending on one's ability to participate in establishing the basis of value, to meet the designated standards, or to perform as if one did.

Female Virtue, Menstruation, and "Dirt"

Elizabeth Roberts's collection of women's oral histories records a similar working-class obsession with respectability but recasts it in distinctly gendered terms. Recalling their childhood years in the earlier part of the century, her respondents return again and again to the demand for decency within their working-class homes. They corroborate the presence of a neighborhood "street standard" enforcing understood rules of behavior and ethics largely through gossip (192–193). (Roberts concludes, "getting a bad, or indeed a good, name mattered immensely to most working-class people.") The collection provides numerous examples of women who found this neighborhood "network" alienating, rather than uplifting, suggesting that it promoted the desire for privacy instead of developing "community" (195–197). The pawn shop, one of the most visible points of intersection between home and neighborhood, is recalled as a particularly shameful place, where one's private deficiencies or problems were exposed to public view (149).

Their memories are dominated, however, by their families' preoccupation with sexual decency. While the fear of sexual "dirtiness" was inculcated in male and female children alike, the concern with female reputation surpassed all others. Working-class girls' virginity seemed continually imperiled and thus in need of constant verification and display. The status of menstruation in working-class communities is in this sense especially important and revealing: although gender *and* class purity would seem to be substantiated by the "evidence" of menstrual blood—that is, non-pregnancy—Roberts's interviewees also suggest that its stain paradoxically signified (the arrival of) sexuality and, hence, finally signified potential class impurity, class defilement. Their discussion registers the existence of an inner/outer, private/public split within conceptualizations of the self, as well as a simultaneous recognition and denial of sexual identity.

A secret, "shameful" (and natural) condition with a nevertheless terrifying potential for visible marking, menstruation carried enormous symbolic significance, a metaphor for working-class culture in itself. As with other sexual matters, working-class girls received little, if any, practical information about this new "event." The silence surrounding sexual intercourse, birth control, and pregnancy significantly extended to the onset of their menstrual period. Though outer cleanliness (hands, neck, face) was insisted upon at all times, there was a striking absence of hygiene surrounding "internal" soiling. Roberts notes that working-class women failed to use sanitary napkins until well after World War II despite their availability for nearly four decades, typically relying on what was a precarious form of protection at best—dark underclothing. The women's recollections subsequently convey a pervasive fear of staining. One observes, "the point was that when you started to menstruate you were just given a pair of navy blue knickers so that it didn't show through" (to be changed once a week!); another "simply hoped her several layers of petticoats and skirts would both absorb the flow and hide it from the outside world" (18). The dual emphases on visible cleanliness and female honor in working-class culture would seem to warrant taking excessive precautions in preventing this type of "dirt" from soaking through. Instead, mothers and daughters refused to acknowledge its existence; only their persistent anxiety about public exposure betrays its reality.

Here, the intersections between the public/private set of relations and the workings of reputation are at their most dense but also their most fruitful in demonstrating the connections—and conflicts—between class shame, class respectability, and gender. Mary Douglas's study *Purity and Danger* reminds us that dirt is typically equated with "disorder," chaos (2). As this chapter and the next will document, working-class male writers often attempted to recuperate such an equation in their narratives of resistance by explicitly associating "dirtiness" with working-class difference and working-class power. But it is a distinctly masculine "stain," achieved through a certain kind of physical labor. Working-class girls and women have no comparable permission to flaunt their class markings. Though middle and upper class men could choose to eroticize the actual dirtiness which also characterized much female working-class labor—Arthur Munby's obsession with domestic servant Hannah Cullwick in the mid-Victorian era is perhaps the most spectacular recorded example[7] —their sexual interest only confirmed the shamefulness of that condition. Dirt and sexuality become conflated, negating the working-class female's femininity. She thus has no recourse but to yearn for a mode of subjectivity which represents a splitting of her self, which allows her to divide her sexual identity along physical and metaphysical lines.

Menstruation ironically encapsulates this dynamic. Douglas's observation that bodily margins and their fluids are often invested with "power" and "danger," as they threaten to "pollute" the culture at large (121), certainly rings true in Roberts's respondents' memories, as well as in the fictional texts themselves. But rather than indicating a concern "to protect the political and cultural unity of a minority group," as she argues about certain body rituals of East Indian caste systems (124), the anxiety surrounding this landmark female rite of passage in British working-class culture points instead to the need for margins or boundaries which distinguish members of the group from each other. The working-class female body represents both the key and barrier to feminine virtue and, hence, to dominant cultural subjectivity.

As the above historians admit, the desire to split the public and the private is ultimately rooted in the desire to claim a distinctly bourgeois ideal/ideology built upon equally distinct gender codes. The male breadwinner model proposed to provide much more than material self-sufficiency and the possibility of better household management; it promised both women and men the status accorded to those having an "Angel in the House." By the turn of the century, wives of the more skilled workers exited the labor market as a sign of the family's respectability, and male trade unionists of all levels, as hinted earlier, began to insist that *their* women's place was also in the home. Unlike women of higher classes, working-class women had a bit more autonomy in that sphere because they typically managed the entire household income; the husband handed over his pay to his wife, who bore complete responsibility for devising a budget and making it suffice. Nevertheless, women lost a considerable degree of freedom when abandoning paid labor. Michele Barrett has been an especially ardent and eloquent critic of the family wage, indicting the labor movement's support by delineating its costs not only for women but for the working classes as a whole.[8]

But, as their testimony and writings demonstrate, working-class women clearly sought to experience the privileges of such a foreign position. Elizabeth Roberts's respondents explicitly balance their pride in a strong work ethic with a wistful envy of those who were able to emulate "ladies of leisure" (52; 137). In Roberts's view, "[t]heir emancipation lay, in their estimation, in the move *away* from work and into the home" (137). In a similar vein, much to the objection of middle-class feminists in this period, working-class women vocalized demands for a front parlor in their homes, defending "their right to a room which expressed their pride in housewifery and which also afforded additional privacy" (*Women in England* 29). As noted earlier, they were equally anxious to prove their viability or worth as mothers as social policy increasingly targeted working-class children's welfare. While they were hardly oblivious to their predicament *as* women, they also sought to convince themselves that they *were* women by writing themselves into a middle-class feminine script.[9] As late twentieth-century feminist scholars exhaustively study that "text" in its ideological and narrative forms, they must acknowledge its desirability, particularly to those it excludes; and they must continue to guard against romanticizing the public sphere, as either the site of emancipation for (largely bourgeois, domesticated) women or of working-class "community."[10]

Working-Class Discourse

While discussing the multiple coping strategies devised by London's working women, Anna Martin makes the following, rather startling, observation: "The English lower classes have so little power of expression, and so often use what language they possess to conceal their thoughts" (29). It is a key perception, though tinged with condescension and susceptible to misinterpretation. The invention and maintenance of a public discourse in working-class communities does, in fact, serve a central protective or masking function, but makes it a powerful form of expression indeed, allowing the working-class speaker the opportunity to conceal, as well as reveal, class meanings. As this study argues, the novels themselves represent one such form of discourse, allowing the writers to shape individual selves in the public arena together with a self-conscious, often excessive, display of their working-class identity. Within the narratives they construct, representations of public and private discourses appear as further emblems of (and tools to enact) the desire to split or fashion distinct worlds, distinct spheres.

The point is important to make, given the myth of an authentic and transparent working-class language which gained increasing validity in these years. That myth relies on well-known, earlier statements such as Wordsworth's preface to *Lyrical Ballads* (1800), which glorifies "common" peasant speech as "true" poetic language capturing the "passions of the heart."[11] It reappears mid-century in Victorian industrial fiction's sympathetic portrayals of the working class: most notably in Elizabeth Gaskell's novels, working-class discourse is frequently valued as a concrete, genuine, transparent language to be contrasted with the duplicitous, fragmented, double-voiced discourse of the bourgeoisie. And as established in my earlier discussion of working-class literary manifestos from the 1920s and 1930s, pride in a separate, uncontaminated, expressive language of class revolt becomes one staple of modern proletarian literary theory. Alec Brown of *Left Review* summed up the view of many in his proclamation, "WRITTEN ENGLISH BEGINS WITH US" (1:3 [Dec. 1934]: 77). Another *Left Review* contributor, lamenting the often stale and convoluted speech of contemporary intellectual radicals, looks back to the "dawning-days of the working-class movement" in the mid-nineteenth century for examples of "flint and steel English" (1 [Jan. 1935]: 130): "brief, clear, pungent . . . straightforward plain English" which "roused the tired worker, gripped him . . . pointed the way to action" (131–132).

As contemporary discourse theories have gained ascendancy, of course, challenges to the notion of a unified, transparent language (of any sort) have become imperative, heavily influencing the direction and development of class cultural studies. Two recent theoretical models of working-class discourse have special relevance to the texts under discussion. The first derives from Basil Bernstein's work during the mid-1960s to early 1970s on the production and reproduction of socio-linguistic codes. Working-class speakers, he contends, utilize language designated as "public" since its meanings generally lack individuation and specificity. Their linguistic form primarily produces general "social symbols" (of their class), relies on "idiomatic, traditional phrases," and tends to use passive, rather than active, voice (46–47). (He also charges that it is "illogical," lacking in causal relationships.) In "public language," meaning is implicit, derived from context rather than content, from nonverbal cues. As Bernstein states, "what is not said is equally and often more important than what is said" (47).

But from his perspective, the "not said" primarily involves individualistic, rather than communal, meanings. Over and over, Bernstein asserts that "*public* language is primarily a means of making *social* not *individual* qualifications" (46). This is "tough" language, incapable of expressing (through words themselves) intimate feelings (48). Its very structure prohibits the articulation of "experiences of difference" (48). By contrast, middle-class speakers have access to a "formal" language "rich in personal, individual qualifications" (28) and characterized by complex, causal connections. They have been trained from an early age to consider, and to speak, their individual needs and desires. The different structuring and values of working and middle-class cultures thus shape quite different modes of communication: rather than needing to extricate themselves from the hegemonic grip of a "master" discourse, working-class people in this model are closed off from it entirely.

Bernstein's formulations would seem to invert the pattern favored by champions of the univocal working-class language theory, even as he echoes their sentiments when extolling the virtues of public language as a medium of *class* meaning: he admits that working-class discourse "contains its own aesthetic," is "emotionally virile, pithy and powerful" and has a "metaphoric range of considerable force and appropriateness" (54). And, more important, he detects a strong "protective function" in such a discourse, shielding the speaker from individual "isolation" with the comforting buffer zone of communal identity. His theory is therefore useful in suggesting how, in the novels themselves, the fear of embracing an individual identity is masked by a public language of shared class meanings. Yet at the very least, he makes questionable assumptions about working-class (not to mention middle-class) culture: his analysis precludes the possibility that individuality could be desired, even as it is suppressed, by working-class speakers and that language could be used to *escape* class subjectivity.

Paul Willis and Philip Corrigan's more recent exploration of working-class cultural forms makes available a much more complicated model of discourse that can help locate the hidden and subversive dimensions of a multiplicitous working-class "language." Responding directly to the new set of assumptions and understandings drawn from semiotics and psychoanalysis, Willis and Corrigan depart from Bernstein's notion of two distinct class languages while also marking out a space for oppositional discursive gestures that "speak" working-class resistance. They accept the poststructuralist premise of a hegemonic discourse that "silences" those who inhabit the margins of dominant culture, yet argue the potential for agency among dominated subjects.[12] Rather than speaking a pure, unadulterated version of "a" working-class language, as in Bernstein's theory, the working classes manipulate the discourses of symbolic systems imposed and privileged by the dominant social order to express their own differing position. Isolated discourses, the authors argue, invariably submit to the authority of capitalist ideology—yet "through specific *intersec-tions,* forms of *reversal* and *combination,* they can generate . . . forms of knowledge which cannot be assimilated back into the dominant contents of any particular 'discourse' in its own right" ("Orders of Experience" 90). In Willis and Corrigan's schema, it is thus *classed* meanings which are produced *im*plicitly by working-class speakers: they engage in their own form of double-voiced or split discourse which simultaneously represses and articulates their rebellion. As with Bernstein, however, the final goal of the working-class subject is presumed to be preservation or protection of class identity. Strug-gling against the neutralization of alternate, potentially interrogative class positions in dominant symbolic systems, he or she searches for ways to register his or her own class-based refusal of hegemonic ideology.

The Willis and Corrigan model allows, then, for the continual me-diation of working-class "language" in a capitalist system, as well as for nascent forms of class consciousness that push through and con-front that system's representation of reality. While not intended for application to *written* discourse, it explains one goal and effect of modern proletarian fiction. As my reading of the hands' discourse in *The Ragged Trousered Philanthropists* demonstrated, it is a model that finds expression directly within, as well as through, the narratives constructed by working-class writers. Yet the novels' representations of discourse also occasionally appear as double-voiced language with a different purpose: to suppress, rather than affirm, class identity. In Tressell's text, though the status of class consciousness is seem-ingly bestowed only upon those who are characterized by a transpar-ent discourse—that is, Owen, not the hands—it is finally granted to those who have the additional, "civilized" capacity to compartmen-talize public and private forms of speaking. Owen is the sole figure to receive multi-dimensional representation in the narrative through an expansive, interior consciousness.

Walter Brierley's *Means-Test Man,* a 1930s depression novel, af-fords perhaps the most dramatic example of this alternative mode of double-voiced discourse. Jack and Jane Cook's style of commu-nication on the one hand resembles Bernstein's "public language," depending almost entirely on nonverbal signs, voice inflections, and context for its operation. Cliches and carefully guarded topics limit the range of verbalized expression and usually succeed in sealing it off from threatening intrusions. Conversation is nevertheless severely fragmented by the running private discourse each maintains. The two watch each other warily but allow themselves unmediated, unfiltered responses in their separate interior consciousnesses. As my later discussion of the novel will help to illustrate, however, their construction of a "public" form of discourse primarily aids them in clinging to the respectable position they believe they have lost through Jack's lay-off. In the face of their obvious material deprivation—and despite several explosive confrontations that erase the line dividing public and private discourses—the Cooks attempt to conceal their shameful lack and "low" status from each other, as well as from their neighbors.

In contrast, Ethel Carnie's *Miss Nobody* and Ellen Wilkinson's *Clash* demonstrate their debt to earlier middle-class social fiction in their representations of working and middle-class discourses: both use the public/private discursive distinction most emphatically to signify the alienation (and corruption) of dominant culture. The conflict between public discourse and private intentions or meanings is a constant feature of middle-class communication. But it also comes to overtake the narratives as a whole as they focus on their female protagonists' struggles with working-class identity. Carnie's Carrie Brown and Wilkinson's Joan Craig adopt an artificial discourse to construct public selves amenable to the middle-class communities they have occasion to join, yet their divided selves remain even after they make sporadic returns to their original working-class spheres. As with the depiction of Frank Owen, the splitting functions to distinguish their difference from other, "average" working-class women in the narrative. On surface, it eventually reads less as a damning bourgeois cultural sign within the plot than as a "universal" hallmark of literary modernity. Yet the mark of modernity is itself finally a protective strategy for the working-class writer: the modernist division of public and private discourses grants their texts legitimacy by creating multi-leveled, complex subjectivity for their characters. Like

James Welsh's plea for artistic autonomy in *Songs of a Miner,* they refuse their exclusion from dominant literary and cultural codes.

The relationship of such discourses to the plotting of public/private spheres in working-class narrative will be addressed in chapter 4. Here, I want to focus upon the specific scenarios and images of exposure they help to create. These latter, localized moments within the fiction are saturated with both the fear of violation and the pronouncement of self-worthlessness. The following sections track their presence, intensifying through the years, in a variety of works. As a modern master narrative of resistance develops, fewer and fewer legitimate outlets for shame can be found, and these increasingly become located in episodes, representations, and themes of revelation or actual exposure. One effect of the conditions governing working-class writing, they tell part of the other tale masked by the public discourse of class consciousness.

II. Exposé as (Self)Exposure in Late Victorian Working-Class Fiction

A Child of the Jago

If *The Ragged Trousered Philanthropists* operates as one kind of master text throughout working-class literary history, then Arthur Morrison's *A Child of the Jago* (1896) surely functions as another, though the term "phantom" text might be more appropriate. For while the former poses as a looming model of modern radical narrative, the latter betrays the specter of open shame "haunting" both writers and critics of working-class texts into the present. *A Child of the Jago* is widely recognized as a preeminent example of the 1890s "slum novel" and represents, as P. J. Keating notes, "a curious mixture of the English social-moralizing tradition and French naturalist objectivity" (*The Working Classes* 179). Of the two, however, its Zola-esque air is more prominent. Morrison's portrayals can scarcely be accused of the romanticism or sentimentality characteristic of much British social fiction. The novel's unflinching view of the Old Nichol ("Jago"), a marginalized area within the already marginalized East End of

London, introduced unforgettably sordid, frightening images of the British working class into public consciousness and refused to offer any relief from their implications.

Though he clearly drew on the work of George Gissing, Walter Besant, and especially Rudyard Kipling for literary depictions of East End life, Morrison is credited with creating a particular type of "realistic" working-class protagonist (rather than aristocrat in disguise) whose life and character are marked by violence (*The Working Classes* 168–171; 180–182).[13] And despite their reformist as well as documentary intent, his images popularized a stereotype of lower class irrationality and brutality many have found insulting and/or destructive. That might explain the critic's tendency (with the exception of Keating) to exclude Morrison's work entirely from discussion of working-class writing or to perceive him as simply another purveyor of the late nineteenth-century middle-class literary project. However, as a working-class writer who felt compelled to mask his class background (to the extent that he invented a fictional biography for himself when he began gaining public attention), Morrison is a most critical figure in the evolving proletarian literary project. His novel serves as an instructive "double" for twentieth-century working-class writing, its shame not muted but fully on display.

Morrison's management of his own working-class identity is fascinating, especially since his firsthand knowledge of East End life became an advantageous, as well as problematic, part of his public persona. Keating's "literary detective work" of the 1960s turned up several crucial biographical details which up to that point had been speculated but unconfirmed: he established that Morrison was born in the East End to working-class parents (his father was an engine-fitter) and was later employed as a low-level clerk for a charity that ran the People's Palace, an East End center for vocational and cultural education, before becoming a full-time journalist. Keating's discoveries conflict with Morrison's own claims of being born into a professional family in Kent and receiving a private, elite education ("Biographical Study" 9–11). But as Keating points out, Morrison was forced to modify his story when he was increasingly pressed to verify the authenticity of his fiction.[14] He eventually disclosed his association with the People's Palace (though he inflated the rank of his position), risking admission of this public identification in order to suppress his more private connection (12). He thus recognized that his class roots were to some degree inescapable, at once the measure and bane of his literary success.

Morrison's preface to the novel's third edition proves to be one revealing source of his embattled attitude toward working-class culture. His own form of deliberate resistance begins to come to light as he discusses his reasons for "repudiating altogether" the term "realism": "I decline the labels of the schoolmen and the sophisters: being a simple writer of tales, who takes whatever means lie to his hand to present life as he sees it; who insists on no process; and who refuses to be bound by any formula or prescription prepared by the cataloguers and the pigeon-holers of literature" (37). He cleverly notes the contradictory objections of the dominant literary press, whose complaints about the text—too didactic or too objective; too real or not real enough—ironically resemble those of contemporary Marxist critics when pinpointing "bourgeois" elements of working-class narratives (including on occasion this one) and of the *Left Review* writing competition reports. Claiming to shun all models and demands, Morrison follows a "realist" path of his own making which admits and denies evidence of authorial intervention. He writes, "A man with the courage of his own vision interprets what he sees in fresh terms, and gives to things a new reality and an immediate presence" (38). Yet at the same time, he pleads journalistic objectivity: "My tale is the tale of my characters, and I have learned better than to thrust myself and my emotions between them and my reader" (40–41).

In the end, however, Morrison's "documentation" of the East End depends upon intimate contact with its conditions and has an avowedly political purpose. He perceives his brand of realism as a "duty," not a "privilege," to inform society of "what it has created." Finessing the extent of his own connections, he announces,

> It was my fate to encounter a place in Shoreditch, where children were born and reared in circumstances which gave them no reasonable chance of living decent lives: where they were born fore-damned to a criminal or semi-criminal career. It was my experience to learn the ways of this place, to know its inhabi-

tants, to talk with them, eat, drink, and work with them. For the existence of this place, and for the evils it engendered, the community was, and is, responsible. (39)

The preface alone suggests that Morrison both desires and refuses to occupy a dominant cultural position. Establishing his own difference from the Jago "criminals" ("them"), he is free to express his concern that they be "seen" and understood. But he is subsequently free as well to unleash his hostility.

In attempting to introduce this alien class to a primarily middle-class audience, the entire narrative of *A Child of the Jago* functions simultaneously as exposé and (self)exposure. It focuses on the exploits and tragic end of young Dicky Perrott struggling to grow up in the Jago's criminal subculture and, as such, clearly engages in social criticism. In a *Daily News* interview, Morrison went so far as to deem the novel the "story of a boy, who, but for his environment, would have become a good citizen."[15] Yet the reader is presented with little evidence to support this prediction, since class subjectivity in the Jago appears grimly static and all too "natural." Admittedly, we see occasional glimpses of tenderness and inherent moral goodness which, if given the chance to flourish, would elevate the characters to a recognizably human level. But while it is established that the inhabitants of Morrison's criminal ghetto can rarely, if ever, outdistance the corrupting influence of their surroundings, they also "breed" their own savagery (and are indeed termed "rats" by the narrator). Morrison's susceptibility to the racist theory of hooliganism, popular in Britain during the late nineteenth century, undoubtedly informed the representation of his characters.[16] His belief that the London working-class community was divided into two actual races, the degenerate and the respectable, and his public support of the building of Penal Settlements to quarantine (and eventually exterminate) the former, reflects the extreme self-loathing and denial embedded within his consciousness.[17] Rather than channeling such shame into select scenes, it pervades his entire text.

The narrative thus operates as a kind of hothouse observatory, allowing us to glimpse the debasement and excess of this "underworld." It opens with a hellish panoramic view:

It was past the mid of a summer night in the Old Jago. The narrow street was all the blacker for the lurid sky; for there was a fire in a farther part of Shoreditch, and the welkin was an infernal coppery glare. Below, the hot, heavy air lay a rank oppression on the contorted forms of those who made for sleep on the pavement: and in it, and through it all, there rose from the foul earth and the grimed walls a close, mingled stink—the odour of the Jago. . . . A square of two hundred and fifty yards or less—that was all there was of the Jago. But in that square the human population swarmed in thousands. . . . What was too vile for Kate Street, Seven Dials, and Ratcliff Highway in its worst day, what was too useless, incapable and corrupt—all that teemed in the Old Jago. (45)

This aerial perspective soon zooms in for a close-up of Dicky's home:

A little heap of guttering grease, not long ago a candle end, stood and spread on the mantlepiece, and gave irregular light from its drooping wick. A thin-railed iron bedstead . . . stood against a wall, and on its murky coverings a half-dressed woman sat and neglected a baby that lay by her, grieving and wheezing. The woman had a long dolorous face, empty of expression and weak of mouth. (49)

The scene is at once particularized and emblematic, the area's squalor and spiritlessness brought further to light. Hannah Perrott's nearly catatonic state proves to be one symptom of Jago culture—surrender to its horrific conditions. But her "exposure" here is not contrived solely for the benefit of the voyeuristic middle-class reader (though that is certainly one effect). For Morrison emphasizes the absence of privacy in this site, its population continually on display to one another. With no respect for, or right to, property, there is little escape from the gaze (as well as noise and physical intrusion) of one's neighbors. The narrator notes, "Front doors were used merely as firewood in the Old Jago . . . If perchance one could have been found still on its hinges, it stood ever open and probably would not shut" (48). As his comment suggests, the Jago inhabitants are themselves partly responsible for this vulnerable—and uncivilized—state.

Rather than fostering community, such crowding and visibility produce antagonism. The countless scenes detailing intra-class violence, both spontaneous and arranged spectacles, are fantastically gruesome. The feuding Leary and Ram families and the High Mobsmen gang are only outdone by Sally Green, the Jago "Amazon." As Gill Davies has also argued (76), she embodies the most primitive characteristics of her class, posing a terrifying combative presence: "Down the middle of Old Jago Street came Sally Green: red-faced, stripped to the waist, dancing, hoarse and triumphant. Nail-scores wide as the finger striped her back, her face, and her throat, and she had a black eye; but in one great hand she dangled a long bunch of clotted hair, as she whooped defiance to the Jago" (64).

Physical violence is compounded by other forms of attack. Despite their obvious isolation from the "normal" middle-class culture of greater London, these Jago-ites reproduce its hidden rapaciousness. They practice their own stark, overtly criminalized brand of capitalist exploitation on each other, as well as on unfortunate outsiders lured into the Jago's borders. Theft is their "trade" and "industry." "Cosh carrying" proves to be one of the more lucrative activities, wherein women (prostitutes and wives alike) seduce respectable men to their home to be assaulted with a blunt object (the "cosh," wielded by the woman's "mate") and subsequently robbed. One household's stolen goods, however, become fair game for another as all make their way to shopkeeper Aaron Weech, the neighborhood racketeer. Weech emerges as a particularly insidious member of the Jago, the greatest emblem of its incorrigibility. He has some means of transforming the area yet subjects its most desperate and downtrodden to extortion. Dicky is only one of his many victims, drawn into increasing debt the more he succeeds in stealing. Weech's bourgeois philosophy—"each man out for himself"—is embraced to greater and lesser degrees by the Jago as a whole, filling the obvious void of class solidarity (except for the refusal to "nark" on one another to the police, which the reader is invited to perceive as a pathetic, rather than encouraging, sign of loyalty). Such mimicry of middle-class existence appears as both a deliberate and unintentional irony within the novel, commenting on the shortcomings of dominant culture yet conflicting with Morrison's other endorsements of that culture as a whole.

Even as the Jago "rats" operate with a survivalist, rather than communal, mentality, they insist upon conformity within their own sphere. Like the Mugsborough rank and file who distrust Frank Owen's alien intellectualism, they refuse to tolerate deviation from "their" system. All visible signs of difference are equated with arrogance. This global rule is illustrated and tested in many forms, ranging from the evident discrimination against Pigeony Poll, the "goodhearted" prostitute despised for her refusal to take on a cosh-carrier, to the mingled fear, admiration, and anger directed at Weech, whose very control of the Jago economy sets him apart and whose self-claimed superiority earns resentment. The greatest hostility, however, is aimed at those who either emphasize their formerly respectable class standing or who simply express a desire to escape the nightmarish Jago existence.[18] Both of Dicky's parents lay claim to "decent" working-class origins: his father was a plasterer before descending to his current criminal state, and his mother was born into an honorable East End neighborhood. Yet it is Hannah Perrott's continual boasting and complaining that singles her out for neighborhood scorn (and later, a particularly vicious attack by Sally Green). According to the narrator's sardonic explanation,

> she was no favourite in the neighborhood at any time. For one thing, her husband did not carry the cosh. Then she was an alien who had never entirely fallen into Jago ways; she had soon grown sluttish and dirty, but she was never drunk, she never quarreled, she did not gossip freely. Also her husband beat her but rarely, and then not with a chair or a poker. Justly irritated by such superiorities as these, the women of the Jago were ill-disposed to brook another: which was, that Hannah Perrott had been married in church. (66–67)

The text finally chides her, however, for having *succumbed* to the Jago's dissolute norm, a fall most evident in her lack of maternal qualities. Hannah's fleeting attempts to provide Dicky with moral standards appear lame at best ("'Dicky, Dicky! you mustn't say sich things!' was all the mother could find to say. . . . 'It's wicked an'—an' low,'" 50), and the death of her youngest child results largely from sheer neglect.

Only the similarly positioned Roper family solicits our genuine sympathy. As recent arrivals from a respectable working-class London neighborhood who make "exceeding use of soap and water," they still take notable pride in their appearance and home and are thus quickly driven out. Their refusal to be associated with this dominated culture becomes "a matter of scandalous arrogance, impudently subversive of Jago custom and precedent" (77) (and conveyed most dramatically by their efforts to shut their door). Significantly, the Ropers' resistance to their squalid surroundings is the sole form of revolt to be recognized and valorized by the novel. An alternative to the others' destructive rampages, their blatant efforts to imitate middle-class behavior are applauded. Morrison's text, then, highlights and validates what future working-class novelists will struggle to conceal or to problematize: the desire to escape membership in an undeniably "dirty," outcast class. The Ropers' longing for *intra*-class difference—asserting and creating boundaries—finally functions within the narrative itself as a sign of respectability, legitimizing them to a (certain kind of) working-class, as well as middle-class, audience. They make explicit Frank Owen's later, more covert, form of resistance.

The Reverend Henry Sturt's privileged presence in the narrative drives home Morrison's rejection of the Jago's alien culture. A scarcely concealed portrait of the Rev. A. Osborne Jay, vicar and self-appointed social reformer within the Old Nichol (and as hinted above, one of Morrison's greatest supporters), Sturt is the sole outsider to survive his excursion into Jago territory. Armed with a striking "self-possession" (91), Sturt lays claim to all that the subhuman criminal class lacks. His first interaction with the Jago population establishes his affiliations, power, and clear superiority: discovering the early stages of an attack on the Ropers, "he flung them back, commanded them, cowed them with his hard, intelligent eyes, like a tamer among beasts. 'Understand this, now,' he went on, with a sharp tap of his stick on the floor. 'This is a sort of thing I will not tolerate in my parish. . . . Go away, and try to be ashamed of yourselves'" (82).

The "rats" confer upon Sturt a mysterious value, unlike the contempt they, and the narrator, level at other middle-class interlopers who undertake their rescue (cf. Morrison's satiric sketch of the "East

End Elevation Mission and Pansophical Institute," hoping to treat the "Uninformed" and the "Hopeless Poor"). Their awe initially stems from his connections to dominant culture's more repressive institutions, such as its police force. Yet the novel stresses the strength of Sturt's inner, moral authority. Finally, the confrontation between the parson and his wayward parishioners throws into relief two conflicting class "knowledges" reminiscent of those in Tressell's text: conscientious consciousness vs. bestial blindness. But the terms are reversed. Unlike the house painters, the Jago-ites are defiantly *proud* of their difference and thus unable to perceive their debasement or understand/control the circumstances that produce it. Associated with a hopelessly distorted, mystifying vision, they possess a "mean cunning" that "saw a mystery and a terror where simple intelligence saw there was none" (83). In this earlier working-class narrative, the command to *adopt,* rather than resist, shame provides the pathway to authentic consciousness ("simple intelligence") and explicitly merges with the authorial voice.

Though claiming to function as a neutral report on London's slums, *A Child of the Jago* all too clearly bears innumerable marks of class humiliation. Morrison's underlying anger at Victorian complacency is superseded by his disgust at the depraved status of this Other-world. In his vision, the Jago population is ultimately victimized not by poverty or dominant ideology but by its own perverseness. The excessive foreignness of the picture only succeeds in laying bare his actual connections to East End life. Gill Davies is thus on the right track when he locates the most vicious, troubling representations of London's late nineteenth-century working class in texts by writers with working-class associations: not only Morrison, but Gissing (who could not claim working-class origins, but for a period of time lived in such districts). His analysis of this phenomenon, however, stops disappointingly short:

> Familiarity certainly breeds contempt, so far as Morrison is concerned. . . . His 'escape' from the class and locality into which he was born . . . —like Gissing's expulsion from his—seem to have exacerbated his fear and hostility. More 'secure' middle class ob-

servers, like Besant, Nevison and Kipling, can permit themselves greater sympathy and enthusiasm for the culture they describe (71–72).

As I have been arguing, Morrison clearly exhibits "fear," "hostility," and "contempt" in his writing. But it derives not so much from "familiarity"—which implies a simple snobbishness—as from a more complex, desiring shame. His indictment of the Jago-ites has as much to do with longings to achieve control over "self"-definition as with claims to superiority. Though Davies seems to equate "escape" with betrayal, Morrison's distancing shares the same source as Tressell's, whom Davies holds in esteem.[19] Only the surface message differs. And as I will now discuss, two other working-class writers of the 1890s, hailing from the North, had already begun taking a decidedly different approach to the representation of working-class culture. They overturned the very images that characterize Morrison's fiction and laid the groundwork for the modern master narrative of resistance.

Miss Grace of All Souls'

Like Morrison, William Tirebuck was born to a "humble" family (in Liverpool), of limited education, and employed in a variety of jobs before discovering journalism (Von Rosenberg 160). Yet his *Miss Grace of All Souls'*, published one year before Morrison's novel, has achieved an altogether different sort of status. A self-titled "Story of the Coalfield," *Miss Grace* has been called "the most important industrial novel to be published in England since *Hard Times . . .* and the most successful portrayal of industrial working-class life since *Mary Barton*" (Keating, *The Working Classes* 235), as well as "the first closely observed and sympathetic view of a mining community in English fiction" (Klaus, "The Strike Novel" 89–90). As Keating's accolade suggests, the novel has ties to earlier middle-class industrial fiction which extend beyond mere attention to class conflict: *Miss Grace* also divides its narrative time between bourgeois and working-class spheres in the northern village Beckerton-Beyond-Brow and links the two through a cross-class romance plot featuring Grace Waide, the vicar's daughter, and Sam Ockleshaw, a quasi-socialist coal miner. At the same time, as Ingrid Von Rosenberg has pointed out, the novel bears equal traces of French naturalism, a more contemporary influence which, as we have seen with Morrison, potentially poses another set of problems for the representation of working-class experience.[20]

Tirebuck, however, managed to produce a different sort of political narrative. While noting ideological divisions among generations of the Ockleshaw family—from the grandfather's passive resignation to the father's rash militancy to the son's reasoned demand for dignity—the novel promotes a lasting image of working-class solidarity. Its coverage of the 1893 "Great Lockout" in the Midlands appeals to the pride of workers themselves, as well as to the conscience of middle-class readers. In addition to its twin emphases on exploitation and impassioned collectivity, *Miss Grace* offers a portrait of the mining class that above all confirms its humanity. The resourcefulness, humor, sensitivity, and altruism of those condemned to live in Brookster's Yard contrasts with the hypocrisy, self-centeredness, and garish excess of the ruling class comfortably ensconced in Beckerton Old Hall. The point is underscored by Tirebuck's unusual manipulation of the romance plot: rather than elevating the working-class partner out of poverty and into another, safer class, or accomplishing a blissful "understanding" between two antagonistic classes, as is typical of the middle-class social novel, the love between Grace and Sam primarily signifies Grace's "conversion" to the miner's movement and eventually to working-class culture itself.

Admittedly, the "ubiquitous goodness" of working-class subjectivity in the text can be equally exasperating to critics. Von Rosenberg, for example, who is mostly concerned with charting structural parallels between *Miss Grace* and *Germinal,* objects to Tirebuck's lack of "realism" in portraying the mining community (and in connection, his lack of a rigorous socialist theoretical analysis) (166). As suggested above, however, most other readers hail the novel's progress in documenting class dignity and agency.[21] Gustav Klaus even locates one of the first examples of the proletarian "collective hero" in *Miss Grace,* calling its "active and resourceful, suffering and yet stubbornly resisting" working-class community the "real protagonist of the novel" ("Strike Novel" 90). And though Tirebuck's association with the ethical socialism of the early Independent Labour Party (ILP) has been cited as much by his detractors as his advocates, it at the very least speaks to his belief in working-class integrity. In an essay entitled "On the verge of change," one of many contributions to the 1894 ILP volume *The New Party,* Tirebuck writes, "Life depends upon Labour. That law alone elevates all necessary labour, however rough, however hard, above degradation. . . . If it is no degradation to walk through clean streets, it is no degradation to brush them" (as quoted in Klaus, 86). But while *Miss Grace* certainly reflects this vision, offering an inspiring alternative to Morrison's often hideous depiction of a "fallen" working class, it contains its own handful of provocative, disturbing images and plot contrivances that undermine its message of class pride.

For all her enchantment with the simplicity and sincerity of the Ockleshaws' existence—and correspondingly, her condemnation of the middle-class way of life—Grace Waide remains the ideal model of subjectivity in the text. She indeed embodies the "grace," refinement, and virtue of a once authentically civilized class. Unlike her father, who has compromised his Christian principles by throwing in his lot with the capitalists, she represents the last uncorrupted vestige of the Victorian bourgeoisie. We particularly admire Grace for having the good sense to reject her intended beau, the frivolous future mine owner Harry Brookster. It is significant, however, that she is attracted to, and eventually wins, the working-class character who is least alien to her own character. Though Sam himself believes that their class differences result in "humiliating comparisons" and thus resists Grace's modest overtures throughout most of the narrative, we are meant to understand that the two are of equal caliber. Sam is yet another version of the self-taught worker-intellectual whose penchant for books brings him as much Culture as socialist propaganda and hence distinguishes him from others living in Brookster's Yard. His "humiliation" is implicitly warranted for the rest of his brother miners, who seem somewhat comical in their simplicity. Although Sam continues to speak in a noticeable working-class dialect (the source of much of his anxiety), his relationship with Grace confirms the underlying difference of his discourse.

Grace's instinctive Christianity is another measure of her greater value in the narrative. Her "troth" to her "deeper, ever Urgent Spirit" parallels the miners' selflessness and charity, but appears as a privileged, sophisticated version, their ideal. In attempting to explain to Harry Brookster the reasons for her class defection, she herself articulates her true function in the novel: "I would be proud to be the means of lifting up one of that class—understand me—not to a better kind of work, however so-called humble or so-called mean, than to simply repeat the old, old kind of marriage with one's so-called superior, and fail to reach any justifying motive either in love or life" (320). Though Keating chooses to interpret her mission as nothing more than an innocuous desire "to inspire Sam to better things for both himself and his class" (*The Working Classes* 238), it signals, it seems to me, a lingering doubt about actual, autonomous working-class virtue. Sam does, after all, experience a literal "fall" through his mining accident—but it is finally a fall *to* (rather than from) "grace," inciting the first visits from the vicar's daughter. Even though she joins his class at the narrative's end, he is in fact elevated to her level through their relationship.

Class shame is most suggestively revealed, however, in those scenes that contrast Grace with working-class women. One early and minor juxtaposition involves Grace and Nance Ockleshaw, Sam's mother: Nance makes her entrance "looking as if she had been born on the shining thin spindles of a loom, and fed into pale sinews on cotton" (7), whereas Grace's "coiled yet loose full and flossy hair was of the shade of certain light marigolds; her face long, delicate, and thoughtful" (11). Nance's daughter Rachel is a much more central figure, positioned as Grace's double throughout the novel. Her romance with miner Britton Lloyd runs parallel to Grace's romance with Sam, but despite her own physical attractiveness and admirable pluckiness, she appears in several quasi-exposure episodes as a nearly monstrous figure.

The first scene occurs when Rachel secretly secures work at the mine to supplement the family's dwindling income (following Sam's accident). After supervising the running of coal trucks on a platform, she emerges from the mine not only exhausted but "dirty, dusty and miry" (100). The narrator attempts to invest this image with pride, stating "and yet she trudged homeward with that spiritual satisfaction of the conscience which labour, at times, even more than worship, seems to have the special prerogative to give." But that qualification is immediately undercut by Rachel's following attempt to *hide* her marks of filth when she arrives home. Though ostensibly performed to keep her employment a secret, the act of concealment equally connotes embarrassment, humiliation. That sense is furthered in subsequent comparisons with Grace and Dora Brookster (the brattish mine owner's daughter who, under Grace's guidance, becomes a mature woman). We discover that while Rachel is at the mine, the latter in their private spheres are simultaneously "working on elevated platforms," but of "thought," "longing"—"platforms on which the spiritual strife was severer in its tension than even the physical strife of Rachel with her trucks" (101–102). The juxtaposition, along with the scene itself, reduces Rachel to a primitive level, her "dirtiness" stamped on her very being. And the marking is accomplished in part by its nullification of any feminine attributes she might have possessed. When she crawls out of the pit, she merges with other masculine and blackened forms, devoid of "grace."

A later episode functions as a stunning companion scene to the one described above and engineers an actual confrontation between working and middle-class womanhood. After the lock-out, Rachel returns to the mine at night in a fury and reenacts her work routine in highly exaggerated movements; when Grace suddenly appears (after following in concern), Rachel turns on her in a fit of apparent madness. On one level, the scene merely works to reveal Rachel's buried class animosity towards Grace, whom she accuses of privilege and collusion. And to some extent, it prompts our sympathy. Yet Rachel's frightening transformation becomes the true focus—a hellion about to devour an undeserving victim. Here, the bestial, irrational dimensions of working-class subjectivity are exposed to middle-class and working-class "spectators"/readers alike, confirming each of their worst fears about the Otherness lurking beneath Rachel's familiar, human exterior. Though shaken, Grace's continued composure and forgiveness only accentuates the disparity between the two.

Rachel's resemblance in this instance to the Jago Amazon Sally Green is striking, underscoring Tirebuck and Morrison's shared anxieties about working-class women's lack, distortion, or perversion of femininity. Though equally concerned with the uncivilized dimensions of their male characters, both writers' desire for a class-coded "normalcy" is most sensationally articulated through the disturbing absence of a fixed gender identity within their proletarian female figures. *Miss Grace* may, as Keating has argued, offer a more celebratory vision of working-class culture by focusing upon an industrial, rather than "outcast," urban area (*The Working Classes* 238–239); but exposure scenes such as this create parallels with *A Child of the Jago* that undercut regional, structural, and ideological intra-class differences.

Lancashire Lasses and Lads

Lancashire Lasses and Lads (1896; 1906), written by Bolton mill worker-turned-journalist C. Allen Clarke, employs a similar strategy for negotiating elements of working-class shame. Clarke is one of the best known representatives of the late nineteenth-century "Lancashire School" of writing, which frequently married regional dialect with socialist convictions.[22] Both Jack Mitchell and P. M. Ashraf have identified *Lasses* as an especially noteworthy precursor to *The Ragged Trousered Philanthropists*, calling attention to the earlier novel's inherent modernity—its forward-looking conceptualization of class subjectivity. And indeed, overall parallels between the two texts certainly hold true.

Much more successfully than Tirebuck and much more akin to Tressell, Clarke attempts to offer a "realistic," expansive look at a particular working-class community (here comprising Lancashire textile workers) by spotlighting its stubborn passivity, as well as its awakening socialist consciousness. His characters do not appear quite as saintly as Tirebuck's, even if his text as a whole is arguably "marred" by other forms of "sentimentality" and "idealism."[23] Mitchell claims to find "signs of a new, more complex and more confident approach to contemporary working-class life" in the novel, invoking Ralph Fox's criteria for modern proletarian realism: "Here at last is that inexhaustible curiosity about the lives of ordinary working-class men *and* women that leads straight into Tressell" ("Tendencies" 64). Ashraf builds her case for comparisons between *Lasses* and *Philanthropists* by noting, "Clarke held up to scathing ridicule the vulgar capitalists who created the hideous stinking town and the workers who accepted it as unalterable" (161). Though the inhabitants of Spindleton are not plagued by the same degree of self-contempt displayed by the Mugsborough hands, they do exhibit signs of humiliation that appear equally regrettable, misguided, and debilitating. Additional points of comparison exist, however, which neither critic acknowledges. For by similarly importing into the narrative an enlightened outsider who attempts to stir the dominated class to rebellion—and by having that bearer of true consciousness be a bona fide member of the dominant class—*Lancashire Lasses and Lads* begins to disclose a similar counter story of class shame.[24]

Exposure functions as both theme and form on several levels in Clarke's novel and impels numerous, linked episodes of unmasking. The primary plot surrounds the public and private effects wrought by Dick Dickinson's entrance into the lives of the Spindleton weavers. The estranged son of a villainous mill owner, Dickinson at once attempts to conceal and erase his class identity by hiring on as a mechanic in the neighboring town and quickly merging into its working-class community. Outraged by the workers' living conditions, and both charmed and frustrated by the culture they have developed in response, he immediately implements short-term charity programs to bring material relief and plans long-term organizing/education measures to foster class consciousness. Dick is handsome, polite, and heroic and thus quickly welcomed, particularly by the Heyes family: he rescues the child Florrie from a mill fire and slowly develops a romantic attachment to her older sister, Hannah. His identity becomes increasingly imperiled, however, as the plot unfolds. Mr. Heyes contrives a bitter revenge plot to "expose" the evil character of Dick's father, who had stolen Heyes's patent for a spinning-mule when they were both young, and begins to question Dick's sudden appearance in Spindleton. Eventually, one of Mr. Dickinson's own thug-like accomplices sent to trail the son discovers his hiding place and reveals his family connections, cutting short his charade as an authentic member of the working class.

On one level, then, the model representative of working-class consciousness is exposed in the narrative itself as an imposter, with true roots in the ruling class. Clarke tries to minimize the damaging implications of this scenario by muddying the lines that divide classes: from the start, we are invited to allow Dick to claim authenticity since he actually becomes a worker, divorced from his father's class both materially and morally. He "is" working class because his allegiances and (current) experiential existence are located in that culture. The exposure also fails to have any lasting repercussions (if anything, it only accentuates his bravery). At the same time, his class identity is clearly a troubling issue for Clarke, who constructs Dick's subjectivity as a mystery in need of revelation/resolution, and who obviously puts stock in the accoutrements of Dick's different class upbringing despite the novel's pride in Lancashire weaving culture. As with Tirebuck, he fails to accept entirely the logic of his developing script, refusing to let that latter culture stand completely on its own as an awakened, and civilized, force of change. His hesitancy, I would argue, is rooted less in his devotion to historical accuracy than in his fascination with Culture.

This exposure plot is replicated as well (in more condensed form) in the narrative's treatment of Hannah. A sweetly beautiful and benevolent weaver, she attempts to conceal her once respectable family's increasing descent into degradation as they struggle to survive on her meager mill wages. Her younger sister Florrie is the emblem of her shame—a dangerously undernourished, overworked child who functions as "living"/dying proof of the Heyes's despair. The episode which introduces both female characters is a suggestive foreshadowing of future exposure scenes in working-class narratives: Dick meets the two on his initial journey into town, and when Florrie admits her "hunger" to the stranger, Hannah "turned round with a pained look at this exposure of the naked poverty of the family" (14). As in Dick's case, this unmasking is quickly deflated, since both female figures appear morally untainted by their revealed material deprivation. They typify the naturally unspoilt "soul" of the workers, to be celebrated rather than hidden in humiliation.

At the same time, like Dick, both are constructed as distinctly atypical representatives of their class community. Florrie emerges as a kind of pre-industrial muse, whose spirit lives on despite her untimely death: her entrance in the narrative is immediately preceded by the appearance of "mad" Harold Bennett, another factory owner's son and poet/philosopher, who is searching for "Her," "the soul of all the flowers, and the voices of all the birds, and the glory of all the trees,

killed by the big town" (10). (It is a measure of his own class blindness
that he fails to recognize the object of his quest in such a common
guise.) And as the paragon of femininity, Hannah poses an instructive contrast to other Spindleton women such as Mrs. Bobbin and
the factory operative Mary Ann. Comic and vulgar, they too are conscious of class status, yet their concern, by comparison, seems merely
amusing. Mary Ann in fact unwittingly reveals the buried class story
of the novel when she confides to Dick, "Wait till I wed a lord an'
then! What are yo' lowfin at, Mester Dickinson? . . . In aw th' factory
tales as I've read th' hero allus turns eawt to be a lord in disguise . . .
an' he faws in love wi' a weaver—never a cardreaum lass; but that
shall be altered, I swear . . . look at me, Mestur Dickinson! Arm't
I a full-blown heeroine?" (224) According to the class and gender
dictates of Clarke's subtextual scheme, the novel indeed demands a
heroine, rather than "heeroine." The narrator may even intervene
to praise Mary Ann's scrappy "independence," which affords her a
"valuable individuality and marketable equality with men" (226). Yet
much like the situation in *Miss Grace,* it is Hannah's form of difference
that guarantees her worthiness to wed this "factory tale's" princely
pauper.

For all its protestations to the contrary, *Lancashire Lasses and Lads*
testifies to the painfulness of revealing one's working-class identity.
The process proves to be nonthreatening only for those who actually have nothing to hide. Not surprisingly, a minor character in the
narrative dies from literal "exposure" to the winter cold, even as
Dick and Hannah emerge unscathed from theirs. An odd disruptive
episode devoted to a late-night storm and shipwreck further registers Clarke's ambivalence, drawing together the story's disparate
ideological strands. Commenting on the eerie moonlight during the
storm, the narrator deems the moon itself "a celestial Cinderella"
bearing "strange light that seems more for the human soul than the
body, the light whose splendour is not in exposing and revealing
like the sun, but rather in fantastically curtaining and half conceal-
ing" (180). While potentially working dark deeds here, the moon's
masking property is nevertheless appreciated, providing a mysterious kind of refuge and suggestively associated with the angelic figure
of Florrie—the "soul" rather than "body" of the working class who,

as it happens, has a particular fondness for the Cinderella tale. She promotes faith in her class's inherent value but a belief in fantasy as well, in the desirability of escape. Both the moon and Florrie demonstrate the powerful appeal of masquerade. But Hannah's living out of the Cinderella myth is the best demonstration of this novel's own camouflaging efforts. With all its favored working-class characters exhibiting a *coveted* difference—and its central couple living happily ever after as the new, compassionate heirs to the Dickinson factory—the text exposes its actual investment in the mystification of working-class reality.

III. Modern Variations

In Chapter 2, I began to explore the convoluted expressions/suppressions of shame in twentieth-century texts which have signified, but also further radicalized, "resistance" in the Tirebuck/Clarke tradition. Despite their warnings, these texts demonstrated that shame has the potential to be more than a purely self-defeating, immobilizing condition. My discussion of Tressell's novel provided one particularly noteworthy example of the way in which shame can serve as an actuating force of revolt: Frank Owen's longing for a "civilized" identity signaled an active refusal to wear the badge of Otherness. In this section, I intend to schematize such modern versions of shame by addressing more localized eruptions in Patrick MacGill's *The Rat-Pit* (1915), The Women's Cooperative Guild's *Life As We Have Known It* (1931), and Walter Greenwood's *Love on the Dole,* and concluding with a more in-depth look at Walter Brierley's *Means-Test Man* (1935). The gendered forms and effects of class shame that begin to appear in the preceding nineteenth-century texts are more prominent here (if less pervasive overall) in select exposure scenes featuring both women and men as protagonists or significant characters.

The Rat-Pit

Though shame typically has a more structural presence in narratives by working-class women themselves, a number of brief images/scenes/vignettes in male and female texts alike similarly register class humiliation in terms of lost femininity or virtue. MacGill's *Rat-Pit,* for instance, quickly associates Norah Ryan's impending shame as a fallen woman with her early, hidden horror at the ugliness and deprivation of poverty. The novel is a sequel of sorts to *Children of the Dead End* (1914), MacGill's more well-known "autobiography of an Irish navvy" (a manual and often itinerant laborer). Enlisting the same characters and many of the same episodes, it essentially retells the earlier narrative of young Irish worker Dermod Flynn, but this time from the perspective of the heroine figure, Norah. Both works foreground the navvy's sense of class pride and are thus cautious in their depictions of shame. The shift to a female point of view in the latter novel complicates matters further, though to some degree the gender distancing relaxes the narrative strictures.

A twelve-year old in turn-of-the-century Donegal, Norah is coded as an innocent girl destined for the nunnery: self-effacing and good-hearted, she appears ever willing to sacrifice her own well-being for the sake of her needy family. Early on she participates in a distinctly female "ritual," racing the "turn of the tide," which requires the crossing of a dangerous inlet in order to beg for yarn at a woolens factory. The event opens the novel and introduces not only Norah but her double in the narrative, Sheila Carroll the "beansho" or "whore." An unwed mother and outcast, Sheila joins the crowd of women who make the treacherous crossing to Greenanore, but she is forced to walk behind them and is particularly distinguished by her "exposed" vulgarity:

> The beansho stood a little apart from the throng. . . : She was bare-footed and did not even wear mairteens, and carried no brogues. . . . The wind constantly lifted her petticoat and exposed her bare legs above the knees. Some of the women sniggered on seeing this, but finally the beansho tightened her petticoat between her legs and thus held it firmly. 'That's the way, woman,' said the old crone who led the party. 'Hold your dress tight, tighter. Keep away from the beansho, Norah Ryan.' (18)

Yet moments later Norah and the others are placed in a similar position, imitating her behavior as they contend with the rising tide. Shoeless and bare-thighed (petticoats tied round the waist), "[t]hey hurried across shouting carelessly, gesticulating violently and laughing loudly. Yet every one of them, with the possible exception of the woman in front, was on the borderland of tears. If they had spoken not they would have wept" (19).

Anticipating the humiliation that awaits them as literal beggars at the factory, this "borderland" encompasses the conflicting directions of the modern proletarian novel: its inhabitants willingly, even defiantly, bare themselves, all the while experiencing pain—an intermingling of fatigue, embarrassment, and bafflement at their revealed lot. The scene's contradictory images of purification and shame further amplify the conflict, illustrating the simultaneous self-healing and self-degradation that marks this location within working-class culture. Though the women seek to preserve their own respectable "difference" from Sheila Carroll, they here recognize their kinship with the *un*desired. Norah's subsequent reaction confirms this fear of self-exposure:

> Norah Ryan, who was the last to enter the water, tucked up her dress and cast a frightening glance at those in front. No one observed her. She lifted the dress higher and entered the icy cold stream which chilled her to the bone. At each successive step the rising water pained her as a knife driven into the flesh might pain her. She raised her eyes and noticed a woman looking back; instantly Norah dropped her clothes and the hem of her petticoat became saturated with water. (19)

While the beansho afterwards interprets the wet cloth as a sign of purely feminine "modesty," Norah's anxiety about being seen by her female companions surely speaks to the shame directed toward her classed, as well as gendered, body. As in menstruation, which similarly represents both purity and defilement, the two become articulated together as an immoral, and seemingly inescapable, condition. Indeed, Norah's eventual fulfillment of that destiny confirms the inherent shamefulness of working-class experience despite, as I will suggest later, MacGill's earlier efforts to deny her class status altogether. Her emergence (and death) as a prostitute seems a fitting final role, the work she was "born" to perform.

Working-Class Women's Autobiography

For the amateur women writers who contributed autobiographical sketches to *Life As We Have Known It,* the tension between class and gender subjectivities, and between shame and pride, proves equally if not more pressing by the early 1930s. Their writing enacts another master narrative of working-class resistance that, as we saw with Ellen Wilkinson's *Clash,* appears even more tenacious and rigid in its demands. Nearly all the narratives share a common set of components: hurtful (as well as heartening) childhood memories that are quickly offset by the writer's family and class loyalty; emphasis on the additional restrictions and marginalizations that sexual difference produces within their class culture; and focus on public, rather than private, experience (where the Women's Cooperative Guild typically enters the story). Frequently invoked as the working-class woman's 'savior,' the guild plays a particularly pivotal role in these life stories. In the words of one writer, "From a shy, nervous woman, the Guild made me a fighter" (49). Guild director and volume editor Margaret Llewelyn Davies describes the entire project as follows: "Besides being primarily a record of individual experiences, the following Memories of Co-operative Women bring out the part that is played by the workers' own Movements in their everyday life. . . . Trade Unionism and Co-operation are woven into the very fabric of the workers' lives" (ix).

Davies accentuates the radical nature of the guild enterprise—and by extension, this particular publication—crying, "Co-operation is the beginning of a great revolution!" (ix) But while ostensibly representing authentic "memories" that pay tribute to the gendered class collectivity made possible by the guild, these often fragmentary texts also contain glimpses of defeat, isolation, and humiliation that cannot be resolved in simple class-conscious terms. Unlike their late Victorian counterparts who, as Julia Swindells has argued, constructed their autobiographical selves as romantic/literary heroines to lend themselves discursive legitimacy, the women here seem compelled to invent other strategies. Their anxieties surrounding femininity itself emerge elsewhere, within exposed vestiges of class shame.[25] Virginia Woolf's sense of a uni-dimensional "narrow plot" in this writing is thus highly ironic, applicable to the surface narrative of pride much more than to the suppressed narrative of "desire."

Mrs. Layton's "Memories of Seventy Years" is by far the most extensive and revealing piece in the collection. Her opening line, "I was born in Bethnal Green, April 9th, 1855, a tiny scrap of humanity" (1), establishes the conflicting sensibilities that surround her "self"-image, pronouncing and disclaiming her existence (and very human-ness). Layton's impulse to cast herself as a diminutive fragment of society is indicative of both her classed and gendered positions and finds outlets throughout her narrative. Interestingly, she accentuates her own *intra*-class difference early on by boasting of her father's middle-class attributes. "Always steady and industrious," he was a government employee in a "situation" whose literal "appearance," she takes pleasure in noting, "was quite out of keeping with the neighborhood we lived in, and when he and my eldest brother came home in the evening I do not think people quite knew what to make of them" (6).

Yet Layton fails to escape the stigma of the East End. Two adjacent scenes capture this nagging self-deprecation, the first a version of the previous "exposure" scenarios:

> I was rather a lazy little girl and not fond of washing myself. I am afraid I often went out in the morning without washing my face. One day when I was alone with my little brother in Victoria Park, a lady spoke to me and asked my age and if I went to school and a lot of other questions. She said I was a bright, intelligent little girl, and asked if I could read a few verses out of a nice Testament she had in her hand. . . . she said she was pleased I could read so nicely and advised me never to miss an opportunity of improving myself. Then she asked me if I had washed myself before I came out that morning. I felt so ashamed when I had to admit that I had not done so. (5)

To be sure, the "lady's" image of respectability is promptly interrogated in the subsequent scene, where the young protagonist searches for temporary domestic work. Turned away by all, she is asked by another ostensibly charitable "lady" to acknowledge her "hunger" and then offered something to eat; the "gift," however, turns out to be "some very dry pieces of bread and some crusts that looked as if they had been nibbled by mice" (9). Upper-class hypocrisy becomes the focal point of both episodes. But the underlying message—scraps for the "scrap of humanity"—remains a counter theme, a recurring apprehension. It materializes again in Layton's nearly obsessive desire for a pastoral existence—specifically, a "longing for clean ground" (15)—and in her professed unworthiness to receive the sacrament of confirmation. Her "dirtiness" is finally registered, however, in her sexualized self once she reaches adolescence. She admits that "at the age of eighteen I was considered a fine strapping young woman" and matter-of-factly notes the circle of men who showed interest. She also notes her sister's immediate anger at her "encouraging" of their attention ("said I ought to be ashamed of myself"). Layton dismisses this charge yet subsequently lists several instances of sexual harrassment that convey a sense of culpability as well as indignation. Though much more politically conscious than MacGill's Norah Ryan, her represented autobiographical self is equally preoccupied with the purity she can never achieve in the eyes of middle-class culture.

Love on the Dole

A critical scene in *Love on the Dole* begins to illustrate the somewhat different positioning of masculinity in these narratives. As seen earlier, Greenwood's novel focuses on the Hanky Park community's inability to articulate its fears, disappointments, and dissatisfactions, "each keeping his discontent in his own bosom as though it were a guilty secret; each putting on a mask of unconcern" (24). But the "guilty secret" extends beyond mere restlessness or disgruntlement. It includes the disgrace reflected in class powerlessness, in lack of control. This has a particular impact on the gender construction of working-class men, whose fixed class identity depends upon, but finally precludes, a fixed gender identity. For in its idealized form, working-class consciousness is equated with masculine symbols and power; yet in daily lived experience, that consciousness can be reduced to impotence or a defeated kind of brutality.

And such a dynamic is strikingly evident in the exposure scene that climaxes the novel's appropriately titled "Overalls" chapter. In that early portion of the narrative, Harry Hardcastle finds himself desperately seeking admission into the circle of adult male workers, admission which he believes is signified most immediately by a pair of overalls (rather than boyish knickers) and by visible streaks of facial grime. For Harry, dirt is a status symbol, rather than a stigma, an emblem of masculine class community. He hopes to attain this sign of distinction through his beginning apprenticeship at the engineering plant, but while he finally gets hold of the pants, he is denied access to the oily machinery that makes "dirtiness" possible. Much to his chagrin, Harry finds himself condemned to deskilled, feminized labor, akin to the pawnshop job he had just escaped.

He thus secretly applies the grease himself one day before walking home, only to be discovered by the Other representative of working-class culture in this narrative: not its idealized masculine valor, but its actual deviancy. Tom Hare, a "foul-mouthed, untidy boy" who "thought nothing of exposing himself in front of the boys" and was "obsessed with matters sexual" (51), sneeringly proceeds to "expose" Harry's charade to the rest of the men by exposing the hidden part of his body which is unmarked—void of grease—and hence seemingly class-*less*. In the process, however, the episode reveals Harry's working-class identity all too clearly:

> They all laughed and closed in on him. Sam Hardie's ape-like arms encompassed him. In a moment he was on his back, struggling impotently, and bawling hysterically. His cries were drowned in the roar of laughter that rose when rough hands tore at his trousers and exposed his nakedness. He screamed, struggled frantically. Somebody ran up with a pot of red paint, a brush and grease; anonymous hands daubed it on him wherever exposed. (52)

The men mock his desire to *be* authentically marked, yet Harry's "impotence" already serves as his true class sign, an altogether different sort of "stain" (and their real target). It becomes a gendered sign as well. Played out like a rape scene, the episode concludes:

> Harry, sobbing, covered his oily painted nakedness, drew on his overalls and retired to the lavatories to wipe away as much of the mess as he could. He felt that never again could he look

any of the apprentices in the face. What would they think of his girlish screaming? of his patched undershirt and ragged shirt lap? Then there was the knickerbockers! They now would know that he wore the abominable things underneath his overall. He shrank, inwardly. What an altogether humiliating episode. . . . This to happen when he wished to identify himself with the boys!

His "nakedness" here is clearly tantamount to his exposed "raggedness." It signifies a lack of respectability that encompasses both poverty and feminization within the social order. But the reader, unable to ignore the passage's own nearly "hysterical" reaction to the "filthiness" of working-class experience, interprets the significance of the attack scene differently than Harry, who afterwards proudly believes he has participated in a type of initiation ritual that ensures "'Y'll be one of us!'" (53) He will be, but to his misfortune. We see that the valorized form of working-class masculinity sought after in the novel *is* nothing more than an ideal or fiction. In the end, the majority of working-class men have no choice but to be Tom Hare.

Unlike Harry, then, the novel itself finally resists the privileging of identifiable working-class markers because they signify debasement, rather than fulfillment or "comradeship" (52). (That is why Larry is its "true" hero.) A later passage underscores this message, featuring an out-of-work Harry dressed in his once prized, now worn, overalls:

You fell into the habit of slouching, of putting your hands into your pockets and keeping them there; of glancing at people, furtively, ashamed of your secret, until you fancied that everybody eyed you with suspicion. You knew that your shabbiness betrayed you; it was apparent for all to see. You prayed for the winter evenings and the kindly darkness. Darkness, poverty's cloak. Breeches backside patched and re-patched; patches on knees, on elbows. Jesus! All bloody patches. Gor' blimey! (169)

Greenwood registers here a longing for the kind of concealment afforded by Clarke's moon in *Lancashire Lasses and Lads*—a "kindly darkness" that keeps shameful markers of difference mercifully hidden.

Means-Test Man

With the final entry of *Means-Test Man* into this discussion, the chapter comes full circle. In many ways, Brierley poses but another, modern version of the Morrison "dilemma" in the working-class literary canon: a writer who often sought to escape his class origins and whose work studies the demoralized, if not debased, spirit of working-class culture. Unlike Morrison, Brierley could claim a "respectable" working-class family background in the North and was more willing to announce the autobiographical basis of his later fiction. Yet his enthusiasm as a WEA, rather than Labour College, student and early disenchantment with life in the mining pit led him to place great value on traditional Culture and to experience continuous displacement as a worker/writer (reminiscent of Lawrence, another product of the Derbyshire coalfields). Early stories, poems, and novels reflected the influence of dominant literary models and for the most part went unnoticed. In fact, Brierley submitted a most "literary," pastoral essay to a 1930 National Miners' Welfare Scholarship competition and lost to the other local contestant, whose essay played up his Nottingham "slum background." His break into the professional literary arena came with recognition from the novelist John Hampson, who responded to Brierley's autobiographical contributions to the locally published series "Memoirs of the Unemployed."[26] Thus Brierley also finally gained notoriety by writing about, rather than around, his class experiences, and by delivering another "realistic," somber portrait.

Though the depiction of working-class culture and consciousness in *Means-Test Man* is far less sensationalized and much more sympathetic than that in *A Child of the Jago,* the novels' reputations have suffered a somewhat similar fate among past and present Left critics. Indeed, *Means-Test Man*'s cool reception by the contemporary radical press verifies the increasing presence and power of an oppositional master narrative by the mid-1930s. The novel's immediate and dramatic commercial success was attributed to its nonthreatening message and decidedly bourgeois literary trappings. (It came to acquire status as an updated "Condition of England" report, seen as required reading for all members of Parliament.) As Andy Croft has established, its nontendentious form and fatalistic theme brought praise from mainstream reviewers of the *Economist* and the *Times Literary Supplement,* who crooned over the novel's "unemphatic manner," "admirable restraint," and "detachment"; and condemnation from such quarters as the *Daily Worker,* who challenged its ostensible realism: "The weakness of the book . . . is that the unemployed worker who sits timidly at home waiting for the investigator is not the rule, but the exception. . . . A book which brought out this fighting spirit of the unemployed would have been a much greater use to the working class" (as quoted in Croft, xiii). Marxist criticism of the 1970s takes a similar, if more accommodating line. Although Brierley is at least acknowledged as a working-class writer worthy of debate, he is still stripped of "authenticity," granted assimilationist rather than "proletarian" status. Roy Johnson, for instance, claims he "represents the working man as the middle-class would like him to be; but not, fortunately, as he often is" ("Walter Brierley"). And while Carole Snee prefers *Means-Test Man* to its obvious counterpart from the period, *Love on the Dole,* she finds Brierley's work in general "self-consciously literary" and an "uncritical" endorsement of "liberal ideology."[27]

Recent critics have been more generous but seem equally to miss the point. As I suggested in the introduction, they have developed methods of coping with the retrograde aspects of realism and in Brierley have found a particularly convenient candidate for illustrating their theories. Both Ramón López Ortega and Graham Holderness make use of the novel's preoccupation with psychological devastation and blending of naturalism with stream-of-consciousness techniques to pinpoint its oppositional stance: Ortega admires Brierley for endowing his protagonist with understanding of "the roots of the social malaise" (129) and for avoiding "facile solutions" in his writing; Holderness perceives a kind of meta-naturalism in the text, its documentary style only a cover—"Each . . . minute detail of empirical observation contains a strange otherworld of dark anxiety and existential terror" so that the novel interrogates the "petty banalities" of dominant reality (27). While such readings have helped a new generation of readers to recognize the social criticism that *Means-Test Man* fosters—and precisely through its desperate governing consciousness—they overcompensate for its deviations and transgressions. The *Daily Worker*'s uneasiness about the novel is somewhat justified: its "otherworld" of "anxiety" and "terror" is not altogether explicable in terms of capitalist critique, exposing certain uncomfortable truths about working-class experience.

At the same time, Andy Croft's quite different defense of Brierley's realism simplifies the motivations and implications of class shame. He insists that "[u]nemployment in the '20s and '30s, as now, destroys people. It does not politicize people," and concludes, "The great strength and importance of the novel is in dramatizing the utter helplessness of Jack and Jane Cook in the face of circumstances they simply do not understand. In this Walter Brierley surely characterized the great majority of the unemployed population in Britain between the Wars" (xv). As I will argue below, the Cooks in fact understand their circumstances very well; their demoralization is often a perceptive, as well as legitimate, response to their condition. But a complicated one. The shame that Jack Cook expresses is finally privileged by the text, intended to "expose" the immorality of the ruling, rather than working class. It is Jane Cook who becomes the explicit agent of a much more problematic shame, the vehicle for Brierley's underlying fears of Otherness. This time, the working-class text directly employs a working-class woman to voice its anxiety about class, and ultimately gender, difference, so that such anxiety can be directly critiqued and ostensibly contained.

Recalling both Morrison's and Greenwood's novels, *Means-Test Man* appears to chart the humiliation caused by a *loss* of working-class identity, or more specifically, of work itself. As a laid-off miner, Jack feels stigmatized within his village, Wingrove, branded by his sudden poverty and "unnatural" domestic arrangement (both he and his wife perform household chores). While the Cooks' fallen position is signified in countless gestures, details, and situations, the most visible emblem of their plight is the monthly visit by the means-test inspector, who monitors their financial condition and need of state assistance. The plot is condensed into one week's (non)activity, leading up to his dreaded appearance. The narrative thus progresses toward one grand "exposure" scene, in which the verification of their lack functions as a "violation" (204) of their home and dignity. Although the

inspector is branded as the nefarious representative of an antagonistic class culture, he also becomes for the couple an extension of
the top strata in their own community. It is their Co-op share book
which becomes "the very calendar of their existence for the last three
years, showing all the steps down in the losing fight against conditions . . . the graph of their fortunes, rising steadily for five years
after the 1926 strike, then falling, falling, falling all the time" (260).
At the instant the book is "bared" to the inspector, so is Jane: "She
felt sick, full of misery and shame, as if she were standing naked before decent men and women" (261). The scene is only a culmination
of recurring references to exposure that in this text almost always
function metaphorically, rather than literally.

Unlike Jane, Jack is capable of turning this shameful condition
to his advantage. Well into the narrative, he discovers that "being
stripped naked and alone for so long a time had made him of fine
consciousness" (162). That is because Jack's class shame appears to be
rooted solely in his inability to labor, in his denied access to work. Jack
joins his wife in desiring many minor material goods, for pleasure as
much as rank, but he mostly desires recovery of his own legitimately
classed body. His "stagnation" and "hopelessness" stem from a lack
of solidity, of strength, of presence:

> He turned on to his side, a movement he always made before get-
> ting out of bed, and spragged his feet for a moment against the
> iron at the foot of the bed. It seemed strange that he had to do
> that to know, to feel that he had a body. When he used to waken
> in the morning after he had been to the pit, his whole frame
> had a fine, almost joyful feeling. He used to smile to himself and
> stretch out his arms and legs, opening his chest and working his
> abdomen, conscious that he had shape and substance and power,
> that his body registered a certain resistance to things. (5)

His uselessness sets him apart from other men within his class, when
all he seemingly seeks is anonymity:

> He was by nature quiet, without strong drive, willing, eager to
> conform to every moral and social lay which the tribe of which
> he was an ordinary member imposed, willing, too, and moreover

thinking it his duty to take his share in the work and continu-
ance of the tribe. But this was denied him, therefore he held
back from free intercourse with his fellows, feeling himself not
whole (98).

What he fails to recognize, of course—and what more militant critics
of the novel decry—is his highly limited notion of class collectivity.
In many ways, Jack resembles the young Harry Hardcastle, along
with other youthful protagonists of the mining novels, or even the
Mugsborough hands, who naively seek wholeness purely through
their (exploited) labor. Without it, "[h]e had no place in the world,
he was nobody" (20). He finds solidarity not in union "brotherhood"
or struggles against an oppressor class, but simply in a common work
activity. He is thus disinterested in protests on behalf of his class. It
never occurs to him to organize the unemployed because he does not
consider them/himself legitimate members of the laboring "tribe."

Despite Jack's fears of isolation within the working-class community, the text finally endorses, it seems to me, a kind of intra-class
difference that is registered through his very desire for definition, for
solidity. In order to sense that he exists—literally and existentially—
he must experience distinctness, separateness, boundaries. Like the
foot against his bed, he seeks "the consciousness of being definite, a
living, independent system moving at ease through a world of varying qualities" (153). As was quoted earlier, such sensation is termed
"resistance" in the text: the physical ability to experience and with-
stand an opposing or separate force of energy/matter. The desire for
self-contained parameters thus becomes both materially and ideologically a resistance to merging. For Jack, the act of labor permits
self-definition but allows him to escape threatening, effacing fusion;
in his utopian vision, "[e]xistence seemed . . . one vast whole embracing the sum of individuals" (208).

While the text on occasion openly acknowledges and supports this
longing for individualism, when framed as actual solitariness it becomes a revelation, a shameful exposure or daring admission. Jack
"could be joyful when alone—few miners could be that, few other
men either; they could be quietly content, but not vividly alive. He
could, but he was ashamed to be caught at it. He did not understand

himself, maybe a touch of lunacy far back in his family accounted
for it" (146). Its shamefulness finally lies, I would argue, in its hier-
archical intent. *Means-Test Man* endorses not mere distinctness or
difference but distinction, difference of quality, of kind. Jack resents
his unemployed status because he believes it specifically marks him
as a failure. His perceived absence of class identity in fact grants him
another, one that he disowns. The very dole line to which he becomes
assigned reflects this dilemma. Though a queue "without a name,"
it is "by far the shabbiest," its "atmosphere . . . shouted that it was
different from all the others." Jack's queue companions are "coarse
and dirty," with "dull, expressionless faces" (167–168). And they lack
much more than money or work: "One thing was common to all the
different types in the queue without a name–to every member of
every type: in some it was stronger than others, but the consciousness
of being below was there–being below the normal level of living in
other senses than the economic" (168). Yet this debasement affixes
itself to most working-class characters in the narrative, both those
who are and who are not unemployed. The women on the bus, the
men at the Social Service Centre, are equally vulgar, "obscene" figures. Jack's subtle, sensitive consciousness actually demonstrates the
degree to which he has escaped their fate, but Brierley is clearly
worried about the slippage that can occur.

In the end, then, this alternately suppressed and revealed desire
for distinction can be glimpsed most directly in the figure of Jane
Cook. While Jack's longing and shame appear nearly noble at times—
the mark of his manly pride—Jane's obsession with (lost) decency
almost always appears small-minded. Time and again, qualitative
comparisons are made between husband and wife which demonstrate
that Jack's intellectual concerns and emotional dissatisfactions are
played out on a much grander scale. Jane "had no levels other than
those of plain uncomplex living" (209), she "had not quite the depth
of thought or feeling that he had—not quite" (185). Her shame derives purely from the decline in status that accompanies a decline in
material prosperity, and as such, she "would never understand the
difference" of Jack's "deprivation": "Hers was mostly the denial of
dignity and decoration, mere superficialities, not touching the real

levels of living; there was a certain aching in the places from where they had been torn, no doubt, but healing could come with sensible thought. His was a vital deprivation; his creative point had been removed" (206). Accordingly, their political sensibilities contrast. Jack has a global outlook: "[H]is hate was general, not based on envy of another . . . his hate was against the big fact that such a system could be"; Jane on the other hand "hated her fellow-beings, her husband included" (66–67). The text never leaves open to question that this is a gendered distinction. Jack "could see and understand Jane's outlook and point of view, the woman was strong in her, it pained her to be compelled to lag behind her kind. . . . [S]he was a wife and a mother, a mistress of a castle and in such realms there were flags to be flown, gay colours to be flaunted" (161).

The working-class woman's preoccupation with reputation is finally deemed less dignified and tolerable because it is assimilationist in the worst sense. Jane's consciousness relishes dominant, "civilized" culture in a way that is only hinted at in Jack's frustrations with his marginalized existence. Like Hannah Perrott, she ultimately longs for her childhood working-class respectability. Whenever we watch her interact with others, she is acutely aware of rank, and of her own inherent, superior worth. On the bus, forced to ride with a "loud-mouthed, brainless slut" who is the wife of another out-of-work miner, "her very being was seared, burning with shame and humiliation; the folk in the bus were disgusted at the coarse, loose-mouthed fool at the back and she, Jane Cook, respectable, honest all her life, was being linked with her" (47–48). Similarly, after a dress price tag at the local Co-op tauntingly reminds her of a "world out of her reach," she considers herself and family unfairly imprisoned behind a "barrier," where "they could look out into the real world and see folk less intelligent, less sensitive, less capable, moving about with even minds and certain feet, taking and giving, choosing and discarding" (55–56). Even late in the narrative, she is still dwelling on her lost opportunities to "be the leading light" in her women's club, "to have received Lady So-and-so."

It is typically Jane who incites Jack's most painful bouts with self-deprecation. When not trying to remain silent, she often at once encourages and condemns his alienation from others. She forbids him to lapse into his natural Northern miners' dialect, for instance—she herself a speaker of standard English due to childhood elocution lessons—yet simultaneously chides him for being out of work. Perhaps most damaging, she casts his class powerlessness in terms of lapsed masculinity, bringing his own buried fears to the surface in an especially cruel manner. Jane charges him with responsibility for the family's lost fortunes and accuses him of preferring domestic work, accentuating his "weakness" to the point that he grows "angry at his impotence" (109). She also hints that he serves as a disappointing role model for their son, John (who, like the house she incessantly cleans, functions as Jane's most visible sign of rightful membership in an elevated class). It is clear that Jack's perceived "failure" as a working-class man ultimately threatens her own viability as a respectable—that is, respectably feminine—working class woman.

Although *Means-Test Man* seems to depart from the trend of earlier texts, which rewarded those female figures who appeared least working class, it still shares their values. Like the common Spindleton women of Clarke's narrative, Jane demonstrates her inherent lack of Culture precisely through her vulgar obsession with it. (Once more, only those who already claim status can afford to ignore or downplay its importance.) Try as she might to prove her own refinement, she cannot help but in the process reveal her "true" coarseness. Jack comes much closer to the mark: his difference appears more authentic, the innocuous result of his wish to reclaim his anonymity within the male "herd." But while one becomes a near parody of the other, both are clearly operating out of the same class-based apprehension about identity. And in their own way, both make use of shame as a kind of class cultural resource. As with their counterparts in earlier works, the class "difference" that they reject is imposed on them, a stigma not of their own making. It subsequently leads them to seek "difference" of another sort, taking them from the "borderland" of Otherness to the coveted inside territory of either class distinction or (seemingly) de-classed individualism. The incorporation of gender difference into this scheme is critical, part and parcel of the private/public differentiation sought after within the narrative. Its association with a conventional domestic arrangement creates one model of such resistance. In the next chapter I will delineate another, exploring the construction of private, gendered selves in the texts through the antithesis of domesticity, romance.

The "Revolt of the Gentle":
Romance and the Politics of Resistance in
Working-Class Writing

■

"Romance, romance, romance," is their monotonous cry. Romance served up in penny batches; romance that depends upon nonsensical scenes, shallow thoughts, spurious philosophy, and unreal life, for its popularity.—James Haslam, The Press and the People; An Estimate of Reading in Working-Class Districts

James Haslam's "estimate" of romance as a particularly insipid, as well as politically insidious, form of popular culture is a familiar one. It anticipates—and reminds us of the connection between—contemporary strains of both low- and high-brow cultural criticism. Himself a working-class writer from the Lancashire area, Haslam could scarcely conceal his disappointment at his neighbors' reading habits, but he was particularly offended by the women's preferences.[1] This chapter is concerned with the "cry" for romance that he and others hear, yet typically regret, dismiss, distort, or deny when they study modern British working-class culture. As it is an explicitly feminized desire, I am especially interested in understanding the often circuitous, often suppressed, route it takes in narratives by working-class women themselves as well as in narratives by men. Romance provides, it seems to me, a most revealing alternate angle of entry into discussions of working-class narrative, functioning as a complex resistance strategy, as well as the more obvious reinscription of a dominant convention governing gender, class, and literary relations. Its radical potential can only be fully appreciated in the context of both feminist and Marxist perspectives on this most pervasive of master narratives.

I. Theoretical Oppositions

The Production of Gender: Feminists "Read the Romance"

Feminist theorists from Mary Wollstonecraft to the present have had a particular and obvious stake in examining heterosexual romance as one linchpin of patriarchal systems. Whether cultural myth, plot device, or popular genre, romance seems a convenient, intimate register of cultural codes, which can either be critiqued as a method of producing feminine subjects or identified as an openly contradictory script and thus a potential site of resistance. Despite the shift away from critique of male texts and toward reclamation of female texts, much feminist criticism in the late 1970s and through the 1980s remained concerned with romance ideology and narrative, centering on the subversion of romance within women's writing or cultural production. Classics in the field, such as Elaine Showalter's *A Literature of Their Own: British Women Novelists From Bronte to Lessing* (1977), Sandra Gilbert and Susan Gubar's *The Madwoman in the Attic: The Woman Writer and the Nineteenth-Century Literary Imagination* (1979), and Judith Lowder Newton's *Women, Power, and Subversion: Social Strategies in British Fiction, 1778–1860* (1981) authenticate and valorize those women's texts that abandon, rewrite, or challenge (however covertly) the romance plot.[2] Rachel Blau DuPlessis's *Writing Beyond the Ending: Narrative Strategies of Twentieth-Century Women Writers* (1985) is an especially good example of this approach, foregrounding the "delegitimation of cultural conventions about male and female, romance and quest, hero and heroine, public and private, individual and collective, *but especially conventions of romance as a trope for the sex-gender system*" within modern women's fiction (ix). The modernist and contemporary writers she studied (Woolf, Richardson, H. D., Rich, Lessing) are related precisely through their "desire to scrutinize the ideological character of the romance plot . . . and to change fiction so that it makes alternative statements about gender and its institutions" (x). DuPlessis herself attacks the paradigmatic romance plot that lingers in nineteenth-century women's narrative on three grounds: its separation of love and quest; its "muffling" of the main female character, who loses her individual agency when she eventually transforms into a heroine; and its privileging of heterosexuality

(5). As with the other studies mentioned, her points of critique have been strategic to work in the field.

Yet alternate trends in feminist scholarship focusing on women as readers and spectators have established that romance is an enormously complex convention, rarely operating in a purely hegemonic mode. Popular culture critics have enabled us to recognize the oppositional possibilities embedded within the romance narrative form itself. Tania Modleski and Janice Radway have both suggested ways in which popular narratives for women–in novels and on television–stir up, though eventually contain, disruptive or subversive feelings in the audience. Modleski's *Loving With A Vengeance: Mass-Produced Fantasies For Women* (1982) begins with the premise that the very "enormous and continuing popularity" of those narratives "suggests that they speak to very real problems and tensions in women's lives" (14). She traces the genealogy of popular "feminine" narratives, moving from eighteenth and nineteenth-century sentimental fiction, Gothic romance, and domestic novels up through Harlequin paperbacks and soap operas, to conclude that "even the contemporary mass-produced narratives for women contain elements of protest and resistance underneath highly 'unorthodox' plots" (25). According to Modleski, that plot is a " 'cover' for anxieties, desires and wishes which if openly expressed would challenge the psychological and social order of things" (30). She argues, for instance, that the Gothic romance "expresses women's most intimate fears . . . about the exceedingly private, even claustrophobic nature of their existence" (20), while the Harlequin romance encourages a female "disappearing act" that registers the "desire to obliterate the consciousness of the self as a[n] [exploited] physical presence" (37).

Radway's work takes a similar bent. Her interviews with contemporary romance readers reveal a desire to escape *and* embrace the gendered self, in the process reconceptualizing the masculine character (123–129). "Reading the romance" through the psychoanalytic theories of Nancy Chodorow, Radway suggests that romance narratives speak to women's deepest longings and anxieties concerning relationships: her interviewees seek both autonomy and a complete erasure of boundaries in their relations with others. They enjoy their emotional commitment to the female world of nurturance, yet seek a man who can in turn fulfill that role as well (135–138). (While men seem incapable of this relational self, the romance narrative demonstrates their potential.) And like Modleski, Radway finally centers on the management of such desires through the texts' narrative strategies.[3]

But even as both critics genuinely work at determining "what constitutes narrative pleasure for women" (Modleski 32), they fail to consider the class divisions among women that might dramatically alter its boundaries. As might be expected, the "selves" that their female readers allegedly recognize and transform through interactions with romance texts appear decidedly middle-class, in flight from pathologically privatized lives. Leslie Rabine's "Romance in the Age of Electronics: Harlequin Enterprises" would seem to take into account this oversight by specifically focusing on the contempoary romance novel's appeal to "working women." She surmises that such readers seek to resolve the split between the "domestic world of love and sentiment" and the "public world of work and business," searching not only for "feminized" relations with men, but change in the world of labor (250). In Rabine's study, one major theme of "revolt and fantasy," then, concerns the depersonalization of automated office space and the related "powerlessness" of the female worker (254): in the Harlequin series, women's work, transported to the professional realm, is meaningful and challenging, allowing the protagonist to win greater control over her circumstances. Another theme concerns the working heroine's demand for recognition of her whole "self" from the hero-boss. As Rabine states, "[i]n addition to acknowledging her sexual attraction and her professional competence, he must also recognize her as a subject," "a unique, exceptional individual" (250). Yet while she begins to differentiate between women readers and recognizes that they might have different needs to be fulfilled by romance narratives, her own reading betrays the same middle-class assumptions that underlie Modleski and Radway's work. Rabine's class orientation is reflected in the "split" she presumes between an ostensibly intimate domestic world and harsh work world, as well as in her proposed fantasized resolution of that split: a love affair with the boss.

Working-Class Women and Romance Ideology

Rarely grounded in a working-class point of view, feminist criticism has a limited perspective of the "problem" to be challenged generally in dominant literary practice and specifically in romance narrative. I suggest that working-class women—as both readers and writers—can never fully conceive of romance as an "intimate" register of cultural practices. They begin at a different place in their relation to that convention and, in a sense, commit a transgressive act merely by desiring the romance script itself: its plot is not a "cover" for other "anxieties" and "desires," as Modleski argues about romance readers generally; it *is* their anxiety and desire. In order to be addressed adequately by feminist studies, their troubled (and no doubt troubling) investment in romance needs to be explored in the specific context of working-class culture and a working-class literary tradition.[4]

During the early decades of the twentieth century in Britain, it was predominantly middle-class women who felt the daily strictures of (and protested against) romantic codes of behavior. Working-class women were typically denied access to those codes by their own cultural experience. Romance functioned as an emblem of privilege and was reserved for others. While the cinema and popular novels encouraged their diverse female audiences to identify with an array of romance heroines, working-class mothers made sure their daughters understood that romance was purely a fantasy with little relevance to their lives and that marriage was primarily an economic relation, rather than fulfillment of love.[5] Unlike their middle- and upper-class counterparts, who frequently suffocated at the hands of fathers, brothers, guardians, and mothers while playing out the real-life role of romance heroine, working-class women suffered chastisement or ridicule within their communities if they merely made attempts to try the role on.

Indeed, in autobiographical writing by working-class women at this time, susceptibility to romance ideology is associated with guilt, danger, and a sense of thrill, as well as outright scorn. Mrs. Layton's memoirs, examined briefly in chapter 3, admit to her fascination as a domestic servant with "trashy" serial tales but add that thoughts of her "dear mother" made her "give up" the habit (*Life* 26–27).[6] (It is interesting that even within Haslam's study, the women respondents' obsession with love stories is qualified by a preference for tales about "proper love" involving aristocrats, rather than workers [16].) And in the fictional texts, female transgression is linked to the pursuit of pleasure in general—entering fair grounds, though forbidden to do so, trespassing on property by freely tumbling down a hill—scenes which significantly impel the romance subplot as well by setting the stage for the lovers' first meeting. Such an impulse cannot be equated entirely with the middle-class woman's wish to privilege pleasure over duty. For as I hope to illustrate in a moment, the presence of romance in working-class women's texts ultimately serves as a means of registering the desire for a seemingly unobtainable individual subjectivity that is posed against an inescapable collectivity. The romance plot comes into play not only to convey a longing for relations based in tenderness, rather than exploitation, but also to represent a utopian private arena in which one is valued for one's *gendered* "self" alone.

Romance and the Working-Class Literary Project

These suggestive connections among romance, pleasure, individualism, and rebellion become equally oppositional in class cultural terms when they serve to unsettle the whole enterprise of working-class writing. As noted earlier, British proletarian fiction traditionally operates as a masculine genre, largely concerned with "public" and transformative experience. The entire private sphere—whether in the form of modernist angst or penny-novel love affairs—soon became branded as both feminine and bourgeois. (In addition to the reviews and manifestos discussed in chapter 1, a seemingly minor *Left Review* piece helps to illustrate this point: in "Factory Library," Ann Gresser contrasts a "boss-run" library, which offered women employees romance and "sex" stories, with a worker-run library, which eliminated romance entirely in favor of books that "helped to make Trade Unionists, Communists, and militant workers."[7])

Contemporary Marxist critics tend to accept and reproduce such criteria, perceiving the romance plots that do exist within earlier working-class novels (male and female) as either a regressive capitulation to popular taste or a sentimental substitute for the "real" political narrative. Choosing the converse of a strictly feminist perspective, they consider romance an entirely alien register, foreign to a genuine working-class subject position. In his praise of Tressell, for instance, Jack Mitchell harangues against the tyranny of the romance plot within the novel's history as a genre, arguing that love "has played a part" in literature "quite disproportionate to its part in social life" ("Early Harvest" 73). He celebrates *The Philanthropists* as a break-through proletarian text precisely because it recenters the novel around work, rather than romance ("Aesthetic Problems" 262). Others, like Carole Snee, Graham Holderness, and P. M. Ashraf, either wince at the clumsy and overblown rendering of romance within novels such as *Love on the Dole* and *Cwmardy* (1937) (and in Snee's case, use it as one yardstick of bourgeois values) or attempt to reread/rewrite the passages or subplots so that they safely promote an alternative message.

Romance thus becomes a forbidden category not only for working-class women who operate generally as female subjects within a specific class culture, but also for those who are producers of class-conscious narratives. Its persistent, if modified, presence in their fiction arguably enacts another kind of transgression, recasting the genre itself. When the working-class woman writer makes use of the private realm, she finally works to reappropriate the master narrative of protest in this body of work by allowing a more self-conscious critique of gender relations, as well as the expression of outlaw desires surrounding those relations. Addressing the oppressive, as well as liberating, effects of "love," the romance plot in women's texts becomes one means of expanding the political terrain of the proletarian novel. While it is hardly an "intimate" category or convention, then, it is also not altogether "alien" either. It provides a recognizable mechanism for addressing a very real component of women's lives. But the incorporation of romance remains quite an anxious operation. As I hinted in my prior discussion of *Clash,* working-class women writers found themselves in a difficult position as they attempted to negotiate an appropriate form for their specific concerns. The pressure to prove their authenticity by adopting (or refashioning) trappings from the masculine narrative model was immense.

This gendered model must also be considered in light of the suggestively gendered conflict between Labour Socialism and Marxism, which served as a critical backdrop to the fiction from the turn-of-the-century on into the thirties: Labour Socialism, considered "ethical" rather than "scientific," and associated with Keir Hardie's slogan "socialism is much more an affair of the heart than of the intellect," was denounced by the British Communist Party as an essentially feminized political movement. Its optimism, and emphasis on winning workers a pleasurable way of life (as well as better wages) appeared naive and reformist.[8] (As will be seen in part 3 of this chapter, the ideological struggle between socialism and Marxism actually becomes narrativized *as* romance in at least two of the male texts from the period: the heroine, a Labour party organizer and the hero, a Marxist trade unionist.) Although women were, in fact, much more attracted to the array of labor, rather than Marxist, parties, the masculinization of the Left, coinciding with the trivialization of "private," "emotional" trends in fiction, created a risky climate for political women writers who departed from the norm. That climate, of course, also affected male writers, who, as I have been arguing, equally felt the pressures of a proletarian master narrative. However, the following readings will suggest that the instability of romance in working-class experience is in some ways made use of more openly and easily by men. They are not quite as implicated in its effects and exclusions and thus enjoy the power to legitimize romance by pressing it to serve a more strictly socialist agenda in their fiction. Along with its suppressed functions, romance operates in their narratives as a self-conscious tool. The female texts, which begin the discussion, convey another kind of vexed relationship to writing and to the romance convention, at once resisting and desiring the very "right" to claim feminine status.

II. Ethel Carnie Holdsworth and Ellen Wilkinson: Writing the "Clash" of Class and Gender

Girlhood glides into womanhood, and one falls in love. (Which shows the innate cheek of the working class, who dare to dream of happiness living from hand to mouth.)—Ethel Carnie, *"The Factory Slave,"* Woman Worker

For God's sake, women, go out and play—Ethel Carnie, "Our Right to Play,"
Woman Worker

While acknowledging the material and ideological conditions that
have severely limited working-class women's opportunities to envision themselves as writers (of any sort), I am less concerned with
probing the particular set of obstacles they faced as they struggled
to record/explain/escape their lives through narrative than with suggesting how obstacles shape the form and substance of their work—
how romance specifically can be viewed as a manifestation of and
response to the parameters surrounding their position as women in
a working-class community and in a fledgling "community" of male
working-class writers. This segment will focus primarily on the work
of Ethel Carnie Holdsworth, the South Lancashire "ex-mill girl" who
was one of the few working-class women novelists in Britain to sustain
an actual writing career. The daughter of a staunch SDF (Social Democratic Federation) member, she became an activist for working-class
causes in her own right, producing more novels, stories, poems, and
journalistic reportage than the majority of her male contemporaries.
Though initially tagged the "Lancashire fairy" by *Woman Worker*'s
prominent editor Robert Blatchford, Carnie Holdsworth quickly put
that title to rest with her gutsy, militant pieces protesting the very
structure and inequities of the capitalist system.[9] In addition to steer-
ing *Woman Worker* in a more radical direction during her short stint
as contributor and editor, she also incorporated her experiences as
a textile worker into narratives that run the gamut from children's
stories to popular novels to proletarian propaganda fiction.

Yet Carnie Holdsworth's literary output has been strikingly
ignored or mishandled by most critics otherwise eager to embrace
working-class writers (and distressed by the absence of women in
those ranks) because it defies their assumptions about working-class
politics and literary practice. (Ironically, she merits a line in Standish
Meacham's historical study, but even there is mistakenly identified as
a "middle-class social worker" due to her "right to play" stance.[10]) Her
writing is difficult to characterize—typically dramatic and passionate but widely varying in form and style, linked primarily by themes

of oppression and romantic love. Its feminist orientation has stimulated some recent interest in her work as a whole: Edmund and Ruth
Frow have published a helpful biographical piece detailing Holdsworth's early political convictions; Gustav Klaus includes reference
to her novel *This Slavery* in his essay on "neglected" 1920s socialist
fiction; and P. M. Ashraf incorporates several extensive readings of
Carnie Holdsworth's novels in her comprehensive survey of British
working-class literature.[11] Much remains to be done, however, to do
justice to the complexity of Carnie Holdsworth's political and literary visions, particularly her sense of the troubled meeting ground
between class and gender. I will explore three of her novels that not
only begin to suggest her range but also demonstrate the expectations
surrounding working-class women's texts. Her uneven relationship
to working-class narrative models will be considered alongside Ellen
Wilkinson's *Clash*.

Miss Nobody

Miss Nobody (1913), Carnie Holdsworth's first novel (published under
her family name), is a fascinating representative of the political
tensions that characterize her work. Juxtaposing urban and pastoral sites, along with realist, proletarian, and folk narrative, it
defies simple categorization. The novel most clearly draws on the
nineteenth-century social narrative model, complete with cross-class
marriage, unexpected inheritance, murder trial, and blissful domes-
tic/political closure. But Carnie Holdsworth's revision of that model
—specifically, her working of the romance plot—is as revealing as
her imitative gestures.

On the one hand, *Miss Nobody* offers a considerable sobering of
romance ideology by focusing on the persistent absence or failure
of romantic love in working-class life. Manchester oyster-shop girl[12]
Carrie Brown spends her spare time absorbed in Tulip novelettes
while surrounded by, and in some cases experiencing, domestic violence, sexual harrassment, and abandonment. Orphaned by a mother
in the workhouse and a roguish father who fled abroad, she has sur-
vived through pragmatism and measured wariness of male promises.
Her character has a distinctly New Womanish air: we immediately
learn of her "bold courage," "original mind," and support for the

suffragettes (1), which is subsequently reflected in her chastisement of male companions on a tram. "Men, aren't you?" she taunts, as they beat an accompanying animal into submission. But though she is capable of viewing popular romances like "The Duchess of Digglemore's Diamonds" with self-conscious amusement, quite aware of the disparity between their heroines' lives and her own, she is unable to shake their appeal as an avenue of momentary escape and transformation ("Instead of the gritty floor of the oyster-shop she trod soft Persian carpets upon which lovers knelt to propose in long-winded poetical sentences as sweet as barley-sugar. . . . Carrie herself was the Duchess for the time being," [6].) Even as she resigns herself to a loveless marriage with Robert Gibson, a prosperous farmer, she continues to read romance fiction with lingering hope.

While Carrie's more naive responses are juxtaposed with the narrator's wry and jaded perceptions, the novel stops short of suggesting that romantic love is an impossibility and/or delusion—it argues only that romance exists in less mythic, inflated forms. *Miss Nobody's* romance plot actually fails to be "romantic" in any conventional sense until the last pages of the narrative. Unlike many middle-class heroines, who often covertly exercise their greatest liberties during the extended period of wooing demanded by the narrative structure, Carrie endures a "courtship" that lasts approximately one week, during which time both parties primarily weigh the material benefits of marriage: Gibson eyes her trim waist and considers her efficiency in the kitchen, while Carrie dwells on her quickly fading good looks and never-ending battle with mountains of oysters. She decides that "to be a good wife . . . in return for the position and freedom he would give her . . . would surely be a fair exchange" (45–46).

Predictably, the marriage soon grows stultifying—Carrie comes to understand the contradictions of life as a "leisured" woman when the "freedom" from her work place becomes burdensome and alienating. Yet in the middle of the narrative, Carnie Holdsworth summarily drops the combined romance/marriage plot and introduces a more recognizably proletarian schema: Carrie abandons the relationship, signs on at a textile factory, and organizes a successful strike for higher wages (the Battle for Ninepence). However, as I will discuss momentarily, this too proves unfulfilling, and eventually she is drawn

back into the marriage—*after* Robert's position is initially weakened
via a murder charge (which instigates his own parallel imprisonment)
and hers strengthened materially via an unlikely inheritance from
her long-lost father. Following this melodramatic turn in the narrative, *Miss Nobody* closes with sincere commitment and understanding between the two, so that love and marriage emerge as neither
a pot-boiler fantasy nor a service contract, but as a rewarding part-
nership between equals. The novel's (uneven) challenge to traditional
romance ideology contests traditional gender roles, but it does not
pretend to deny the importance of love itself.

This reconfiguration of the romance trope also complements the
critique of *middle-class* culture suggestively launched by the novel
through its periodic pastoral settings. Carnie Holdsworth goes to
great lengths to indict the isolating effects of rural middle-class existence, which valorizes propriety (along with property). The country
village of Greenmeads, home to Carrie's sister Clara and her own
future husband, is profoundly insular and sterile, an ironic contrast
to her daydreams. On her initial crowded tram ride out of Manchester, Greenmeads represents the utopian possibility of an expansive and private state:

> Looking through the window, splashed with the rain of the pre-
> vious day, she saw fields of waving meadow grass, infinite spaces
> of tender blue sky bending down to them. The sky fascinated
> Carrie. It looked so different here in the country from the nar-
> row, hand's-breadth between the grey houses as she viewed it in
> slack moments from the door of the oyster-shop. . . . 'To think of
> all that space being here, and none of us knowing of it,' she said
> aloud, then, being a practical person, looked into her shabby
> purse of the uncertain clasp to see if her ticket was quite safe. (7)

Carrie's self-conscious anxiety about legitimately crossing this border
is well taken, for once married and settled there, she continually experiences displacement, permanently branded with an alien status.
She initially seeks out such an existence in order to escape the monotony of her own class territory, yet once settled into Greenmeads,
she achieves an individual subjectivity very different from the one
for which she had literally "bargained." She is indeed set apart, but

precisely because she continues to experience herself as an ostracized *class* subject. Her only friend is another outcast, the village idiot Peter Moss, who like many in his position of child-like innocence is wiser than most. Her stint as a union organizer at the textile factory, then—the role she adopts after her flight from the Gibson farm—reacquaints her with the potentially empowering dimensions of communal experience (and introduces another kind of utopian space):

> Some thirty girls and women worked in the long, white-washed rooms, and when they were really serious, singing some old hymn tune, or a popular ditty of the day, there was a sense of brave, beautiful fellowship about them, transforming them from so many cranks in a mighty machine into living souls. . . . Carrie loved this life better than domestic service. She felt herself one of many—weak and insignificant enough alone, but wonderful, strong, beautiful, along with them. (160; 166)

On one level, Carrie's transformation in the text from would-be bourgeois romance heroine to working-class hero sets the seal on Carnie Holdsworth's privileging of proletarian experience.

The plot's further machinations, however, create another ideological twist by short-circuiting this transformation. In the end, Carrie deliberately forfeits her hero status to emerge finally as a (compromised) heroine: Carnie Holdsworth's own narrative in effect completes the novelette Carrie leaves behind in Greenmeads with the page still turned down, resuming and finishing off its disrupted story. Though she enjoys the solidarity she builds with other women workers, Carrie grows tired of the work itself; her subsequent firing and brief but grueling experience at a Christmas-card factory lead her once again to flee Manchester. On her way back to the country, she encounters several other options which, if acted upon, would dramatically alter both her own life and Holdsworth's narrative model: a vagabond, for instance, invites her to join him on the road, yet she rejects this picaresque role as too dangerous and solitary for a woman. Directly afterwards, a socialist in a laundry van offers her a ride and enigmatic political rhetoric, both of which she also rejects.

What she accepts, as outlined above, is the position of fulfilled wife and mother in an entirely different class community. Hardly an antidote to popular romance, the novel thus finally reinscribes a great deal of its underlying fictions, at least concerning class mobility. For romance functions as both utopian and realistic fantasy, a dream of what could exist within the present system but outside Carrie's own particular class-bound world. In some senses, *Miss Nobody* most obviously endorses the vision of the middle-class social novel it often imitates, engineering romance and marriage between classes to stave off radical change. Safely ensconced in the countryside by the narrative's end, Carrie exits from the oppressive industrial economy without having to dismantle it. She settles for individual escape by gaining another, ultimately more desirable, class subjectivity—becomes Mrs. Somebody.

Viable as it is, the above critique will not get us very far if we fail to recognize that Carrie's choice can be viewed as an act of transgression as much as of regression. While *Miss Nobody* clearly predates the period of more self-consciously prescriptive working-class fiction, it displays the beginning tensions running through early twentieth-century efforts. The text's unorthodox privileging of individualism, combined with (and primarily articulated through) its valorization of romance, purposefully resists the dictates of working-class culture. But its rebellion is accomplished with some degree of uneasiness. Carnie Holdsworth creates a taboo script that tries to have it all ways. The novel incorporates a composite of episodes from evolving male working-class narrative forms as if to establish its own validity before commenting on the latter's incompatibility with female working-class narrative strategies. Overrun with contradictions, Holdsworth's text insistently opens up new possibilities of opposition while foreclosing on others; its protagonist exercises the right to create a different set of class borders for herself, problematic as they may be. *Miss Nobody*'s concluding situation and line, "Are not our dreams the lamps on a rainy road?," represent a difficult plot choice: to celebrate cross-class love over working-class unity.

Helen of Four Gates

Carnie Holdsworth's next major novel, *Helen of Four Gates* (1917), represents the mode of her fiction that is least recognizable as "political" writing and, as a result, perhaps the most perplexing (or merely aggravating) to critics. Like *The Taming of Nan* (1919), it concerns itself with the alternately suppressed and irrepressible passions that mark the lives of country "folk." On surface, the novel seems to have only the slightest relation to working-class life: it traffics in the outcast, the marginal, the contained. And like all of her work, it views that experience through a female lens, centering the narrative around a particularly strong-willed female protagonist. Helen Mason is one of her most exotic, most extreme women characters—the Heathcliff of the modern working-class literary tradition. (And one of her most popular, if judged by the novel's best-seller status and transformation into film.) *Helen* is, in fact, more than a bit of *Wuthering Heights* revisited, set in a wild country area of North England named Brungerly and shot through with similar acts of sadism, madness, violence, and forbidden love. Its sensationalist dimensions include supernaturalism: the area has a history of witchcraft, where "[n]ight with a laugh of anarchy blotted out the symbols of law and order, . . . reclaimed for a short time the wild that was half tame, and lent a sense that here fierce dark deeds had been done, and might be done again" (3). (Helen herself is also likened to a witch numerous times in the narrative.) Like Brontë's text, Carnie Holdsworth's narrative also finally reworks its Gothic formula, but as with *Miss Nobody*, her revision or adaptation speaks to the specific needs and desires connected with her distinct class (and gender) position.

The very foreignness of the setting allows Carnie Holdsworth to address and displace issues of class identity and solidarity. Similar to the prior novel, *Helen* makes oblique attacks on privatized social structures, affirming collective experience by demonstrating the price of its absence. Flung to the edges of urban reality, Brungerly and its companion village, Little Moreton, represent a horrifying lack of community. The narrative opens with a tramping scenario, its two principal male rivals, Fielding Day and Martin Scott, coincidentally thrown together in their aimless wanderings for food and shelter. While Little Moreton seems a mecca for all those like Day and Scott— "received into its arms of crooked streets the weak, the broken, the incapable, the unwanted, and, anon, the rebellious" (5)—it also harbors savagery. Four Gates Farm, squatting on the town's border, emerges as a perverse mockery of all dominant social norms. Its household thrives on exploitation, unspeakable cruelty, and misery. Abel Mason, a physically and emotionally crippled old man, avenges the humiliating loss of his lover (who leaves him to marry another and eventually dies) by adopting and punishing her daughter, Helen.

Though his abuse takes a myriad of forms, ranging from small acts of torture to virtual life-long enslavement to the farm, Abel's most hideous triumph entails the poisoning of Helen's great love affair with Scott. Unable to bear the possibility of her potential happiness (as well as the resurrection of love), he frightens Martin away from the farm by fabricating a family history of mental illness, an act whose consequences have indeed pitched Helen into a kind of madness by the time the narrative begins. After Day and Scott arrive (months later) at the Four Gates doorstep, and Mason observes Day's own instant and intense hatred of Helen, he offers the man money in exchange for marriage to his "daughter" (thereby ensuring an even greater escalation of her pain). The rest of the narrative responds in kind with an escalation in (melo)drama: after Martin abandons Helen for the second time, unable to bear the horror of her existence, she succumbs to her father's force and enters into a sadistic marriage which leaves her brutalized and pregnant. After Martin suffers a ravaging illness that awakens his spirit, he returns to Four Gates to reclaim her and he finds a woman "dead" to herself and to even the most desperate of his interventionist measures. But in the final pages of the novel, a series of other timely deaths (stillborn child, Day, and father) revive and liberate Helen, allowing her to achieve a "Love Triumphant" with Martin and reintegration into the town community.

As the above plot summary suggests, however, there is more than a hint of fascination with this wild, outcast universe. By creating a chaotic version of social relations within an alien sphere, the text can at once praise and condemn working-class existence—show its lack as well as its virtue. While Four Gates creates a series of overlapping subject positions for Helen that are primarily incapacitating—mad woman, witch, frenzied lover—it also fosters a unique strength and self-possession which is allowed the greatest articulation through the overlaid romance plot. Her obsession with Scott is her most significant transgression, not only because it taunts her father but because it marks her as a passionate woman of intense power. Hardly a demure, virginal figure at the outset, she emerges as an increasingly masculinized, aggressive lover, continually pursuing Scott through sheer psychic force (even as he escapes in body). She literally erupts into the text as a stunning presence: "borne aloft on the maddening wings of ambitious ecstacy" (4), Helen "might have been some high priestess of Nature's—imbued with the holiness of life and its aspirations, and scorn of those who ran from its battles. From every tone, look, from every inch of her tall form, issued a majestic pride, defiance, and dignity" (157).

But her own "laugh of anarchy" involves not so much a rejection of the traditional romantic heroine role, as enacted by other now infamous "mad women" of middle-class women's texts—Bertha Mason, Martha Quest, Anna Wulf as a modified embracement of it. Helen's position as an active, desiring subject is most valued by the text for its ability to convert her into a desired object. As readers, we constantly watch her being watched and wanted by men (including Fielding Day), who are alternately repulsed and fascinated by her enigmatic and sensuous presence. And it is finally when she is most tamed that she is most alluring. The eventual fulfillment of Helen's tortured romance with Martin is, I would argue, Carnie Holdsworth's most anarchistic, rather than conventional, move as a working-class writer—what she would find most daring. Like Carrie, Helen develops an individual identity that defies all strictures to achieve her goal, the consummation of love. Carnie Holdsworth's handful of admirers all remark on the "independence" of her female protagonists, yet it must be stressed that that independence should be read as a specific *kind* of autonomy that actually signals the ability to detach oneself from class markers and confinements. For this Other-world might also in the end permit a veiled, less threatening critique of her own class culture's debased and violent tendencies.

Four Gates farm may represent a privatized culture, but the pathology of the Mason family recalls, to an exaggerated degree, working-class families in other Carnie Holdsworth narratives (the Browns, the Martins) which are similarly marred by illegitimacy, fragmentation, deprivation, and abusive, as well as nurturing, bonds. And while on the surface Helen always remains the text's valorized figure, her very "difference"—strength of will, passion, and "savagery" (156)—equally proves to be the source of her shame. Her sexuality and "virility" together become coded as a troubling lack of femininity. In the heat of an argument, Martin calls attention to her exposed body:

> "Look! What would Lizzie Trip and' a' o' them think o' thee" he asked, pointing at the open coat, the bare gleam of her neck. He averted his eyes. Slowly the woman's eyes travelled down to that strip of bared flesh—the flesh she had forgotten. . . . All the blood of her body swept into her face. Red-hot needles of shame seemed to stab her through. The sob of a helpless child came into her throat, whilst she cowered down into the coat. (142)

Helen's later conversation with Lizzie confirms the implications of this incident: "My father didn't bring me up like a turtle-dove. . . . I'm made the other way, somehow—allus th'other way—runnin' after what should run after me, runnin' awa' fro' what I should run to. I feel like creepin' into a dark hole, an' ne'er comin' out agen—like I were *disgraced*" (195). The narrator attempts to counter such pronouncements with admiring references to Helen's "elemental purity" (142) and character, but her stigma as a "curst" woman (156) is only laid to rest by inscription into a successful romance (which, notably, makes Helen "feel clean" [283]). This strain of her fiction allows Carnie Holdsworth another method of working out her complex response to working-class subjectivity, expressing resistance as well as sympathy and loyalty, without the same degree of exposure or self-implication.

But Helen's desire to escape the "master" within, rather than outside, the household suggestively extends the novel's critique to relations between men and women in that culture, for *Helen of Four Gates* is most dramatically "about" male power. The novel depicts a series of attacks on women—Mason's sadistic treatment of his ward (as noted earlier, inspired by memory of another woman) is only the most vivid and emblematic. Day, of course, becomes his surrogate in further attacks on Helen, but other women such as Aunt Milly Mason, along with the ghosts of the persecuted witches themselves, suffer abuse. In a world repulsed by its own marginality, men either look for other seemingly weaker outcasts to victimize, as do Mason and Day, or they launch quieter assaults out of self-loathing, like Martin Scott. The latter's own cowardice leads him to commit perhaps the greatest offense by abandoning Helen, refusing to acknowledge her worthiness by refusing to validate her "un"-natural strength of character. Helen's final ascendancy thus rewrites the dominant working-class script on several fronts. As "love triumphs," so does the individual spirit; and if Helen is "tamed" in the process, so is the tyrannical masculine spirit at Four Gates farm.

This Slavery

The apprehension that marks Carnie Holdsworth's early fiction is more fully evident in her later novel *This Slavery* (1925), precisely because it makes such a strikingly dramatic concession to proletarian literary expectations.[13] A "propaganda" text which stirred debate in the labor press, the novel is at once her most compliant and resistant effort. Here, she offers a direct, fairly predictable treatment of urban working-class life, charting the effects of economic depression and a bitter strike on a textile mill community. The dedication page sets the tone for the novel as a whole: "To my Mother and Father, slaves *and* rebels, with a Daughter's affection and a Comrade's greetings." While maintaining Carnie Holdsworth's focus on female experience, *This Slavery* contains and aligns that experience much more in accordance with a masculine narrative model. The novelist's trademark independent women are this time strong-minded about the "right" issue: class warfare. Sisters Hester and Rachel Martin may respond differently to the pressures of working-class life, but both emerge as the novel's most committed worker-rebels. Carnie Holdsworth's manipulation of the romance plot, however, continues to interrogate, as well as facilitate, her class-conscious agenda. In this text, cross-class romance represents an out-and-out betrayal of working-class values, clearly remedying the prior novels' political slippages. Nevertheless, the novel succeeds in subverting its own surface narrative of class defiance.

This Slavery lends itself easily enough to affirmative Left readings which virtually ignore the romance subplots in favor of its more recognizable political concerns. P. M. Ashraf, for example, argues that the novel's significance lies in its sophisticated treatment and foregrounding of revolutionary practice: "In *This Slavery,* the problems of political education, of a mature leadership, of reformism, of mastering revolutionary theory and the lessons of a sharpening conflict in industry are not character traits but part of the story" (195). She centers her analysis on Rachel, who actually recedes into the background over a portion of the narrative but is the more openly (and traditionally) militant of the two sisters. From her perspective, Rachel "is much the most serious rank and file leader in this period of fiction" with "at least some notion of the dialectic of class struggle" (195, 194).[14] I, too, applaud Rachel's refreshing role as a speaker and strike leader who courageously confronts the mill owner, struggles to read *Das Kapital,* and spends time in prison for the cause—especially as she so clearly supersedes the prototypical socialist/union figure, Jack Baines. But in the haste to claim Rachel as a new improved version of the proletarian fictional hero, Ashraf neglects to mention other more problematic aspects of her character, specifically her involvement in a love triangle that includes Baines and Hester. This omission creates a distorted picture not only of Rachel *as* a female figure, but also of the novel as a whole, whose political and romantic plots are undeniably interwoven.

To address that connection most productively, attention must shift to the other protagonist, Hester. Her role in the text's most substantial romance plot ostensibly works to illustrate another dimension or sphere of class struggle. An erstwhile painter and classical musician, Hester is the sensitive, artistic member of the family who initially succumbs much more readily than Rachel to the bleakness of working-class existence. A romantic entanglement with Baines gets thwarted early on, leaving her vulnerable and alone. Much like Carrie Brown, she accepts a wealthy businessman's marriage proposal in a desperate attempt to "gain freedom," only to discover that she prefers her own class-bound world. Even worse, she is rendered powerless to act on that class's behalf: the "Socialist Dream" of which she murmurs in her sleep (inspired by Morris's *News From Nowhere*) is given birth in crippled form through her son Stephen, who dies in childhood. Her marital relationship lacks even a hint of sincere affection and soon thrives on antipathy as she is forced to become part of the enemy class in her husband Sandy's war on the millhands. Yet this heroine also gradually transforms into a hero of her own kind, and unlike her counterpart in *Miss Nobody*, never turns back: Hester becomes a spy within her home, surreptitiously helping the strikers rebel against her husband and eventually openly joining their fight. (Among other methods of sabotage, she writes the "doggerel" that the striking workers sing to pass on information from the inside.) Whereas Carrie unapologetically reaps the benefits of cross-class romance, Hester revels in her reclaimed working-class solidarity—and as proof dies by police bullets, a martyr to her people. Her seemingly more legitimate romance with Baines, which works to frame the narrative as a whole, is simultaneously resolved in the closing chapter (though in a compromised way and with an obviously compromised future) to confirm her class loyalty.

The novel accomplishes much more, however, than Carnie Holdsworth's testimony to working-class women's revolutionary mettle. It becomes the constellation site for an alternate set of classed and gendered meanings that rewrite its classic story of resistance: "this slavery" turns out to be quite a pervasive condition triggered by, but not limited to, an exploitative capitalist system. To begin with, the romance plots take on the additional function of gender critique in *both* class spheres. Carnie Holdsworth's condemnation of courtship/ marriage as a patriarchal, as well as bourgeois, institution distinctly *harmful to women* is more clearly laid out in the scenes involving Sandy, who treats Hester as one of countless prize possessions to be displayed and controlled. His condescending impulse to rehabilitate the town's "diamond in the rough," together with his smothering household of material goods, eventually imprison Hester as much as Rachel's jail cell confines her (for street agitation) during the same portion of the narrative. Their marriage represents far more than a symbolic "defection" on Hester's part, as Ashraf surmises. In much the same way, Baines prizes her seeming "difference" from other working-class women while simultaneously pressing her to conform to his own ideal. From the start, he seeks to make her a particular kind of proletarian object of desire which the course of the narrative brilliantly deconstructs. He clearly prefers Hester's ethereal, traditionally feminine qualities to Rachel's tougher character, but when she appears to decline his offer of marriage—and soon after becomes Sandy's wife—he scorns her "softness." Holdsworth's political daring in this regard is most evident in the strike negotiation scene: drawing the two together again as representatives of opposing camps, the episode reads like a confrontation between the stock male working-class hero and an entirely new female model. Baines condemns her class betrayal, sputtering "You have lost any chance of striking the tiniest blow for the working classes. *I am a member of a defensive organization which may turn into an attacking vanguard.* You—are lost!" (144). Yet she proves to represent the true vanguard by branding his trade union politics another form of sell-out, including among its strategies the scarcely disguised subjugation of women (along with petty wage increases and trade union hero worship).

At the same time, the analysis that Hester begins to spin out as she constructs her self-defense speaks to a final, much more muted strain of critique in the novel, one that betrays Carnie Holdsworth's own fascination with romance ideology and, in connection, her lingering sense of shamefulness surrounding working-class identity. *This Slavery*'s working-class tableau is punctuated by moments of enormous yearning and deprivation that finally seem to endorse Hester's bid for individualism, even as her attempt to achieve it through class mobility is questioned and ultimately undermined. The novel opens with an exposure scene combining three characteristic elements: a wish, a gap, and a stain. Longing for the spare time to paint, and despairing over her weary fate as a "working girl," Hester sits by the dying fire repairing a "tremendous hole" in her sock which she had attempted to hide earlier but "had found peeping over her clog-top" (6). When Baines makes a surprise visit and the light is suddenly turned on, she is caught not only with a bare leg exposed (the ostensible comic focus of the scene), but more importantly, with her winder's belt still wrapped around her body and a damning "smudge of blacklead on one soft, delicate curve of . . . pale cheek" (9). Hester is repulsed by both the fundamental dirtiness of her class world and the persistent struggle necessary to survive and change it. She confides to Rachel, "It's all so sickening. . . . To have to fight for everything—bread, love, everything—like beasts" (18).

The narrative's final turns clearly invite us to join Rachel in finding such a perspective unsatisfactory. We are also, I would argue, asked to understand it, and, further, to envision it as another valid form of class resistance—to borrow a term from the novel, "the revolt of the gentle" (19) against their own enforced degradation. Hester's shame derives from "a sensitive perception that to be poor amongst the poor was to have the soul slain, bit by bit, until nothing was left to creep on the earth but a bent body from which the light had faded" (33). (As she herself states one page later, "I sometimes feel like a dis-souled body. . . . We're like a set of pigs kept grovelling on the ground.") Rachel hopes that this "fine sensitive disdain" will eventually "break" so that her sister will demonstrate that "surrender is not infinite and that the revolt of the gentle is more to be feared than that which spends itself" (19). But Hester's faith in a self-determined, singular, and privileged identity—"I . . . am still—Hester Martin, wild though crushed, solitary though jostled and herded" (38)—is already in itself a kind of rebellion, posing a counter-voice in the text which does in fact bear out those middle-class readings of her character, such as Sandy's, that the narrative so derides: Hester indeed seems a "sensitive plant" who should not "class" herself "with them" (86). Her self-styled role as thwarted artist cannot shake all of its associations with bourgeois, bohemian culture because the promises afforded by that culture clearly remain compelling to the writer of this novel. Despite Carnie Holdsworth's periodic attempts to recast the role so that Hester embodies the "Soul of the People" (243), she cannot conceal its inherent attractiveness as a *valued* position of difference.

It seems entirely fitting, then, that Hester serves as the vehicle for romantic daydreams that also become tentatively validated over the course of the narrative, underwriting the text's covert theme of individualism. Although she tries to deny her susceptibility to romance's seductions and later lives out its contradictions, she cannot bear to have the ideal sullied, calling it "the great primitive, sacred impulse, the only romance that touches with angel-hands the grovelling ignominy of a slave's life" (16). The novel thereby naturalizes heterosexual love, suggesting that it is not a mere patriarchal or capitalist "plot." The discourse creating Hester and Baines's single love scene makes a similar point: they "said in the vernacular . . . things that had been said in Babylon, classic Greece. . . . They stepped over the borders of a county into the universal land of poetry" (13–14). To be sure, such observations are immediately prefaced by a considerably grimmer view of male and female relations ("Nature made her inexorable appeal, in the sordid trap of monotonous streets where slaves lived, eager to let none escape her" [10]). But Hester's evolving presence justifies the longing for freedom from "sordid" class ties that romance ideally guarantees. Her mother provides perhaps the most persuasive endorsement of the romance myth when she offers the following interpretation of a love poem: "[W]e are only ourselves, and know ourselves, when somebody loves us—just for ourselves—and we feel free, then" (225). The voice of working-class pragmatism and opponent of romance ideology throughout most of the narrative, Mrs. Martin comes to recognize the connection between romance and subjectivity quite late in the novel; though the final turn of events quickly overshadows it, her declaration makes all too clear the relationship between gender construction and the seductive illusion of self-determination.

Hester's link to the character Bob Stiner, another marginalized member of Brayton's working-class community, supplies the final pieces to this counter-narrative. Stiner is distinguished not so much by aesthetic refinement as by an extreme, violent anger about his existence (along with a penchant for poetry and alcohol). Another closet romantic, he emerges as a revealing "mad" double for Hester, clinging stubbornly to his outcast status within his own class culture while also seeking collectivity. He roams the town muttering to himself, occasionally scrawling revolutionary messages on sidewalks and walls, and is shunned by most of his class (excepting Rachel and Hester) for his inexplicable flights of fancy. His repeated chance meetings with Hester play up their relation as "soul mates." But their tie is most dramatically exposed in his fateful search for a bouquet of violets: a measure of Stiner's alternately pathetic and endearing efforts to romance his estranged wife, the search represents another mode of resistance that, like Hester's, violates norms of working-class experience. The ragged bouquet he chooses indeed mocks his aspirations. Both his wife's and Mrs. Martin's "unsentimental" taunts seem to echo throughout the scene, sneering at his efforts to adopt a different class cultural code. When tragically killed on his way home in a scuffle between a policeman and a striker, Stiner finally demonstrates the larger tragedy of the parameters that confine working-class practices (and are maintained from within as well as without). His aborted mission registers dissatisfaction with, and despair at ever escaping, a burdensome class existence. That transgression ultimately explains the "indirect and ironic relation" posed between his "quest of violets" and the policeman's simultaneous "quest of trouble" (198): in working-class culture and its accompanying fictional texts, the quest for romance is, quite assuredly, a "quest of trouble" that disrupts established conventions.

This Slavery thus haltingly weaves together another story that cannot help but conflict with its own larger project, continually calling into question its very interpretation and validation of working-class experience. When the novel was critiqued by the *Sunday Worker* for making the "usual love situation" serve as "the pivot of the machinery of the whole tale," Carnie Holdsworth herself retorted that love, like "the bread struggle," is central to existence.[15] To her credit, she publicly defended romance (and all that it represents) as a viable political issue in working-class fiction. Yet she also clearly felt a need to mask or offset those dimensions which threatened her own status as a class-conscious woman and writer. As Hester says when Sandy mocks working-class people's propensity to "tell all sorts of yarns"— "[p]erhaps the true story they don't tell would be less popular but more terrible" (86).

Clash

The conflicts within *This Slavery* that articulate problems of desire, ideology, and form also characterize Ellen Wilkinson's *Clash*—the other overtly "political" novel written by a working-class woman during this period. *Clash* is typically billed as an autobiographical novel about the 1926 General Strike from a woman's perspective. As I noted in chapter 2, in some respects it is indeed by far the most imitative of the male working-class texts, substituting a female protagonist as the central trade union organizer who alternately makes spellbinding speeches and suffers disillusionment in the struggle to lead her people to victory. Unlike Carnie Holdsworth's women activists, who either adopt the role only briefly or periodically drop out of narrative sight, Wilkinson's Joan Craig retains her union status while remaining the central focus of the drama. At the same time, the different gendering of the conventional narrative in itself allows Wilkinson's explicit feminist politics to mark her text and ultimately reshape, as well as reinscribe, the masculine literary pattern. Joan discovers that her efficacy as class hero and specific attempts to organize working-class women are often limited by the sexual politics pervading a largely male trade-union world. The novel's critique, on that score, is made abundantly clear. But it is Wilkinson's incorporation of the cross-class romance plot into this official narrative that is most crucial to the working out of her feminist, as well as proletarian, agenda. And once again, it is also the vehicle for a different sort of subtextual class agenda that allows expression of the novel's most urgent, if finally suppressed, voice. As I will discuss, the text's closure is a tenuous achievement at best, resolving the "clash" between class and gender politics at the expense of other persistent, transgressive, desires.

Even more so than *This Slavery, Clash* self-consciously foregrounds the ideological functions of cross-class romance. The romance plot most dramatically facilitates the text's concern as a whole with the opposition between "false" and "true" class consciousness examined earlier. Joan's dilemma as protagonist extends beyond the immediate political difficulties surrounding the strike. Her increasingly uncomfortable role as liaison between her working-class community in the North and the union leadership in London who eventually sell them out reflects her greater, personal struggle to remain true to her class roots. In the opening pages, she appears a worn-out union activist who "[a]t the age of twenty-six . . . had begun to think of her fellows simply as pink faces before a platform, or as lines of dark figures into whose hands she thrust meeting bills" (7). Her journey to London to monitor the strike decision becomes a journey of temptation. With all its sophistication and material luxuries, bourgeois London emerges (at times too pointedly) as Joan's Garden of Eden. And Anthony Dacre, a sensual, married writer who is part of the Bloomsbury literati, is her demon.

In contrast to *This Slavery*'s cross-class romantic configuration, Joan's relationship with Tony is founded in genuine love and initially appears much less objectionable on political grounds: Dacre is a seemingly harmless Fabian, rather than cold-hearted capitalist, who gradually becomes as smitten with the workers' cause as he is with Joan herself. Yet it is precisely the attractiveness of his packaging which Wilkinson targets for exploration and condemnation. Like all forms of ideology, his smooth exterior conceals dangerous contradictions. The narrative wastes little time in exposing the brutality that underlies the ostensibly civilized surface of left-wing middle-class intellectualism. The Gordon Square crowd eagerly assist the strike effort so long as it fails to impinge upon their theatre productions, coal dividends, or love affairs. Joan instinctively dismisses the political efficacy of this community early on, understanding that the North actually serves as the center of authentic resistance (and increasingly, of reality), but her reserve ebbs away under Tony's caresses. Wilkinson, however, demonstrates her own unquestioned allegiance to working-class values by at least modifying, if not entirely rejecting, a middle-class narrative solution: A competing romantic interest from the working-class arena soon enters the story—an ex-war hero whose crippled, scarred body can scarcely contain the militant energy brimming inside it. A plain and impotent rival, Gerry Blain offers Joan comradeship, rather than passion, an assured position in the next round of class warfare. "Romance" in its most typical guise is thus distinctly equated with dominant culture and functions primarily as a corrupting force in Joan's life. Gerry's offer of a marriage based on "brains rather than love," in which she would be "on the stretch all the time, working at top speed," is the only feasible option for a working-class woman.

The politics surrounding Joan's romantic choice, however, go well beyond the testing of her class loyalties. Ultimately, her crisis with Tony rests on his need to split her "private" position as woman from her "public" position as organizer/leader—to transform her from hero to heroine. As their relationship intensifies, he increasingly resents Joan's dedication to her work. Her decision to run for a vacant Parliament seat leads him to issue a familiar ultimatum, career versus love, offering to set her up in a flat in exchange for her undivided attention. To her credit, Wilkinson acknowledges the attractiveness of such a position for a woman who has never experienced this dilemma (either materially or emotionally). When he frames the situation crudely, of course, Joan initially challenges his double standards: "[A] woman can't have everything Joan. I know it seems a hard choice, but the choice is there and it's got to be faced. How shall I put it? . . . Loving your mate and bearing his children and bringing them up is a whole-time job." " 'Kirk, kinder, and kitchen,' mocked Joan. 'I didn't expect this Victorianism from you, Tony' " (179–180). But his subsequent attempt to mystify this relation proves more seductive, even as the text clearly relishes the irony (and dark comedy) of his suggestions. The passage is worth quoting at length:

> "No, Joan, perhaps I am thinking a bit ahead—to a time when equality is unquestioned, as it is now among intelligent men and women. Given that, a . . . worthwhile woman with the brains and the power that you have, Joan, has to make a choice. . . . [T]he women I am thinking of, the woman I believe you are, Joan, may find their mate. . . . Such women, Joan, could be great lovers and great creators. The wealth of spiritual power that could raise them to a great career could give a new meaning to marriage. In the ecstasy of their passion they would create wonderful children and train them finely. To their husbands they would bring fulfillment and the peace that passeth understanding. These men could do great things for the world. They would express not merely themselves but the inspiration of their union. Does that seem a narrow life to you, Joan, a choice not worth reckoning in the scale with Parliament or leading movements?" Joan's eyes had filled. She looked at Tony with a new admiration. . . . She wanted to rise to his level. "I'm not sure that I am worthy to walk that road, Tony." (180–181)

Her relief work in a particularly destitute, but spirited, northern mining community quickly brings her to her senses, however. She discovers that she is glad to "be in the thick of it again" and recalls the exhilaration she both feels and inspires as a "living red flag, the spirit of revolution." While she admits to herself that Gerry can never substitute as a lover, she looks forward to the equality that he will allow her.

Though Joan's desire for romance is recognized as one authentic component of her experience, forming part of the "clash" that structures the narrative, it is clearly associated with a cultural program that seeks to control women. As the above passages attest, Wilkinson's use of the romance plot to challenge gender, as well as class, relations is more than obvious, even if the text's solution retreats from the real problem at hand. But as with Carnie Holdsworth, her own evident investment in its fictions remains and functions as another, far more interesting, cry of protest. Wilkinson's own peculiar position as a popular symbol of working-class and feminist radicalism made her dissent all the more risky: as one of the few women leaders of Britain's trade-union movement during this time and an outspoken Labour M.P., she was a "celebrity" valued for her uncompromising stand on workers' and women's issues. Whereas Carnie Holdsworth made a modest name for herself as a writer of both romantic tales and political tracts, Wilkinson became an increasingly public figure whose journalistic pieces were strictly incendiary. In fact, her own 1926 *Plebs* article, treating contemporary British and Russian fiction, explicitly condemns the Western literary obsession with personal experience (specifically "sex") and praises the Soviet focus on "a literature of the job."[16] *Clash* presumably represents a stab in that direction, yet it cannot dictate or hold all of her narrative's conflicting energies. Carnie Holdsworth's dangerous interest in passion, privacy, and control—privileged modes of experience seemingly out of the reach of most working-class women of her time—emerges with equal intensity here. And much more directly than in her texts, Wilkinson's novel relays that fascination largely through references to, and representations of, sexuality.

Despite its final message of moderation, the novel continually valorizes individual, ostensibly self-indulgent, moments of disruption and disorder. From the beginning, Joan's sexuality is the most overwhelming of her powers yet seemingly unavailable to her consciousness. It is at once absent and present:

She sat on the arm of the chair like a bird poised for flight. Much too thin, with wiry black hair that stood away from her face, and quick black eyes, Joan Craig always gave an impression of excessive energy. Her horse-power was too big for her body, her

> gear ratio too high. People trying to describe her features found
> they couldn't. . . . She left the impression of a breeze rather than
> a woman. The men she had worked with during the crowded
> years since 1918 had often tried to reach the woman, but Joan
> eluded them. Personal contacts wearied her. Family or friends
> were carelessly shed if something exciting in the way or a strike
> or a good organizing row called her to any distant town. (11)

In this way, the text itself endorses Dacre's separation of the public
and the private, insisting that Joan's eroticism be noticeable (and ir-
resistible) to everyone but herself while engaged in political activity.
Wilkinson plays it both ways: she establishes Joan's qualifications as
a trade union leader through her "virile" character (76) while also
establishing her qualifications as a woman.

Passages like the following document her desirability to even the
most resistant male spectator: "Though his own marriage was a perfectly happy and peaceful one, the wild strain in Joan appealed to
deep fires in Royd's nature. . . . Joan always declared that she hated
women who used sex appeal in business relations, being magnifi-
cently unconscious that she could no more help her sex appealing
to men like Royd than she could help breathing" (13–15). Yet such
statements must be read against another set of images that reveal and
announce Joan's "dirtiness." She is frequently caught unwashed and
"soiled," dismissing herself shamefully as a "dirty pig" (131). Such
exposure scenes happen most critically when in the midst of Helen
Dacre, Joan's rival and the epitome of asexuality and Culture. Not
surprisingly, then, the disturbing implications of Joan's "excessive
energy" are also often neutralized by counter images that emphasize
her own *a*sexual, child-like innocence. The narrator often describes
her as a "golliwog," an "elf." It seems vitally important to the novel's
ideological intentions that Joan remain "one of those women who
isn't always remembering she *is* a woman" (55), even as we are constantly reminded that she is.

Frequent references to Joan of Arc contribute to this complicated
embedded narrative as well, since they work both to condemn and
confirm the novel's overarching theme of working-class sacrifice. As
suggested, Joan is more than willing to become a class martyr, giving

up her chance to enter the bourgeois world of excess and individualism. ("Sacrifice her on the altar! Her whole being contracted to one passionate, intense wish that she might be worthy." [61]) But while this "wish" indeed verifies her "worthiness," the role itself seems suspect when enthusiastically encouraged by the Bloomsbury women—particularly when they cast Joan as a feminist martyr. Her London confidante Mary Maud worries about the romance with Dacre because she believes it will thwart Joan's political ambitions. She tells Gerry Blain, "I want Joan to grow to all she might be by herself," arguing that her forfeiting of "personal happiness" will be necessary for her own fulfillment as well as her "greater" cause: "[W]hat I mean is that now so much has been won, the vote, open professions, and all that, there must be some women in this generation who will put their job first and who will tackle some of these problems that are left lying around" (97).

Blain, however, questions her perspective, offering another that continues to have relevance for contemporary critical discussions about working-class incorporation and opposition: "After all the blurb about sacrifice during the War, I want to give that word a rest for a bit. . . . [M]ost self-sacrifice is the line of least resistance, passively suffering something, instead of using one's brains to alter things so that sacrifice is unnecessary. . . . [I]f some one says 'Sacrifice for what?' then you go all mystic and talk about the Higher Good" (96–97). It is in fact Gerry who typically revives the "Joan of Arc" nickname throughout the narrative, but with deliberate satiric intent. The narrator, too, alters characterization of Joan as the novel draws to a close, stating, "[t]here was very little pose about Joan Craig. She didn't strike a mental attitude and declare that everything should be sacrificed to her life's work. She was a very human, practical person who didn't want to do any sacrificing at all if she could help it" (220).

Yet by ending up in Gerry's arms, Joan in effect accomplishes her martyrdom. Her future "public" success comes at the price of her complete forfeiture of erotic experience. She only appears to win all by combining an authentic working-class identity with a stable gender identity (a "good" working-class woman rebel). As will be true in the male texts, the sexualized female body here emerges as the locus of both class shame and individual pleasure—which is why Joan, who in the text's master narrative attempts to recover, rather than escape, her collective self, must relinquish her body in the end. She seems a (considerably) tamer version of Helen Mason, whose very embodiment of sexuality is similarly undermined by the stigma it suggests, and seemingly allowed only because it is situated outside a recognizable working-class setting. Both Wilkinson and Carnie Holdsworth are clearly rejecting the typical dominant script for working-class women by denying their protagonists a sexualized status. (All, in one way or another, are "miss" "no-body.") But the final suppression of their interest in sexuality, and separation of the romantic and the erotic, ultimately complies with another dominant ideal for women, limiting the expanse of their desire.

These women's texts reflect, from another vantage point, the enormous pressures shaping working-class cultural production. I have attempted to demonstrate that romance serves as one underestimated and crucial component of resistance in working-class women's writing, accomplished with considerable ambivalence and seeming sleight of hand. They seek, as it were, a "right to play" that for women can represent either liberation or confinement (or both), depending upon class positioning. More than a deliberate intervention into gender relations and a gendered literary practice, romance serves the critical function of making possible a more veiled critique of working-class subjectivity through its alternate expressions of dissatisfaction, longing, and refusal. It is ultimately in the *intersection* of such gestures and desires that romance helps to rewrite the master narrative of working-class politics.

III. Laboring to Love: Working-Class Men Write the Romance

> *I know not the sweets of the rose,*
> *Bend, grind and labour I must—*
> *Wind 'mong the pines never blows*
> *For me—only wild storms of lust*
> *Surge through my big, hulking frame,*
> *(Love for me never was meant)*
> *Braised by their force and their flame,*

Tamed only when they are spent. (II. 9–16)
—James Welsh, "Labour" (1917)

These silly girls with their synthetic Hollywood
dreams, their pathetic silk stockings and lipsticks,
their foolish strivings to escape from the cramped
monotony of their lives, are the raw material of
history. When their moment of deep discontent comes
to them in a mass, taking form in the words of their
class leader, then there are revolutions.
—John Sommerfield, May Day (1936)

Working-class male writers have a no-less-complicated relationship to the romance convention, in some ways equally caught between alienation and intimacy. As members of working-class communities, they, too, can experience romance as a forbidden cultural practice and genre. Why, then, would they risk the taint of a bourgeois, feminized form in their writing? Or more to the point, how might romance function as transgressive desire in their particular context? Though they enjoy a bit more autonomy in the various spheres of working-class culture, men share with women a striking, if often suppressed, longing for private space, for the private sphere. The romance plot also serves in their narratives, then, as a means of registering the conflict between individual and collective subjectivity.

However, that plot functions differently within the shame/exposure dynamic. As I will demonstrate, romance becomes bracketed off from the domestic/public compound of relations in the male texts ultimately by its potential to circumvent the humiliating objectification experienced in both the workplace and the family: the work arena is associated with the exploitation of the laboring, classed body, while the domestic arena is associated not only with a similar loss of autonomy and privacy, but often with exploitation and degradation of the sexual body. The romantic relationship comes to represent the (momentary) possibility of a disembodied, classless self—one in which sexuality is certainly stimulated but ultimately deferred. At the same time, another agenda can be detected which finally controls both the function and form of the romance subplot(s) in these narratives—for working-class men have an additional, "intimate" relation to romance due to its patriarchal effectivity. Their incorporation of romance works to reaffirm dominant ideologies of sexuality and of gender that, as witnessed in the texts by women writers, restrict working-class women's agency. In the process, this masculinist use of romance plotting helps to mask the shame that it initially expresses or permits.

The Knobstick

C. Allen Clarke's early novel *The Knobstick: A Story of Love and Labour* (1893), originally serialized in his labor paper *Teddy Ashton's Northern Weekly*, sets a somewhat anomalous precedent for the presence of romance in twentieth-century male texts. As in *Lancashire Lasses and Lads*, the romance plot serves as a central structuring device: The title itself indicates that romantic love becomes profoundly bound up with class politics and class loyalties in this narrative ("knobstick" is a term for strikebreaker). Although Clarke draws upon the 1887–88 Bolton engineering strike as a primary source for the story—and as Ashraf notes, makes faithful and groundbreaking use of "factual" detail—personal relationships quickly become the narrative focus.[17] Henry Belton, the out-of-work engineer who arrives in Spindleton with a half-starved son and despondent spirit, eventually emerges as a model worker and strike leader with socialist aspirations. However, his clandestine romance with Lizzie Banks, the town's most virtuous "mill-girl," takes center stage and creates most of the energy within the text. Their love is barred not by class difference or conflict, as in the women's novels, but by the existence of Belton's estranged wife, Alice Meyers, a former milliner who deserted her husband and son for another man. As long as she remains alive, Belton is prevented from pursuing an honorable relationship with another woman. Their marriage also impacts upon the plot when Alice later murders her lover but escapes prosecution due to Belton's generosity (he heroically accepts responsibility for the crime to save her). In purely sentimental terms, the romance plot thus comes into play to underscore Belton's inherent goodness. Amidst his considerable deprivation and unjust treatment, love represents a tantalizing possibility and eventual reward, to which he is clearly entitled.

Romance, in fact, serves to endorse the vision proposed by Lizzie's father—"Let's tak pleasure while it's here. It met be gone into another street an left no address when we want it" (118). As will be true in twentieth-century male texts, romantic scenes primarily take place in extraordinary, utopian spheres. Love blossoms at the annual carnival (in the center of town), in the woods, and at the Blackpool seaside, symbolizing a more privileged mode of being which both is, and is not, out of reach. But romance also conveniently allows distinctions to be made between "correct" and "incorrect" forms of pleasure by addressing working-class female sexuality. The Victorian virgin-whore dichotomy unquestionably informs Clarke's text. Like Hannah Heyes, Lizzie's appeal as a working-class heroine rests largely on her passivity, on *un*conscious charms that transform her into an object of desire.

And much like *Jane Eyre*'s Bertha Mason, Belton's wife looms large in the narrative though she is absent throughout most of it, another monstrous specter of excess who contrasts with Lizzie's virginal, controlled, and above all, "natural," femininity. In addition to her occasional violent rampages, Alice "was vain and shallow, and housework didn't harmonise with her ideas at all. All she thought of was dress and admiration. She used to sit in bed reading novelettes" (64). Such dangerous habits lead her to ignore her child (unlike Lizzie, who creates an instant maternal bond with Belton's son) and into promiscuity, pursuing a passionate affair with the "knobstick" of the title. Her (delusory) middle-class aspirations finally reach their apex in her relationship with a literal betrayer of the working class (and interestingly, the man whom she eventually murders because he betrays *her*). The morality lesson becomes even clearer by the novel's end: Alice dies in the workhouse while delivering a still-born child, appropriately repentant and confessing her guilt (on all levels), which clears the way for the legal consummation of Belton and Lizzie's love. Their pointedly *legitimate* pleasure is in turn accomplished and writ large in the greater climactic success of the community, the engineering strike.

Romance thus assumes the forefront in *The Knobstick*, but does so much less apologetically than in the later women's texts and serves a somewhat different political purpose. To begin, the novel's romantic and political narratives finally work together to promote a decidedly middle-class ethic in a Christian socialist guise: disapproving of class hatred, the novel recognizes character (honesty, goodness, trust) rather than (impersonal) social forces in its depiction of class strife. Clarke has not yet made the transition to the quasi-Marxist perspective of his future work. His emphasis on individual morality finds its greatest outlet in the realm of personal relations. Romance helps to establish the capacity for working-class people to express and desire intimacy, as well as testing their caliber.

In addition, however, the romance plot sets limits on working-class women's power within the culture itself. While there is a faint suggestion that Lizzie matures intellectually and politically over the course of the narrative, she does so expressly under Belton's tutelage, and as his bride essentially remains a decorous helpmate—hardly the respected, equal "comrade" that Ashraf portrays in her brief treatment of their relationship (157–158). She is reminiscent of those earlier working-class heroines like Disraeli's Sybil or Gaskell's Ruth, women of refined beauty who actually possess or suggest upper-class roots, values, and manners. More ordinary working-class female types such as Alice are represented as oversexed, self-centered harridans whose actual dominance in day-to-day existence leads to their own ruination. In contrast to Carnie Holdsworth's and Wilkinson's protagonists, both types of women in Clarke's novel are completely disqualified from any position of self-determination.[18]

Children of the Dead End

In Patrick MacGill's *Children of the Dead End* (1914), we begin to discern new possibilities for working-class narrative form in its more ambivalent approach to romance, representing though it does a rather odd mixture of class-conscious autobiography and courtly, rather than popular, romance. The novel's anxiously claimed "veracity," offering a truthful report on the Irish navvy's daily existence, jars with the highly contrived romantic quest plot that increasingly takes over. More than the other novelists, MacGill betrays an overbearing self-consciousness about his text's autobiographical dimensions, interrupting the narrative with "bulletins" to the reader: "In this true story, as in real life, men and women crop up for a moment . . . then go away and probably never reappear again. In my story there is no train of events or sequence of incidents leading up to a desired end" (111). Such authorial statements, however, become highly questionable since the narrative's seemingly aimless bent, following the protagonist through his series of odd jobs, is in fact governed by another, imported, form.

That form serves several functions. The first-person narrator, Dermod Flynn, quickly comes to perceive himself as a member of an outcast, itinerant class, the "navvy." From the age of twelve, when he is sent out into the world by his mother to "push his fortune," he experiences a series of degradations as an exploited manual laborer that both reinforce his pride in his class identity and incite a resistance to it. His body is a particular source of apprehension—the locus of his oppression but also his power, since it is the measure of his masculinity. Dermod develops the persona of knight/love poet in an effort to resist objectification and quickly discovers an appropriate muse. Childhood companion Norah Ryan (of *The Rat Pit*) comes to represent an unsullied ideal, as all other illusions and ideologies—including Celtic legend, Catholicism, and the capitalist work ethic—are gradually stripped away. In this novel, Norah embodies a "sacred" femininity which contrasts with the vulgar sexuality and materialism of other women in the text (his mother, other workers, prostitutes). She allows Dermod to uphold a vision of "pure" love in the midst of "filth," of "squalid poverty": "It was a love without any corporal end; its greatest desire did not turn to the illusive delights of the marriage bed. My love had none of the hunger of lust. . . . [I]t was something far holier and more enduring. To me Norah represented a poetical ideal; she was a saint, the angel of my dreams . . . [who] was too beautiful and pure to be degraded by anything in the world" (268). An extreme example of the formula that will be seen in later novels, the romantic relationship here depends on complete denial of the body—in fact, it largely remains a fantasy.

Spurred on by his mission to find Norah (from whom he becomes separated) and make her a "great lady," this fantasy allows Dermod to suspend his class subjectivity. He dares to imagine an existence in which he functions as "heart and soul" rather than "article of exchange" (37)—a vision as utopian as it is arguably bourgeois. It also disrupts the increasingly prized bond he shares with another navvy, Moleskin Joe. Joe is a key figure in the text, a raffish, ostensibly endearing representative of traditional masculinity who in some ways operates as a substitute father for Dermod. He deflates Dermod's romantic idealism, particularly his adoration of the feminine, setting up a counter tension in the narrative by pulling him back towards a more collective mode of consciousness. Under Joe's influence, Dermod begins to question the elitist and effeminate nature of his poetry (as well as other journalistic projects he attempts); more than ever, he values physical strength, the ability to settle arguments and engage in self-expression with his brawn rather than his brain.

Equally important, their relationship has a distinct homoerotic dimension. Even as Dermod repeatedly claims that the navvy class lacks a "sex instinct," his continued celebration of the naked male body, combined with the arousal he experiences as both a spectator of and participant in fights, suggests its deflected presence. Joe's body attracts particular attention, "a fine figure when stripped. His flesh was pure white below the brown of his neck and the long muscles of his arms stood out in clearly defined ridges. When he stretched his arms his well developed biceps rose and fell in graceful unison with every movement of his perfectly-shaped chest" (199). And in an ostensibly minor scene, we watch Dermod impulsively but secretly run his hands over the "rippling muscles" of a fellow potato harvester who has fallen asleep. Undermining the narrator's rejection of the entire arena of sexuality, the male body in this instance becomes another kind of class sign (and site) in the novel that seemingly reconciles individual with collective desires. (It also obviously complicates the courtly romance framework.)

Dermod's pursuit of individual subjectivity through Norah thus competes with the reality of his class-based existence. The split between fantasy and reality appears to remain unresolved, like the political narrative itself: Dermod becomes consciously converted to socialism and continues to enjoy his solidarity with various navvies, but actual strikes and other protest actions ultimately prove unsuccessful. A sense of fragmentation and disjunction finally threatens to reign (one sticking point for critics who have charged MacGill with "selling out" as a working-class writer.[19]) The narrator's continuing

obsession with Norah is crucial, then, to our mapping out of the ideological and formal tensions at work in the text, since she remains
a totalizing ideal even after he finds her as a prostitute much later.
Although Norah's sexualized status deflates his myth of femininity,
the novel maintains her innocence, reinscribing the myth as a whole.
Like Hardy's Tess, Norah is "still pure" in Dermod's eyes ("I knew
that there was no stain on the soul of her," 296). Seduced by a wealthy
farmer's son, she was, he insists, a "child" who had been "betrayed"
and "easily led astray" (268). Through the illusion of wholeness and
inviolability that Norah embodies, the romance plot accomplishes
a kind of closure by binding together the narrative's contradictory
moments and threads, maintaining the possibility of another, less
stigmatized, existence.

But since there are suggestions scattered throughout *Children* and
The Rat Pit that Norah is in fact the *source* of sexual knowledge,
another significant aspect of that closure involves the resolution of
women's sexuality (and hence one aspect of their power). Through
a series of brief, fragmented references, it emerges that Norah and
Dermod's brief period of courting as emigrés during the Scottish harvesting season comes to an end as a result of her impatience with his
sexual ignorance; while he remains content to imagine himself as her
knight, she longs for direct sexual experience and becomes attracted
to Alec Morrison (by whom she later became pregnant). Conflating
love and sexuality, she threatens Dermod's fiction of the feminine,
and her presence is accordingly removed from the remainder of
the narrative until the end, where her image stubbornly upholds his
myth. And as in *The Rat Pit,* she is also linked suggestively in this
earlier novel with a "withered and wrinkled harridan" (74) named
Gourock Ellen who is unashamed of her status as ex-prostitute and
despite her proverbial "heart of gold," the epitome of vulgarity in the
text. Branded as a witch, Ellen defies cultural norms and becomes
Norah's only trusted companion. Good intentions and virtuous acts
aside, both bear out Moleskin Joe's warning about women's demoralized nature—"They're all the same" (220).

By transforming Norah from a desiring sexual subject into the
reified object of romantic quest, the novel raises and then manages

the threat of female agency. It is especially useful in throwing into relief the complexities surrounding the linkage of romance with a privileged subjectivity in these texts (at least for women). *Children* may attempt to rescue working-class women from stereotyping, allowing them to adopt a position from which they are typically barred, but the strain involved in incorporating both versions of Norah's story is telling. Both, in the end, punish her.

Love on the Dole

By the 1930s, the romance plot tends to be more clearly subordinated in male texts (when appearing at all) and at least on the surface serves a more self-consciously oppositional function by furthering the texts' critiques of capitalism. But the anxieties surrounding class difference that remain in these narratives also become managed (in part) through representations of private relations between men and women. As we have already seen, Greenwood's *Love on the Dole* is an enormously complex novel that has a difficult time stabilizing its master narrative of class pride and revolt. Despite its deliberate parody of popular romance narrative, it is one of the few texts from the decade to completely endorse the desire for individualism conveyed through its romance subplots.

As Roger Webster has similarly noted, chapter titles such as "Take A Pair of Sparkling Eyes . . ." and "The Villain Still Pursues Her" contest the romance genre, and call attention to the disparity between fiction and reality (53–54). Hanky Park cannot help but yield principally ironic romantic heroes and heroines. Lacking privacy, energy, and money, the novel's two central couples—Helen and Harry, Sally and Larry—find it impossible to sustain their relationships and eventually their very illusions about romance. Greenwood is quite clear on the role that popular culture plays in fostering those illusions. Helen Hawkins comes to the realization that "[a]ll was a tangle; reality was too hideous to look upon: it could not be shrouded or titivated for long by the reading of cheap novelettes or the spectacle of films of spacious lives. They were only opiates and left a keener edge on hunger, made more loathsome reality's sores" (65). And while captivating men and women alike, romance is represented in the text as a particularly feminine weakness, the neighborhood women "prey to romantic notions whose potent toxin was to become part of the fabric of their brains" (31).

Despite its criticism, however, *Love on the Dole* finally validates the pursuit of romance. It becomes part and parcel of the text's socialist vision while simultaneously exposing, as Meath's character does generally, the alien nature of working-class culture. The failure of romance in working-class lives becomes a measure of its value, something that could be accessible under a different social system that meets material needs but equally allows for "civilized" bonds of intimacy. In a revealing interview with the *Manchester Evening News,* Greenwood said of the novel's purpose, "I have tried to show what life means to a young man living under the shadow of the dole, the tragedy of a lost generation who are denied consummation, *in decency,* of the natural hopes and desires of youth."[20] Restoration of the public/private split thus becomes central to his text's multiple, somewhat conflicting, messages about working-class experience. Those in the narrative seeking romantic relations are ultimately seeking retreat from a class subjectivity associated largely with oppression: hemmed in by both numbing factory work (until their jobs are lost entirely) and an overcrowded, often violent household that merges with others, they attempt to mark out individual identities, individual spaces, that remain inviolate.

The home emerges as the site of a particularly horrific, animalistic sexuality. Tom Hare's crude jokes about the local girls, for instance, lead quickly to a painful discussion of the working-class family:

"... They're all the same, her and th' old man. . . . So're all of 'em as is married. That's what they get married for . . . Your ma and' pa . . ."

"Shut it, Hare," snapped Harry, white, a threatening stare in his eyes: "You leave me ma and pa out of it . . ."

"Yaaah," Tom mumbled: "You're just daft, that's all." He glanced, furtively, at the others who were staring at their toes in silence. Their demeanors abashed him. He sensed he had overstepped the mark, and accustomed as he was to have their attention only at the expense of relating the behaviour of his parents, in whose bedroom, owing to pressure on the accommodation, he slept, he laughed forcedly and said: "Aw, y' get t' think nowt at all about it when y' get used to it . . . Why, on'y last night they came home drunk, and he . . ." (61–62)

Tom's story is followed by Helen's independent realization about "the staring horror of her home" (65):

No, that dirty, misshapen, half-naked child who had stood on the kerb a moment ago was not a character out of an absurd nightmare. His name was Tim Hawkins, one of a swarm, which lived, somehow, in the littered, mouldering kitchen which defied all efforts to keep clean. He and all that was associated with him; the unmentionable things, her parents' shamelessness which she herself dared not believe; these shut the door to idle dreaming and left her companioned only by her sole self. (65)

Afterwards, Helen's mother appears in the doorway to offer living proof of such bestiality—"a pot-bellied, middle-aged woman, teeth missing, hair in disarray about her face, her gait that of premature decrepitude. 'Hey,' she growled, and her stomach convulsed with the exclamation: 'Hey, come on wi'that there dinner, will y'. How long're y' gonna stand there gassin?" (66) Her behavior produces such shame in Helen that it is ironically romance that allows her to be "her sole self." It is important in this narrative, as in others, that the romantic sphere defer the consummation of sexual desire, allowing relations to occur between individual subjects, rather than objects. Helen and Harry's rare seaside holiday (bought with their racetrack winnings) emerges as the novel's primary utopian scenario on a number of levels: in a pastoral space beyond the reaches of the textile mill, they escape the production/consumption circuit; and playing husband and wife without actually engaging in sex, they experience intimacy without reducing it to a bodily function. The vacation neatly encompasses all that Larry Meath promises in his sidewalk speeches.

Ultimately, then, *Love on the Dole* reproduces the script of romance itself. The novel establishes careful structural links between the romantic and political narratives, so that the former not only deflates hopes but also provides solace within the latter. Florid passages of passion are embedded within, but are not entirely engulfed by, the languages of naturalism and satire. And for all her exposed delusions about love, Sally Hardcastle does achieve the status of traditional romance heroine in the text. Her extraordinary beauty attracts the most desirable man in the community—Larry—and her own romance "plot" is foiled finally by economic forces, rather than any kind of awakening proto-feminist consciousness (cf. Carrie, Helen, Joan). But if the novel's indulgence in romance fantasy transgresses several class-based boundaries, it also works hand in hand with a more typical masculine narrative. Depression-era novels such as Greenwood's almost inevitably feature the domestic arena as the new dominant sphere of activity (supplemented by political activity such as the Means-Test protest), which is depicted as an unnatural, unfamiliar space for men, unsettling gender roles and threatening to engulf the entire social structure.

Though both work and family relations in Hanky Park are typically marked by the loss of individual control, the community as a whole appears to be run by women. They continually undermine men's power and eventually imperil their very masculinity, whether at the pawnshop—where an imposing female "mob" needs to be restrained by force—at home governing the family budget, or, significantly, in the labor force itself, retaining or replacing positions while more costly male workers shift to the unemployment line and demeaning domestic duties. As explored earlier, the lingering fear of impotence pervading the narrative is linked to the increasingly effeminate character of the "de-skilled" labor available at public work sites, as well as that required at home.

And it is notably women—indeed, their very sexuality—that ultimately impel the plot as a whole. While the men lose their jobs, Helen's pregnancy and Sally's "prostitution" (after Larry's death) create more dramatic resolutions, as well as entrapments, at once furthering and (temporarily) disrupting the nightmarish narrative of want, exploitation, and weariness. (The women characters' actions also help us to interpret Greenwood's rather curious prefatory note in the novel's first edition about his use of the term "tart." Claiming regional specificity, he explains that in the North "tart" is a "general term for all femininity.") Women tend to adopt a dominant role in the romance subplots as well, placing men in another feminized position:

in love, women are the aggressors and men become the uncomfortable objects of *their* gaze. They are, however, considerably softened in that arena, as a rule seeking harmony rather than hegemony. Sally and Helen may press their lovers to adopt unfamiliar, constricting roles, yet they also seek to perform traditional feminine acts of comfort and nurturance. Serving a digressive as well as central function, the romance plot here displaces female power to a less threatening sphere, even as women continue to exercise some measure of control.

Mining Narratives: Harold Heslop and Lewis Jones

In chapter 2, I began to examine linkages between *The Gate of A Strange Field* and Greenwood's novel, focusing on their shared representations of worker-intellectuals. Those connections are deepened by their similar uses of romance subplots. But *Gate* is also one of a well-known set of Welsh mining novels from the 1930s including Heslop's *Last Cage Down* (1935) and Lewis Jones's *Cwmardy* (1937) and *We Live* (1939)—all of which in many ways appear to be more model revolutionary texts. While they allow romance to represent the search for individual subjectivity, they include the private sphere of relations in their narratives primarily to demonstrate its properly marginal position within the social system. And as with *Love on the Dole,* romance equally serves as an arena for their commentary on gender relations.

Of the four, only *The Gate of A Strange Field* comes to reject romance entirely as a legitimate desire or experience within working-class culture. At first glance, the novel appears to include romantic love as an integral part of its utopian vision. As the narrative opens, Joe Tarrant yearns to extricate himself from the dehumanizing world of home, as well as mine. I earlier sketched out his dissatisfactions as a young laborer. But we also learn early on, with the lead-in warning "[m]ining leads to excess," that Joe's parents "had instincts no higher than the animals, and they lived lives of utter sexual carelessness" (6). Their home is filthy and supremely disordered. ("Joe could not remember a time when there had not been a bed in the kitchen.") His adolescent romance with Molly Grahame initially provides him with an escape.

Played out in abandoned fields and carnivals, their relationship comes to be associated specifically with pleasure, and soon, with a seemingly classless identity. Joe "was losing himself and finding himself again—with her" (56). Their romance also allows for brief enjoyment of sexuality, but Molly's pregnancy forces an untimely marriage which quickly plunges their relationship into the same "pit" of "foulness" associated with his family. His mother's "disfigured" and "monstrous" body (6) merges with his wife's, reacquainting him with "sexual horror." This transformation is in fact prefigured during his first meeting with Molly at the carnival: with its crowd of "huge black men, curly-headed and brutish-looking . . . Chinese and Japanese, and over-sexed Arabs" (18), the fair is the site of racial exoticism and excess. Once the romantic becomes contaminated by the sexual, and henceforth figured into the domestic, Joe's class identity is sealed.

As his self-education process gains him notoriety and a respected union leadership position, he finds solace in an increasingly militant and "scientific" Marxism. But it is his illicit love affair with Emily Rutter, an organizer for the Independent Labour Party (ILP), which offers him true (momentary) fulfillment. Much different from his youthful romance with Molly, their relationship is mature, intellectual. The passages detailing their growing infatuation (on occasion sounding much like the "cheap novelettes" scorned by these writers) have the effect of endorsing Emily's feminized brand of radical politics—the "ambition to restore to the world its lost potion—Love" (144). The attachment provides Joe with a new, "corrected" vision of life. Emily's ILP affiliation itself usually appears as reformist: she "went her blissful way agitating for a more powerful Labor Government, strong in her simple faith, grubbing about like a mole" (184), and later speaks out against the strike. Yet even as Joe critiques her naive idealism, his "hard materialism" becomes challenged.

However, that challenge proves erroneous and finally dangerous. Throughout the text, the public and private plots reflect and reinforce one another: a critical mining accident occurs simultaneously with news of Molly's pregnancy; Joe's disillusionment with his Marxist education matches his disillusionment with his marriage; and most dramatically, the collapse of the General Strike parallels the collapse of Joe and Emily's love. Unlike Greenwood's text, the unsatisfactory resolution of both plots here serves less as a critique of capitalist culture—which keeps the working class at a subhuman, oppressed level—than a criticism of the pursuit of individualism in both arenas. The ability to escape a collective subjectivity, even momentarily, is exposed as an illusion. Joe's aspiration to rise above the rank and file as a union official comes to symbolize the problems with union leadership as a whole: the struggle for individual glory undermines mass solidarity and ultimately betrays the aims of the strike effort itself. Similarly, his search for an individual "self" with Emily becomes dismissed by the narrator as mere "cupidity" and vanity. The intermingling of romance and socialism, which she represents, is finally supplanted by a more masculine Marxist vision in which "the counsel of the mind . . . overrule[s] the wisdom of the heart" (281). Joe thus undergoes a kind of rebirth as a collective subject in the closing pages of the narrative when he is rescued from a life-threatening mine flood by his fellow (male) workers—the dawn breaks over a revitalized class community.

The other three novels of this sub-genre organize similar episodic features around the actions of a central male protagonist, which include strikes, mining accidents, disillusioning trade-union politics, and romantic liaisons. Yet trappings of romance subplots in this case work to acknowledge and legitimize individual desires, though they are clearly perceived as complementing and furthering the more strategic, pressing interests of a class-based identity. In *Last Cage Down,* Heslop's later novel, self-centered mining leader James Cameron is posed against the text's true hero, Joe Frost, an ascetic, benevolent worker-intellectual who embodies the ideals of the Communist party. Like Joe Tarrant, Cameron must learn over the course of the narrative to subordinate his individual gratifications, which include both an obsession with his own leadership role and an intense sexual interest in a barmaid named Betty. But much more than Tarrant, Cameron abuses or exploits his personal drives, so that *Last Cage Down* primarily counsels balance: in the end, he must simultaneously become Frost's political ally and the barmaid's husband when she's discovered pregnant. He comes to recognize Betty as an individual, rather than an object, whose love can nurture their (presumably) common class goals.

Once again, however, this romantic closure works specifically to indict women's sexuality, which here proves to be especially trouble-some and repulsive. In this Heslop text, the female body and its desires are directly associated with the oppressive, fearful, and rank nature of the mine itself. Franton Colliery, for instance, is "dirty, unkempt and horrible, like some old woman who has forgotten the bloom of her youth and is unmindful of her dirt. The black, panting pithead cast its dark shadows over everything" (47). And the orifice called "the goaf"—"the space between the floor of the mine and the roof when all the coal has been extracted"—is an exceptionally "vile place": "A miner's fight is always with the dreaded thing. . . . It grins eternally within its abysmal home, and like a savage animal it can wait a long time for its prey" (8–9). The sex scenes involving Betty evoke such a fight, with Betty herself bearing a phenomenal likeness to a "savage animal" waiting to strike; Bridget, another woman in the novel, is dismissed as "a great hopeless lump of child-bearing woman-hood, a gigantic queen bee" (132). Such images strikingly contrast with Heslop's celebration of the solitary male body when it is free of "the shackles of toil": Jim "gazed at himself. . . . He loved himself for what he was, a big noble fellow, a fine piece of humanity. . . . He clapped his great, hard muscles, felt them, pressed his lips against them, said loving things to himself, and remembered. . . . Cover up beauty!" (19)

Through most of the novel, women's power is at once recognized and devalued—precisely through representations of female sexu-ality. Their bodies are ironically linked with the capitalist system but also with the primitive and the retrograde, and as such, with the power of eroticism. The fleeting romantic sensibility appearing near the narrative's end seems a small attempt to contain working-class women by legitimizing them. Transformed from temptresses into nurturing political partners, they recede into the background as the prized symbol of "intimacy."

Thanks to the enthusiasm of contemporary critics like Graham Holderness and Carole Snee, Jones's *Cwmardy* and its sequel, *We Live*, have gained special notoriety within the British working-class literary canon as post-Tressell texts which more successfully than others defy the bourgeois dictates of the novel form—and specifi-cally through their handling of personal/public, individual/collective tensions. Though these readers tend to inflate the role of the mining community, Cwmardy, as the actual "protagonist" and underestimate the frequency or significance of private scenes involving individual characters, their overall assessment seems fair enough: the novels indeed privilege collectivity, carefully orchestrating private experiences to accentuate the magnitude and importance of mass action, mass identity.[21] The romance/marriage between miner and union leader Len Roberts (arguably the central figure in both narratives) and Mary Jones serves as the most prominent representative of that private realm. Their affection is tested by numerous obstacles, including Len's resentment of Mary's expanding role in politics, but proves to be a mainstay for both as they further the Communist party's goals.

One passage in particular, favored by nearly all of Jones's commentators, illustrates the novel's harmonious blending of individual and collective relationships. During a march protesting the General Strike sell-out, "Len kept close to Mary all the way, pressing her closely to his side in the crunch. 'This is life,' she whispered, stretching herself to bring her lips near his ear. 'Yes,' Len replied, 'because it shows the way to revolution and freedom' " (*We Live* 139). The mingling of intimacy and solidarity here may seem somewhat forced, but the vignette at least recognizes the multidimensionality of human emotions. However, another demonstration scene which focuses exclusively on Len conveys virtually the same message: "Len momentarily felt himself like a weak straw drifting in and out with the surge of bodies. Then something powerful swept through his being as the mass soaked its strength into him, and he realised that the strength of them all was the measure of his own, that his existence and power as an individual was buried in that of the mass now pregnant with motion behind him" (*We Live* 243). From the start, Len and Mary's love is completely and positively rooted in the historical destiny of their class. Their relationship thrives on embracing, rather than rejecting or escaping, their communal identity. Len's letter to Mary from Spain, depicted as the locale of the latest class war, extends that community globally in a way few working-class writers had managed before. Written in his dying moments, it delivers the narrative's final pronouncement on the personal and the political: "Sleep happy in the knowledge that our lives have been class lives, and our love something buried so deep in the Party that it can never die" (332).

Len's pronouncement remains problematic, however, on several grounds, smoothing over tension areas within both texts. For romance also represents a refuge from the shame of those "class lives"; and despite the novel's striking feminist sympathies, working-class women bear the brunt of Jones's anxieties about class difference. The incest sub-theme running throughout *Cwmardy*—the shameful secret of working-class experience hinted at in other novels' horrific pictures of sexuality—serves as one symptom of his fears. Len's sexual longings for his sister Jane are inspired first by glimpses of her maturing body, but later by her own seeming advances. Her dangerous desires swiftly lead her to pregnancy out of wedlock with a local boy and death during childbirth. Jane's "dirtiness" is in turn but an extension of her mother's, who had never married the children's father and who frequently asks him to "clean" her through a legal bond. Mary and her father form a second, though not so explicit, incestuous relationship within the novel. Though we occasionally witness sexual pleasure between Len and Mary throughout their romance and marriage, such experiences in both their pasts suggestively force sexuality into a forbidden zone. Their sickly, debilitated bodies (a combination of malnourishment, sensitivity, and traces of consumption) ensure that they rarely cross the line. As with Dermod and Norah in MacGill's fiction, their love transcends the material world. While the romance subplot primarily testifies to the compatibility of private and public interests, it also exposes the friction between them that precludes any final resolution.

A Scots Quair

The three novels that comprise Gibbon's trilogy are perhaps the most provocative in my discussion. Their treatment of romance and subjectivity, centered around a female protagonist, departs significantly from the shared conventions of other male texts, yet they have also been consistently well received by a range of readers. In one sense, Gibbon's approach reaches back to Clarke's, establishing a suppressed point of continuity within the male working-class literary tradition.

Like Clarke, Gibbon concentrates on the private sphere in his narrative, with the same apparent ease. But the comparison ends there, for his texts also reach forward into a distinctly modern aesthetic, as well as political, sensibility. His revealing *Left Review* commentary, for instance, explicitly lashes out against the dictates of proletarian realism. While defending his own radical credentials—"I hate capitalism; all my books are explicit or implicit propaganda"—he objects to the "misapprehension and ignorance" of the Writer's International statement of purpose:

> With a little bad Marxian patter and the single adjective 'bourgeois' in their vocabularies they proceed (in the literary pages of the *Daily Worker* and like organs) to such displays of spiteful exhibitionism as warrant the attentions of a psycho-analyst. From their own innate second-rateness they hate and despise good work just as they look upon any measure of success accruing to a book (not written by one of their own intimate circle) with a moronic envy. (1:5 [Feb. 1935]: 179)

His unorthodox style and devotion to "quality" have helped him develop a flawless critical reputation. More than any other writer since Tressell, whose secure foothold in working-class literary history seems as much upheld by sentimentality as by scholarly admiration, Gibbon has emerged as the favorite son of this genre. And as with Tressell, his popularity with contemporary critics is partly due to his experimental, quasi-modernist style. Ramón López Ortega speaks for many when he boasts that Gibbon "ranks with major twentieth-century writers," including no less than T. S. Eliot (whose own praise of Gibbon, which Ortega mentions "incidentally," further authenticates his stature) (139; 141). Recently, however, feminists have also begun paying attention. Deirdre Burton has argued that *A Scots Quair* bears a striking resemblance to contemporary women's texts, employing similar stylistic devices and demonstrating unusual sensitivity to women's issues. She points to such features in the narrative as nurturing friendships between women, recognition of the materialist base of marriage, and especially "the recurrent representation of Chris's awareness of her own split subjectivity and contradictory social and psychological positions" (36).[22] But if the trilogy in fact has a more predictably "feminine" stamp than the novels of the period by working-class women themselves, I'd like to focus specifically on its uses of romance plotting to explore why this writer is granted much more respect than women writers of the period generally command.

Although *A Scots Quair* begins with an epic/mythic history of the people and their land, and builds toward an escalating multiplicity of viewpoints and voices, it allows one woman's consciousness to dominate throughout. The novels follow Chris Guthrie from adolescence through middle age as one (highly individual) representative of her class. (The first novel in the trilogy, *Sunset Song,* is a particularly self-conscious feminine epic, its narrative merging the parallel rhythms of Chris's body and of the harvesting season.) And unlike the male texts examined above, these works focus on women's labor, openly celebrate private emotion, and valorize the body (both male and female). Furthermore, the sexual, the romantic, the political, and the domestic all surprisingly merge here. Sexuality does take an excessive and oppressive form in Chris's childhood—both she and her mother are terrorized by her father's brutish, self-centered attacks (though Chris is mostly threatened, rather than actually victimized). Her mother's subsequent suicide and her father's continuing incestuous desires both play parts in shaping her consciousness. Yet she achieves a fulfilling and quite aggressive sexuality in all three of her marriages—each of which mark the successive volumes—and wins varying kinds of love. As I will detail below, courtship and marriage serve a different *class* function in these texts.

At the same time, the sexual/romantic/domestic triad breaks down intermittently, with the possibility, but not the guarantee, of resolution. The waning of love and/or desire, the collapse of private relationships, appears both natural and cultural, the outcome of forces: Chris's first and most passionate marriage with the crofter Ewan Tavandale is destroyed by World War I; her second marriage to the socialist minister Robert Colquohoun founders as a result of his political despair as well as Chris's resistance to her own gentrification; her third brief marriage to Ake Ogilvie, while representing a shift to the urban environment of Duncairn, fails not because of alienation or economic limitations but due to simple boredom. As in *Miss Nobody,* popular romance narrative becomes satirized here for its absurd valuing of female chastity, its rags-to-riches morality, and its idealized closure, rather than for its belief in the power of love itself.[23]

Despite these departures from the twentieth-century working-class narrative model, however, *A Scots Quair* still registers conflict between individual and collective subjectivity and does so by explicitly addressing working-class shame. As constructed, Chris's split consciousness appears predominantly rooted in class rather than gender. Though Deirdre Burton's feminist analysis of the trilogy is useful, she misreads Chris's struggle with "contradictory subject positions" as a universal "dilemma" of "female experience" (39). Gibbon's female protagonist always experiences gender from a classed position, and the basis of the primary division within her consciousness emphasizes that position. The body/mind split cited by Burton is actually particularized in the narrative as a conflict surrounding the "real," peasant Chris, who feels one with the earth, and the "English Chris"—the intellectual, asexual self that seeks the same sort of classless identity secretly prized in the other novels. Shifting between second and third person, the text represents the division as a split between nature and culture—significantly, between native and oppressor discourses:

> So that was Chris and her reading and schooling, two Chrisses there were that fought for her heart and tormented her. You hated the land and the coarse speak of the folk and learning was brave and fine one day and the next you'd waken with the peewits crying across the hills, deep and deep, crying in the heart of you and the smell of the earth in your face, almost you'd cry for that, the beauty of it and the sweetness of the Scottish land and skies. You saw their faces in firelight, father's and mother's and the neighbors' . . . you wanted the words they'd known and used, . . . Scots words to tell to your heart, how they wrung it and held it, the toil of their days and unendingly their fight. And the next minute that passed from you, you were English, back to the English words so sharp and clean and true. (37)

Overturning the male texts' common formula, romance in this set of narratives begins as, and continues to be, one means of actually *restoring* Chris to her peasant consciousness, since it reinforces and revives her sensuality. All three relationships with men remind Chris in varying ways of her class loyalties, which she registers through her body. But romance also provides another kind of pathway to a "separate" self in the sense that she becomes completely immersed in the tumult of personal experience, deliberately shutting out the changes and needs of her class community. This is not so apparent in *Sunset Song*, where Blawearie Farm, the Guthrie homestead, serves as the intersection point of individual and class experience. In *Cloud Howe* and *Grey Granite*, however, Chris begins to pull away from her class as it becomes proletarianized, and develops noteworthy differences. It seems to have less and less to do with her; she grows nostalgic for its (reconstructed) past. Her attempt to extricate herself from that class through private, intimate bonds proves increasingly unsuccessful, however, so that Chris's attempt to maintain a separation between private and public worlds—arguably part of what Burton calls her "female vision" of community and of culture—is finally thrown into question. Her solitary return to Blawearie at the end of *Grey Granite* (sans men or her son) emerges as a problematic, rather than laudatory, act of defiance.[24]

But if the trilogy uses romance plotting to interrogate Chris's interpretation of class politics, it also serves to critique her son's equally imbalanced vulgar Marxist views, which deny the validity of individualism. As he becomes radicalized by his experience as a laborer at the Duncairn metal works plant, Ewan greatly prizes his class consciousness and fears the dilution that occurs through his romantic/sexual entanglement with an English schoolteacher, Ellen Johns. Ellen's Labour Socialist convictions initially elicit Ewan's attention and admiration, yet his growing militancy soon places a wedge in their relationship. And that wedge is driven deeper by sexuality. Unlike his mother, Ewan lacks the freedom to celebrate his body. His fear and revulsion stem from the torture he experiences in jail during a police round-up of "Reds." His body becomes a communal symbol of oppression. [After the police did] "shameful things to his body,"

he lay still with a strange mist boiling, blinding his eyes, not Ewan Tavandale at all any more but lost and be-bloodied in a hundred broken and tortured bodies all over the world, in Scotland, in

England, . . . a livid, twisted thing in the prisons where they tortured the Nanking Communists, a Negro boy in an Alabama cell while they thrust razors into his flesh, castrating with a lingering cruelty and care. He was one with them all, a long wail of sobbing mouths and wrung flesh, tortured and tormented by the world's Masters while those Masters lied about Progress through Peace, Democracy, Justice, the Heritage of Culture. (452)

Rather than functioning purely as an inspirational image of solidarity, however, the passage also exposes the limitations of Ewan's conclusions. For the "boiling mist" of the opening line indeed "blinds" him to the healing possibilities of private relationships, private desires. After the jail incident, Ellen takes him into the woods and by "seducing" him momentarily enacts his reawakening: he is "hallowed and clean and made whole again" (466). But it is a brief rebirth, stunted by his return to the brotherhood of the Communist party. Though the trilogy closes with the heroic image of Ewan leading his dramatic hunger march, his failed relationship with Ellen notably undercuts his political achievements. He appears only a shell of a man. Rejecting both complete withdrawal and complete immersion, *A Scots Quair* finally seems to endorse a vision which could imagine a fruitful tension between individual and collective subjectivity, between private and public relations.[25]

The trilogy's incorporation of the romance plot thus accomplishes explicit ideological ends, calling attention to, rather than attempting to suppress or critique, the legitimacy of "self"-hood. It champions, as David Smith suggests, "life rather than dogma" (127). And as Burton adds, it certainly broadens the representation of women in the male working-class text. Gibbon's narrative recognizes working-class women's autonomy and supports (if not altogether privileges) one kind of feminized standpoint. But while the script of romance, sex, and marriage gets revised considerably here from a gender perspective—with woman emerging as the positive dominant force in all three—there is another, potentially disturbing, tendency to construct Chris throughout the trilogy as a sexual object, not only for her lovers', but for the reader's consumption. The countless scenes in which she undresses alone before a mirror and gazes at her reflection suggest that she experiences herself as an object of desire (as well as desiring subject), something separate from herself—undoubtedly one aspect of female subjectivity, as Burton's essay points out. Those scenes serve as one marker of the passing years, during which she alternately anticipates and dwells on male appreciation of her body. However, Chris's gaze is mirrored by ours. We are invited to adopt a specifically voyeuristic position, fetishizing (along with Chris) her various "parts":

> But it was only for a second she thought of that, . . . and slowly took off her clothes, looking at herself in the long glass that had once stood in mother's room. She was growing up limber and sweet, not bonny, perhaps, her cheek-bones were over high and her nose over short for that. . . . So she saw herself and her teeth clean-cut and even. . . . And below face and neck now her clothes were off was the glimmer of shoulders and breast and there her skin was like satin, it tickled her touching herself. Below the tilt of her left breast was a dimple, she saw it and bent to look at it. . . . And she straightened as the moonlight grew and looked at the rest of herself, and thought herself sweet and cool and fit for that lover who would some day come and kiss her and hold her, so. (63–64)

Some time later, Chris again looks

> at herself naked as though she looked at some other than herself, a statue like that of the folk of olden time that they set in the picture galleries. And she saw the light white on the satin of her smooth skin then, and the long, smooth lines that lay from waist to thigh, thigh to knee, and was glad her legs were long from knee to the ankle, that made legs seem stumbling and stumpy, shortness there. And still impersonally she bent to see if that dimple still hid there under her left breast, it did, it was deep as ever. (116)

Such episodes recall the ostensibly tongue-in-cheek scene involving the village's prurient minister—also named Gibbon—whose erotic

Song of Solomon sermon similarly lingers over descriptions of a woman's breasts and thighs. In both contexts, it seems to me, the audience is allowed to have its "bit pleasure by proxy" (53).

While Chris thus enjoys her body in ways unimaginable to the other writers—male and female alike—she also increasingly *becomes* her sexuality, reduces herself to her body. Although this process is critiqued (obliquely) from a class position, as suggested earlier, it appears to be naturalized in gender terms. At times, she is uncomfortably reminiscent of Lawrencian women like Anna Brangwen, whose celebration of fertility and ties to the land appear nearly depraved.[26] Gibbon's portrayal of Chris is clearly informed by a much more sympathetic interest in women's cultural and social positioning, but susceptible to similar distortion and masculinist assumptions. For as the narrative unfolds, heterosexuality itself receives special attention: the "love between a childe [man] and quean [woman]" joins class struggle as the "other" prime mover of history, "a tale so old— oh, old as the Howe, everlasting near as the granite hills, this thing that brought men and women together, to bring new life, to seek new birth, on and on since the world had begun" (320). At once enriching and limiting her possibilities as an active agent within the narrative, Chris's eroticization suggests another dimension to Gibbon's ideological agenda. His deployment of the private sphere can be enormously useful for readers who are trying to perceive more clearly the complicated operation of romance in working-class writing, as well as for other writers wishing to push the limits. The trilogy's insights, however, free of the shame haunting other texts, come at the expense of a certain distance from working-class women's actual experiencing of romance as oppression, as well as bourgeois luxury.

In many ways, romance serves as the very foundation of the alternate scheme of resistance strategies developed over the course of this study, the representative disrupter of most critical equations or formulas seeking to define "opposition." By focusing on the intersection of class and gender relations (within and between classes), this "private" sphere becomes the place where we can glimpse the greatest anxieties and longings concerning working-class culture and writing—where we can begin to track the debilitating, as well as empowering, effects of both marginality and incorporation. The adoption, modification, and suppression of the romance convention provides perhaps the best vantage point from which to view the bared outlines of a master literary framework because it is *in* those instances that the framework is so clearly being negotiated; it is in those instances that assumptions about class authenticity and agency are alternately reaffirmed and challenged. Arguably the most visible arena in which the master narrative of class conflicts with the master narrative of gender, romance at once forces and allows writers of both sexes to confront the significance of their exclusion from (an assortment of) dominant scripts.

A F T E R W O R D

Getting Their Own Back

■

Poor and working peoples have always found ways to get the best of those who have power over them—to win back a momentary sense of autonomy and self-respect. I have suggested that between the turn of the century and World War II, writers who emerged from various working-class communities throughout the United Kingdom— from London's East End to the Derbyshire coal fields, from the Welsh mining villages to Lancashire's textile towns—contributed to a broad developing structure of feeling about the meaning of both working-class identity and working-class resistance. In their narratives, Spindleton's weavers, Mugsborough's hands, Manchester's shop girls, and Cwmardy's miners share a sensibility (if not a slogan) that encompasses rage, shame, and desire. Accentuating defiance, they still cannot conceal the profound distress that surrounds their abject position in dominant culture.

A suspect motto in *The Ragged Trousered Philanthropists,* "gettin' your own back" actually reveals the aim—and final achievement— of these texts all too clearly: its very phrasing registers the urge not simply to act, to claim agency, but to acquire a self of one's "own" that conflates individualist and collective consciousnesses. In their bid for privacy, pleasure, and inclusion, which both competes with and complements their mission of class solidarity, they create a model of subjectivity that ultimately falls into neither bourgeois nor Marxist categories. Helen Lynd's study of late nineteenth-century England looked forward to the future development of such subjectivity, calling it "positive freedom." As noted earlier, she distrusted the rigidity of turn-of-the-century Labourism, since in her estimation its collectivist philosophy offered "salvation in narrowly conceived blueprints of a new social order" (*England* 430) rather than a "new method of analysis" (428) to understand individual workers' relationship to culture. Envisioning individuality as "something to be wrought out in a rich social setting" (430), Lynd had only to consult the working-class fictional texts of the subsequent period to glimpse her theory worked out in narrative form.

Tressell's Frank Owen, Holdsworth's Hester Martin, and Brierley's Jack Cook serve as particularly striking examples of this hybrid consciousness. Through their negotiations of public and private arenas, they on one level certainly reveal their affiliations with the introspective, sealed off psyches of avant garde literature. Yet their privileged difference from other working-class figures never goes all the way; it is always mediated or balanced by their shared material class positioning and, finally, their class allegiance. Shame dictates their desire to escape the working-class "mass," but they know they cannot. And most importantly, should not. At times, the narratives may fall short in making this prized, quasi-individualist identity work toward radical ends. Frank, Hester, and Jack perhaps "fail" as transformative agents in conventional utopian terms. But that's ultimately not the point. In the end, the result of such ideological and formal tensions is an amalgam representing nothing less than a new class subject and cultural form.

In the opening chapters of this study, I went to considerable lengths to document the rehabilitation efforts of working-class studies—from post–World War II to poststructuralism. Intent on acknowledging and/or preserving the emancipatory aspects of working-class culture(s), theorists as diverse as Hoggart and Hall have forever changed our sense of the possibilities offered by the conceptual and lived position of "class." A reading strategy attentive to the multiple forms and representations of class shame can contribute to that project by re-envisioning neglected or stigmatized cultural practices. These novels demonstrate that the notion of a reproduction-resistance "circuit" operating within dominated cultures may appear functional, but on closer examination, is disrupted by interior "static." The conflicting pressures and desires encompassing works by Clarke, Wilkin-

son, Greenwood, and the others give new meaning to the process of
"struggle and contestation," as well as to concepts such as "militancy,"
"recuperation," "self-indulgence," and "indignation." Their very inability to choose between a strictly bourgeois individualism and a
strictly socialist or Marxist collectivism is not a symptom of cultural
reproduction, but rather a dramatization of the current limitations
of reproduction as a theoretical and analytic category.

The brief autobiographical reminiscences of one Mrs. Scott, the
"Felt Hat Worker" of the Women's Cooperative Guild volume *Life As
We Have Known It*, represent a rather remarkable crystallization of
this dynamic as it takes up (and necessarily implicates) both gender
and class. She begins with two observations which become interwoven
on several levels: (1) the significance of gender difference and, by
extension, differently gendered spaces; and (2) the necessity of independent vision. Opening her piece with the memory of a violent
sexual crime committed near her home when she was three years old,
she proudly recalls her response to her mother's warning that the
hollow "was not safe for little girls": "I remember getting something
to drag behind me and asking one or two more children to venture
with me, and going down to the hollow to see if anything really did
happen to you. . . . This I suppose was the beginning of my habit
of testing things for myself and not taking facts and opinions ready-
made" (81). Mrs. Scott proceeds to praise the Women's Cooperative
Guild as a working-class institution which encourages such a "habit,"
"placing the facts before [its] members, and letting them judge for
themselves whether to accept or reject" (81). Denying the very notion
or strictures of a master narrative, she writes her life along ostensibly
individualized lines, focusing on reading, work, and political activism. One anecdote offers a particularly striking glimpse of her hopes
for the future, inspired by a "deeply religious" library book she had
borrowed:

The husband told the wife if she built a town, it would be all
baths, kitchens and washhouses, and she retorted that if he built
one, it would be all art galleries, museums and parks. I won-
dered why they could not be combined, and I have sat hours at

work planning a city, fitting in beautiful homes and everything
to make life beautiful and happy, instead of sordid and ugly like
our factory towns. (84)

Mrs. Scott's socialist utopia recognizes the necessity of both public
and private spheres and appears to be endorsed by the guild—her
last paragraph thanks the wcg for helping her and other working women to "see the City Beautiful" (101). Yet, like the narrative by Mrs. Layton examined in chapter 3, this text subscribes to a
formula which increasingly conflates those spheres, clearly subordinating individual to collective desires. Her own fleeting romantic history becomes a tale of the ilp's Clarion Fellowship group, where she
and her future husband discover a haven of "real comradeship" [89].
Finally, this writer's confident autonomy is both strengthened and
compromised by her sense of working-class narrative conventions.
As with the hollow of her youth, they prove "unsafe" for women.
Only the "horror of debt" (82) documented in her early years begins to suggest the power, as well as fear, of longings which remain
unfulfilled.

The narratives' imbrication of sexual and class differences can be
most valuable, it seems to me, to the newly revitalized body of materialist feminist theory. Cora Kaplan's work in that field over the
past decade began a "sea change" in the right direction by reclaiming fantasy and pleasure as crucial topics in the study of gender
and class. Arguing for a "historically appropriate use" of psychoanalysis in feminist criticism, she was one of the first to note and
critique socialist feminism's avoidance of the private sphere, particularly sexuality. Its "deep commitment to the rational and . . . mistrust
of emotion" (*Sea Changes* 4), inherited from orthodox Marxism, kept
women's material oppression in focus but precluded the necessary
exploration of their desires and needs. Kaplan's reinterpretation of
that founding slogan of feminism, "the personal is political," together
with her use of postmodern methodologies, has set a new agenda for
theorizing class and gender subjectivity.[1]

Old habits, however, and older political maxims, die hard. Rosemary Hennessey's recent contribution to materialist feminist theory,

for instance, breaks with tradition on many fronts but maintains a cautious approach to the private sphere, reducing women's sexuality to ideological "sexualization."[2] Indeed, throughout the writing of this book I found it difficult to suppress my own nagging misgivings about the women novelists' longings for the most conventional of pleasures. They and I both appeared to be making fatal transgressions. Their texts serve, then, as especially useful reminders that feminist and Marxist schools of thought can become mired in shared versions of authentic rebellion and must be shaken up, dislocated from prior models or formulas.

At the same time, these vestiges of an ascetic Marxist/feminist "tradition" have been offset by a Bakhtinian trend to embrace the "excess" and sensuality of subordinated cultures. Bakhtin's notion of pleasure as a potentially liberating and disruptive state, distilled into his writings on carnival, has become a staple of postmodern thought.[3] When linked to the iconography of the peasant, lower class, or "grotesque" body, it informs recent feminist work in body politics as well. Susan Bordo's studies of eating disorders and Laura Kipnis's essay on *Hustler* magazine are just two examples which champion working-class culture as an oppositional sphere defiantly exulting in low, "profane" gestures and practices. Though taking different avenues, each explores what Bordo calls the "management of desire" (96) in contemporary capitalist culture by favorably contrasting the excessively massive or uncontrolled working-class body with the excessively thin and puritanical middle- or upper-class body. Such tropes are invoked precisely to address class divisions among women, with the effect (if not intent) of *re*dressing socialist feminism's prior limitations.[4]

Once again, however, working-class writing itself makes the most compelling case for a more moderate approach to these questions and issues. The classed and gendered bodies within these narratives can never figure as exclusive symbols of either power or oppression. The novels' interconnected sensibilities of shame and pride should make us wary of polarities and prescriptions. They insistently invoke a middle ground. I close by suggesting that we neither revere the past and the class that such fictions can be drafted to represent, nor, as Carolyn Steedman finally advises, "consign" their "impossible, secret stories" to the "dark" (144). When we allow those exposed "stories" in turn to reveal (and often counter) our own, they have the potential to set contemporary cultural theories of class on a new (convergence of) path(s).

Introduction

1   See chapter 1 for a detailed discussion of the debates surrounding this assertion. For specific histories of the early twentieth-century Labour College movement, see Kelly; Ree; and J. P. Millar, *The Labour College Movement* (National Council of Labour Colleges, 1979).

2   The following novels serve as examples, though their fame or notoriety is clearly relative to the utter obscurity of the texts I focus upon: George Bernard Shaw, *An Unsocial Socialist* (New York: Brentano, 1901); Clementina Black, *An Agitator* (New York: Harper, 1895); Isabella Ford, *On the Threshold* (London: Arnold, 1895); Gertrude Dix, *The Image Breakers* (London: N. Heinemann, 1900); Margaret Harkness, *A City Girl* (London: n.p., 1887); Henry Green, *Living* (London: Hogarth Press, 1948).

3   For the standard works of reproduction theory, see the following: Althusser; Basil Bernstein, *Class, Codes and Control*, Vol. 3, *Towards a Theory of Educational Transmission*, 2nd ed. (London: Routledge, 1977); Bourdieu and Passeron; Bourdieu, *Outline of A Theory of Practice;* selections from Bourdieu's *Distinction;* Bowles; Bowles and Gintis.

4   See his *Learning to Labour.*

5   See "The Emergence of Cultural Studies," especially 11–12.

6   For an enormously useful overview of the cccs's work, see *Culture, Media, Language,* Ed. Stuart Hall et al., especially Hall's introductory piece, "Cultural Studies and the Centre: Some Problematics and Problems," 15–47, as well as his later "Cultural Studies and its Theoretical Legacies," *Cultural Studies,* Ed. Lawrence Grossberg et al. (New York: Routledge, 1992), 277–294. Also see the following studies and/or collections: Hall and Jefferson; *Working Class Culture: Studies in History and Theory,* Ed. John Clarke et al. (London: Hutchinson, 1979); *Women Take Issue,* Ed. Women's Studies Group, Centre For Contemporary Cultural Studies (London: Routledge, 1978); McRobbie, "Settling Accounts with Subcultures"; Hebdige; Batsleer et al.; Widdowson; Willis and Corrigan, "Cultural Forms and

Class Mediations"; Willis, "Cultural Production"; Willis, *Learning to Labour;* Willis and Corrigan, "Orders of Experience"; Willis, *Profane Culture.*

7 See, for instance, Hakken; John Fiske, *Television Culture* (New York: Routledge, 1987); J. Fiske, "British Cultural Studies and Television," *Channels of Discourse: Television and Contemporary Criticism,* Ed. R. Allen (Chapel Hill: U of North Carolina P, 1987); Simon Frith, *Music For Pleasure: Essays in the Sociology of Pop* (New York: Routledge, 1987); Laura Kipnis, "Refunctioning Reconsidered: Toward a Left Popular Culture," *High Culture/Low Theory,* Ed. Colin MacCabe (New York: St. Martin's, 1986), 29–31; and McRobbie, ed., *Zoot Suits.*

8 Willis and Corrigan, "Orders of Experience," especially 85–86.

9 See *Women Take Issue*; and other more recent relevant works such as Swindells and Jardine.

10 Similarly, his co-authored essay with David Shumway, Paul Smith, and James Sosnoski encourages teachers to help students become "agents in the production of social practices" by "fostering forms of resistance" which "promote . . . analysis of the underlying ideological interests at stake in the text" (482), yet those "interests" to be "resisted" seem exclusively hegemonic or canonical. See Giroux, "The Need for Cultural Studies." Also see Giroux and Aronowitz; and Giroux, *Teachers as Intellectuals,* and "Resisting Differences."

11 My conception of such a circuit is independent of that sketched out by Richard Johnson in his essay "What is Cultural Studies Anyway?" which represents "a circuit of the production, circulation, and consumption of cultural products" (46), but they do share certain commonalities. In the effort to both describe and critique various assumptions and methodologies operating within cultural studies scholarship, Johnson's diagram illustrates the actual relationship between "moments" of capitalist production, capitalist reproduction, and the production of "new" cultural forms. Arguing that these "moments" are never truly separated, he contends that in certain cases, "the circuit is, at one and the same time, a circuit of capital and its expanded reproduction *and* a circuit of the production and circulation of subjective forms" (47). He appears, however, to be accentuating the need to perceive these seemingly public and private spheres in active, transformative relation, rather than to redefine the underlying concepts themselves, which I do.

12 Ranciere.

13 See Sennett and Cobb. At one point Steedman herself mentions Sennett and Cobb's work in relation to her own, but emphasizes their differences: she argues that they focus on the "systematic exclusions" produced by the structuring of labor and school systems, which she believes overlooks the more subtle senses of "injury"—particularly as they are experienced by women. I agree with Steedman's evaluation of the gender-blindness in Sennett and Cobb's study, yet find more similarities between the two approaches than gaps. See Steedman 113.

14 Hooks. Specifically, hooks speaks of "depths of longing": "Those without money long to find a way to get rid of the endless sense of deprivation. Those with

money wonder why so much feels so meaningless and long to find the site of 'meaning.' Witnessing the genocidal ravages of drug addiction in black families and communities, I began to 'hear' that longing for a substance as, in part, a displacement for the longed-for liberation—the freedom to control one's destiny" (12). She concludes, "All too often our political desire for change is seen as separate from longings and passions that consume lots of time and energy in daily life. . . . Surely our desire for radical change is intimately linked with the desire to experience pleasure, erotic fulfillment, and a host of other passions" (12–13).

15 For the former, see Freud's *Three Essays on the Theory of Sexuality* (Standard Ed., 7:125–243. London: Hogarth Press, 1953) and *On Narcissism: An Introduction* (Standard Ed., 14:67–102. London: Hogarth Press, 1957); O. Fenichel, *The Psychoanalytic Theory of Neurosis* (New York: Norton, 1972); E. Jacobson, *The Self and the Object World* (New York: International UP, 1964); H. Nunberg, *Principles of Psychoanalysis* (New York: International UP, 1955); even, to some degree, L. Wurmser's *The Mask of Shame* (Baltimore: Johns Hopkins, 1981). For the latter, the best known is E. H. Erikson's work such as *Childhood and Society* (New York: Norton, 1963). Also see G. Kaufman, *Shame: The Power of Caring* (Cambridge, Mass.: Schenkman, 1985) and S. Levin, "The Psychology of Shame," *International Journal of Psychoanalysis* 52 (1971): 355–362.

16 Broucek comments, "Shame frequently has to do with experiencing oneself being treated as an object when one is attempting to relate to the other in a intersubjective mode. . . . In the state of sudden, unsought, or undesired self-objectification the immediate experience of one's actuality of being may be lost, resulting in shame and a disorienting transformation of the interpersonal and phenomenal world" (39–40). This theory becomes concretized in a later segment focusing on a stripper named "Olympia"; in that chapter, Broucek cites John Berger's famous passage in *Ways of Seeing* about women as "self-surveyors." See Broucek 37–42.

17 Her theory of "field dependence" also goes as far as identifying gender as a determining category of experience: reminiscent of Nancy Chodorow's claims, she notes that field-dependent patients—"self-effacing," "readily merging . . . with the surround" (36)—are frequently women. See "The Role of Shame in Depression Over the Life Span," in Helen Block Lewis, 29–50.

18 See Benedict's *The Chrysanthemum and the Sword* (Boston: Houghton, 1946), 222–224.

19 Helen Lewis notes that shame is often equated with infantile narcissism. See Lewis 1–5; 30–32.

20 Geertz's own well-known work on Balinese culture, as well as Milton Singer's examination of the University of Chicago's Indian Education Project conducted during the 1940s, are just two anthropological studies which directly challenge Benedict's shame/guilt thesis. See Geertz's *The Interpretation of Cultures* (New York: Basic Books, 1973); and Gerhart Piers and Milton Singer's *Shame and Guilt* (New York: W. W. Norton, 1953, 1971), 71–95. The enormous body of post-structuralist anthropological theory, of course, has abandoned this line of inquiry entirely,

rejecting its racist assumptions and naive methodology. For one example of the latter, see James Clifford and George Marcus, Eds., *Writing Culture: the Poetics and Politics of Ethnography* (Berkeley: California, 1986).

21   I have consulted a number of psychoanalytic texts concerned with shame. Lynd's work is frequently cited but noted for its general concern with identity and the relationship between shame and guilt. See, for instance, Morrison 8–9 and 45–46; Broucek 19–20; Helen Lewis 30, 37; Steinberg 658.

22   She warns, the "attempt of psychology and social science to exclude history in the interests of abstract method, logical completeness, and a timeless objectivity may result in missing the concrete realities that these disciplines are attempting to understand." But history, also, must be historicized and recognized as constructed narrative: "The historian inevitably selects the problems and the data that seem to him most significant and classifies them in the way that seems most significant. His conception of what is important reflects the concerns of his particular environment, his class, and his own period of history" (112).

23   Clark Wissler, foreword to Lynd and Lynd vi.

24   Interestingly, the book's acknowledgments page thanks the Hammonds, prolific labor historians, and her "friends" the Webbs.

25   I am fully aware that such a "period" is a construct and encompasses several traditional "sub"-periods (Edwardian, Between the Wars, the Twenties, the Thirties, and so on), each of which generates particularized studies of British working-class culture and history. I am arguing that it has taken on a kind of shorthand referential status for historians and cultural theorists when discussing proposed contrasts between Britain's pre– and post–World War II working class, as well as for some literary critics working with this "canon" of modern working-class texts.

26   See the discussion, in chapter 1, of the position taken by Robert Roberts in his autobiography (Roberts), and by Gareth Stedman Jones (Jones).

27   As with Giroux's search for "authentic" resistance, it makes little sense for critics to distinguish between "working-class" texts with a merely "descriptive" purpose, and "proletarian" texts with a "radical," "interrogative" purpose; the writing in some senses always mingles description and contestation. For one argument that seeks to preserve such distinctions (with qualifications), see Williams, "Working-Class, Proletarian, Socialist."

28   Also see Jameson's *Marxism and Form* (Princeton, N.J.: Princeton UP, 1972), 327–331.

29   Thanks to Nancy Armstrong for her assistance in clarifying my intentions here.

30   For one discussion of such projects, see Ken Worpole's *Dockers and Detectives* (London: Verso, 1983).

31   The former argues that the nonnaturalism present in works such as *Sons and Lovers* actually helps to foster a utopian vision (i.e., by showing that "reality" is *not* natural, the text shows what can be changed); the latter proposes that Greenwood's text is a self-reflexive work that exposes and "mythicizes" the bourgeois novel's very process of naturalization. See Holderness; and Webster.

32 See his *Working-Class Fiction in Theory and Practice: A Reading of Alan Sillitoe* (Ann Arbor: UMI, 1989).

33 The term is employed by Alf Louvre (Louvre, 34).

34 I am grateful to Evan Watkins for helping me to think through this aspect of my argument.

35 Hawthorn's prefatory essay makes note of this narrow interest, "regretting" that the volume fails to address texts by working-class women, but quickly settles for an easy—and highly questionable—out: shifting the discussion to the representation of women in men's texts, he suggests that writing was often conceived of as a "feminine" practice by the working-class (quoting Sid Chaplin here), and hence, occasionally allowed for "positive" depiction of women's lives. See *The British Working-Class Novel in the Twentieth Century* (London: Arnold, 1984), viii.

36 See Gagnier, especially 6–11 and 31–40; Landry, especially 3–10, where she discusses "ventriloquism" as a tactic, and 18, where she warns, "There is a danger . . . in reading as texts of liberation texts that encode merely more subtle forms of subjection"; and Armstrong, especially pp. 23–26 where she alludes to "genuine" subversion.

   For an admirable feminist study of conservatism and middle-class culture in England during the 1920s and 1930s, see Light.

37 See her "Introductory Letter to Margaret Llewelyn Davies," *Life As We Have Known It*, Ed. Margaret Llewelyn Davies (London: Hogarth, 1931), xxv.

38 For other feminist critiques of Woolf's elitism here, see Gagnier, 36–38; and Swindells, 190–192.

1 Rehabilitating Working-Class Cultural and Literary History

1 See Goldthorpe et al. To their credit, Goldthorpe et al. express considerable skepticism toward the "embourgeoisement" thesis itself and in their exhaustive empirical research merely attempt to test the claims made by Mark Abrams and Ferdynand Zweig about recently "affluent" sectors of the working-class population. For one critique of their study, see Chas Critcher, "Sociology, Cultural Studies and the Post-War Working Class," in *Working-Class Culture: Studies in History and Theory*, Ed. John Clarke, et al. (London: Hutchinson, 1979).

2 Within this general context, Julia Swindells and Lisa Jardine offer one particularly interesting overview of the debates within contemporary British Marxism involving E. P. Thompson, Raymond Williams, and Perry Anderson. See Swindells and Jardine.

3 Patrick Joyce's excellent *Visions of the People: Industrial England and the Question of Class, 1848–1914* is interested in similar questions. It appeared in print after the bulk of my own study was written, and while his definitions of "class" and of "resistance" are different—even more cautionary—than mine, I wish to acknowledge our shared inclinations.

4 Broadly speaking, such studies abound, including Henry Pellings's *A Short His-*

tory of the Labour Party and the *New Left Review* publication, *Towards Socialism,* Ed. Perry Anderson and Robin Blackburn (Ithaca: Cornell UP, 1966). More recent versions are Burgess; Hinton; and Winter.

5   Standish Meacham's study of working-class culture in the Edwardian era is one exception to this rule, uninterested in contrasting current conservative trends with a radical past. See Meacham.

6   See Vicinus's chapter on music hall culture, which she believes swiftly degenerated from "a class to a mass entertainment," in Vicinus.

7   In his 1983 introduction to *Languages of Class,* Jones looks with some hindsight on his earlier argument here and attempts to reformulate, if not retract, it. He concedes, for instance, that he overemphasized the waning of artisan culture as one linchpin of this class culture's "depoliticization." Yet the thrust of his revision remains problematic since he in turn veers back to a renewed emphasis on "institutional," rather than "cultural," forms of political mobilization. See Jones 10–11.

8   The term is Carolyn Steedman's in *Landscape For A Good Woman,* 22.

9   Reference to title of book by Jeremy Seabrook, published by Gollancz in 1978.

10   Cronin cites as his source here the 1939 Mass-Observation survey.

11   *The Equipment of the Workers* is a particularly difficult source to judge, since most of the survey responses are published in the form of survey takers' notes—much paraphrasing and selection of bit quotes, combined with on-the-spot evaluation of the interviewees. Moreover, the YMCA's "Reconstruction" program divided the "Well-equipped," the "Inadequately-equipped," and the "Mal-equipped" manual laborers according to their degree of "spiritual awakening."

12   For a similar critique of this feminization thesis, see Alexander. In her essay, Alexander seeks to "query the use of the epithet 'feminine' to denigrate both the new consumer industries and the human needs they evoke" (246) and instead probes the "fantasies of desire and loss" suggested by young working-class women's fascination with material goods.

13   See, for example, Stearns; also Standish Meacham's treatment of working-class women in the same period, which perhaps *over*emphasizes the "dull," "narrow" outlook of their lives.

14   Taylor. This article challenges the notion that domestic service declined and changed drastically by the inter-war period, arguing that "domestic service remained a central experience for working-class women and especially for girls" (121). Despite training in "self-lessness," they experienced enormous alienation and loneliness.

15   This is less evident in Ross's most recent studies of working-class mothering. In "Labour and Love: Rediscovering London's Working-Class Mothers, 1870–1918," she emphatically states in her opening paragraph, "I want neither to celebrate nor to judge mothers, but to make them historical subjects" (73). The essay concentrates on the often painful relationships between working-class mothers and

their children, documenting the sense of deprivation and neglect experienced by both parties. Also see *Love and Toil: Motherhood in Outcast London.*

16 See Alexander.

17 Such rhetoric is most notable in *Rewriting English,* which offers only predictable, if defensible, criticisms of the WEA's function. It can also be found in other, more comprehensive studies of British working-class history, such as Stuart Mac-Intyre's work.

18 See Mansbridge.

19 As stated in the league pamphlet *What Does Education Mean to the Workers?* (Oxford: Kemp Hall, 1917), 8.

20 An earlier article entitled "The Romantic Revival in Poetry and Historical Materialism" illustrates such principles in its economic analysis of Romanticism. See *Plebs* 10: 3 (April 1918): 54–56.

21 See, for example, the sets of instructions and "results" in 1:3 (Dec. 1934): 71–74; 1:7 (April 1935); 1:10 (July 1935): 418–420; 2:4 (Jan. 1936): 177; and 2 (November 1936): 680.

22 See O'Rourke. Though I think she gives into the grim implications of her question too easily, O'Rourke's essay offers some helpful speculations about the difference of working-class women's experiences.

23 For statistics concerning enrollment in both classes, see Ree 21.

2 The Ragged Trousered Philanthropists and After

1 See Mitchell, *Robert Tressell* 21–23, where Mitchell notes Tressell's "apparent" lack of interest in "colossal class battles, . . . lock-outs, demonstrations, police and military violence, organisational ferment . . . [and] the problems of building an effective revolutionary party" (210).

2 The novel has been lauded as "the book that won the '45 election for Labour" (Alan Sillitoe, Introduction, *The Ragged Trousered Philanthropists* [Lawrence & Wishart, 1955; 1964, 1]), a true form of popular culture: it was "handed around and read and reread until it literally fell to pieces" among World War II soldiers (Mitchell, *Robert Tressell* 2). As Jack Beeching claimed in the 1955 *Marxist Quarterly,* "Go into any meeting room of the working-class movement in Britain and you will probably find at least one man present, who could say: 'That book brought me into the movement. That book made me a convinced socialist. That book altered the whole course and direction of my life'" (as quoted in Mitchell, *Robert Tressell* 1). See Miles for a lengthier discussion of Tressell's wide and devoted readership.

3 See, for example, the quite divergent analyses offered by Mayne; and Neetens.

4 Noting that Pope shifted Owen's thoughts of suicide to the end of the narrative (creating a conclusion of "maudlin pessimism"), and arguing that she excised the "most bitter" social commentary from the original text, Brian Mayne calls her editorial job not only "bowdlerisation," but "sabotage" (77–78).

5   In his essay "Tendencies in Narrative Fiction in the London-Based Socialist Press of the 1880s and 1890s," Jack Mitchell describes short stories and journalistic pieces in such Social Democratic Federation-affiliated publications as *Justice* and *Social Democrat* which thrive on "dark" and "claustrophobic" moods of "increasing misery" in their portrayals of working-class life. He argues that the tales "mock" workers' efforts to organize collectively and dwell on their ignorance largely as a way to explain or justify the SDF's "own isolation from the wellsprings of proletarian life and culture" (70). Mitchell subsequently acknowledges connections between these stories and Tressell's novel, but contends that they have quite different political ends (and visions).

6   Miles 10, 6.

7   See in particular Mayne, 75–76.

8   Such is the position maintained by both Mitchell and F. C. Ball. See Mitchell, *Robert Tressell*, 23–24 and most of chapter 3; and Ball, *Tressell of Mugsborough* (London: Lawrence, 1951), 222.

9   I am indebted to Bruce Robbins's fine analysis of servant discourse in the eighteenth- and nineteenth-century British novel for this observation. See *The Servant's Hand: English Fiction From Below* (Durham: Duke UP, 1993).

10   Tressell's own name reflects a similar act of appropriation: a pseudonym (also spelled "Tressall"), it puns on the term "trestle," one of the most common items of the building trade. His real name, as Ball's biography establishes, was Robert Noonan.

11   The final example is problematic, since it, even more so than the others, finally satirizes the workers themselves. But it still reflects, it seems to me, a highly complicated sense of class "consciousness." After Harlow complains to the other hands about receiving a churlish note from one of the supervisors ("worded in much the same way in which one would speak to a dog"), they laugh behind his back at seeking any kind of respect and proceed to write the following mock note:

> Mister Harlow,
> Dear sir: wood you kinely oblige me bi cummin to
> the paint shop as soon as you can make it
> convenient as there is a sealin' to be wite-woshed
> hoppin this is not trubbling you to much
> I remane
> Yours respeckfully
> Pontius Pilate.

12   See Neetens, 81–89.

13   Again, see Mitchell for a discussion that links Tressell, Carlyle, Ruskin, and Morris in *Robert Tressell*, 150–162.

14   See Thompson, *William Morris*, especially pp. 717–730.

15   George Barrington's presence in the novel further exposes the true political underpinnings of Owen's character. A wealthy, educated socialist "experimenting" with manual labor, he remains a shadowy figure in the narrative (and is

eliminated entirely in Pope's version) until the pivotal Great Oration scene, where in the original edition he becomes the mouthpiece for the socialist future. Though considered by some critics a *deus ex machina*, he functions as a critical figure in Tressell's schema of class agency, accentuating the elite cultural foundation of the Great Oration vision.

16   For two classic discussions, see Heidi Hartmann; and Barrett.

17   See, for instance, Johnson ("The Proletarian Novel" 84–95) and Snee's (*Culture and Crisis* 170–176) biting critiques of the novel's "bourgeois" form.

3   On the "Borderland of Tears"

1   See Rowan 60–62; and Thane 57–62.

2   Again, see Rowan 67–73, for discussion of the Guild Campaign. For working-class women's contributions to the suffrage movement in the North of England, see Liddington and Norris.

3   For contemporary feminist critiques of the family wage concept, see Barrett and McIntosh; and Hartmann. Also see the specific debate concerning domestic labor that links up with the above articles: Seccombe; and Coulson et al.

4   Jane Lewis offers as illustration the following excerpts from pertinent historical documents: in his speech to the TUC Annual Conference in 1877, one man implores "men and husbands to use their utmost efforts to bring about a condition of things, where their wives should be in their proper sphere at home, instead of being dragged into competition for livelihood against the great and strong men of the world"; another, testifying before the Royal Commission of Labour in 1894, stated that he was "very loth to see mothers of families working in factories at all . . . their employment has nearly always a very prejudicial effect on the wages of the male worker." See "The Working-Class Wife," 103.

5   As argued by Humphries.

6   Rowan writes that even though "the tendency of the class as a whole was to defend the status quo" regarding the family wage, "agreement" among working-class women's groups "was struggled over for many years, and it was not until the First World War that the movement's ambivalence, shown in the debates about school meals and state maintenance, was finally overcome" (67).

7   For a superb overview of this case, see Davidoff. Also see Liz Stanley's introduction to *The Diaries of Hannah Cullwick, Victorian Maidservant*, Liz Stanley, ed. (New Brunswick, N.J.: Rutgers UP, 1984), 1–28.

8   See her essay with Mary McIntosh, above; also, *Women's Oppression Today, Problems in Marxist Feminist Analysis*, esp. chapters 5, 6, and 7.

9   Several sociological studies of British working-class women conducted in the 1970s have discovered similar, lasting impulses to split the public and the private that reflect both a challenge to, and longing for, a different class/gender arrangement. Porter (*Home, Work and Class Consciousness*) and Pollert (*Girls, Wives, Factory Lives*) investigate attitudes toward women's labor and conceptions of gendered

subjectivity among women and men. Porter's study tends to emphasize the oppositional dimension of working-class women's desire to preserve the home as their domain, perceiving their alienation from the public work space as a rejection of the total encompassing logic of capitalism. In contrast, Pollert's study of women factory workers reveals their continued enthusiasm for the Angel in the House ideology itself.

10 Ellen Ross, "Survival Networks," particularly notes the wistful observations of West End social workers and philanthropists visiting the East End who were "fascinated" by its public mode of existence, "themselves locked in isolating middle-class 'privacy'" (9).

11 See his Preface to the Second Edition of the *Lyrical Ballads, English Romantic Writers*, Ed. David Perkins (New York: Harcourt, 1967), 321.

12 As discussed in the introductory chapter, while fully acknowledging the strictures imposed upon working-class culture within the capitalist social order, they take issue with much contemporary poststructuralist theory. See "The Orders of Experience," 85–86.

13 See Gissing's *The Nether World* (London: J. M. Dent, 1889); Besant's *All Sorts and Conditions of Men* (New York: Harper & Bros., 1899); and Kipling's story "The Record of Bedalia Herodsfoot" (1890) in his *Many Inventions* (New York: Macmillan, 1893).

14 The *St. James Gazette* review of the novel in December, 1896 essentially accused Morrison of plagiarism, comparing his descriptions of the Jago with those of the Rev. Osborne Jay's in *Life in Darkest London* (1891). The review was entitled "How Realistic Fiction is Written" and claimed to demonstrate "how fiction is worked up out of a nucleus of fact" when the writer is "ignorant of the subject" ("Biographical Study" 27). Keating notes that Jay swiftly came to Morrison's defense and "completely exonerated" him.

15 As quoted in Keating's *The Working Classes in Victorian Fiction*, 179.

16 The concept of hooliganism was one offshoot of Britain's imperialist ventures: immigrants from its colonized countries were tagged with animalistic behavior and furor, seen to "infect" marginal areas. See Gill Davies's "Foreign Bodies: Images of the London Working Class at the End of the 19th Century," 67–68. Also see Geoffrey Pearson's extensive study, *Hooligan: A History of Respectable Fears*.

17 Keating documents Morrison's support of the Penal Settlements (originally proposed by Jay himself) and makes reference to an article of Morrison's, "Hooliganism," which describes the hooligan as a "mere unlicked cub of a peculiarly vicious type, . . . [who] flourishes more openly of late by reason of his long immunity from licking" ("Biographical Study" 32).

18 Pierre Bourdieu writes of this phenomenon in French working-class culture: "Whereas great class differences may pass unnoticed and are in any case very well tolerated . . . because they are seen as based on differences of nature, . . . not the slightest deviation is permitted to those who belong to the same class (or

originate from it), because in this case difference could only arise from the desire to distinguish oneself, that is, from refusal or repudiation of the group" (381). See his chapter on working-class cultural 'taste' in *Distinction*, 372–396.

19 Davies favorably compares Tressell's novel with Henry Nevinson's collection of stories *Neighbours of Ours* (1894), both of which he claims 'legitimize' and "celebrate" working-class culture (68–69).

20 See Von Rosenberg.

21 Kiernan Ryan, for instance, admires the novel's "truly heroic marriage, which cuts across class divisions and convincingly prefigures the real human possibilities beyond them in a manner unparalleled by . . . other novels" (such as Constance Howell's *A More Excellent Way* (1888) and George Bernard Shaw's *An Unsocial Socialist* [1884]). See his "Citizens of Centuries to Come: The Ruling-Class Rebel in Socialist Fiction," in Klaus, *Rise of Socialist Fiction*, 16.

22 For biographical information and a brief overview of the Lancashire School, see Paul Salveson, "Allen Clarke and the Lancashire School of Working-Class Novelists," in Klaus, *Rise of Socialist Fiction*, 172–202. For a more complex discussion of the School and of dialect literature, see Joyce 279–304.

23 See Ashraf's discussion of lyricism in Clarke's writing as a whole (163–168).

24 Patrick Joyce takes an equally cautious approach to Clarke's work. Though acknowledging his bona fide socialist politics, Joyce situates Clarke in the context of dialect literature, which he considers "populist" rather than class conscious. See Joyce, 290; 301–302.

25 See Swindells 140–151.

26 As documented in Andy Croft's introduction to the 1983 edition of *Means-Test Man*, vii–x.

27 Snee "Working-Class Literature," 180–181. She goes so far as to complain that in Brierley's second novel, *Sandwich Man* (1937), the protagonist "is trying to educate himself out of the pits and indeed out of the working class, and Brierley records that attempt uncritically and indeed approvingly. . . . There is no suggestion from Brierley that Arthur's concept of education as material and intellectual *self* improvement is in any way reprehensible" (180). (Snee also bristles at his obvious hagiography of Lawrence in that text, concluding "and in the end one feels that as he obviously had nothing to say which Lawrence had not already said he should not have written the book, for Lawrence says it so much better"!)

4   The "Revolt of the Gentle"

1 Haslam's outlook in this study seems far more Arnoldian than Marxist—seeking to make available, as well as encourage, the "best" literature to working-class readers. At the same time, he believes in specifically promoting reading materials that can induce social change. He is thus distressed to discover from one female news agent in Ancoats that, truth to be told, her readers have little interest in books or tales about social welfare: "What they wants here is love an' romance."

He proceeds to contrast his sense of romance—Chaucer and Sir Walter Scott—with hers: Cinderella. See *The Press and the People*, 5–6; 15–16.

2   While these studies are by now so well known that they need little summary, it should perhaps be noted that they do take somewhat different tacks. With her "Feminine," "Feminist," and "Female" typology of British women's writing, Showalter privileges those female texts that break entirely with masculine cultural forms. Gilbert and Gubar offer their "palimpsestic" text as a model, in which nineteenth-century women writers surreptitiously revise male plots by employing the traditional female archetypes of angel and monster for their own purposes. Lowder Newton undertakes a more materialist study of women's subversive strategies, focusing on the shifting historical situation producing women writers of the period and examining ways in which they rebel against gender ideology (redefining power in female terms and adopting a female quest narrative).

3   Radway focuses on the function of the romance's "mythic ending," which "undercuts the realism of its novelistic rendering of an individual woman's story" (208). Also see her essay, "The Utopian Impulse in Popular Literature," which examines the conflicting functions of narrative "middles" and "ends": according to Radway, the middle of the Gothic narrative incites dissatisfaction with the status-quo, only to be de-fused by the closure.

4   Jean Franco has demonstrated the importance of considering such cultural and class differences in her study of Mexican romance fiction and comic-strip novels: the former, directed at middle- and upper-class women readers, wholly encourage identification with the traditional romance heroine; but the latter, directed at working-class women, encourage their readers to substitute work for romance, portraying romance as a deceptive ideology and *as something alien to their social position*. (Franco concludes, "These novels suggest that 'love' is a luxury, a fantasy not of all women but of middle and upper class women seeking the complementary male who will heal the split in their personalities," 137).

   Also, see once again Alexander. Though Alexander does not focus on romance, she does recognize it as one mode of "rebellion" (262) among young working-class women in the inter-war years.

5   Jane Lewis notes the pervasive lack of enthusiasm surrounding the marriage ceremony in many working-class neighborhoods and suggests that the ideology of motherhood, which received such a renewed boost in the Edwardian period, was due in part to bourgeois anxiety regarding frequent common-law marriages and separations among the working class. See *Women in England*, 11.

6   For a contemporary look at the relation between romance and working-class women, see McRobbie. While focusing on the "girls'" desire for romance, she also notes their mothers' influence in subverting romance ideology.

7   *Left Review* I:5 (Feb. 1935): 177–178.

8   This issue could, of course, constitute another study in itself. See Stuart MacIntyre's extensive discussion of the splits between Labour Socialism and Marxism

among sectors of the British working class in MacIntyre 47–65; 106–126. Mac-Intyre's research offers suggestive evidence of the gendered dimension to this conflict, but he himself fails to pursue the implications.

9 See "Factory Intelligence," March 1909, "The Factory Slave," March 1909, and "The Tree of Knowledge," December 1909, as well as her ardent feminist pieces, "Our Right to Play," April 1909, and "Modern Womanhood," August 1909. For a brief account of Carnie Holdsworth's years with the *Woman Worker,* see Frow and Frow.

10 See Meacham 28.

11 See Frow and Frow; Klaus's "Silhouettes of Revolution," especially 94–97; and Ashraf 176–195.

12 Though the shop is quite modest, Carrie apparently owns it. This places her among the more "respectable" in her class, even as it fails to bring her any real economic security.

13 Despite the novel's publication date, Gustav Klaus speculates that *This Slavery* was written a decade or so earlier, noting its occasional references to pre-war historical events and political figures, and interestingly, what he perceives to be a "strong emphasis on suffering and brutalisation" associated with a "distinctly prewar working-class sensibility" ("Silhouettes of Revolution," 94). But as my discussion will argue, the novel is most dramatically marked by a faith in working-class solidarity and a narrative structure characteristic of later, class-conscious fiction.

14 Ashraf specifically contrasts Rachel here with Tressell's Frank Owen, claiming that Rachel is much more "tolerant" of the rank and file and does not rely on pat speeches.

15 *Sunday Worker,* 5 and 26 July 1925. I am indebted to Gustav Klaus's essay, "Silhouettes of Revolution," for bringing this crucial exchange to my attention.

16 *Plebs* 19:5 (May 1926): 178.

17 Ashraf 148–156.

18 Clarke also offers little positive commentary on women factory workers in his non-fictional report, *The Effects of the Factory System.* He particularly objects to those women who seek to continue working while pregnant, noting "[t]his age of competition makes them grabbingly selfish in the struggle for existence." (Interestingly enough, in the same section he points with distaste to the "exposure" of women's genitals due to the placement of male and female toilets in the factories, which he believes leads to their "indecency.")

19 See Mitchell's "Early Harvest," 75–81. Mitchell claims that the novel's success "was used against" MacGill "and his class," converting him "into a kind of 'official' working-class writer to put across the propaganda of the ruling class in the language and idiom of the workers themselves" (75). Though Mitchell praises *Children,* he objects to its lack of "scientific socialism" and points specifically to its unsatisfactory closure: "It is true that near the close Dermod does have a fleeting

realisation of the inadequacy of 'one man's fist,' but there is no lead on to participation in the organised class struggle and so the book entirely lacks a practical
revolutionary perspective" (79).

20   As quoted in Constantine 235.

21   See Holderness 27–29; and Snee 181–190.

22   Burton begins her essay by stating, "Reading Lewis Grassic Gibbon's famous
trilogy in the early 1980s, I found I was having to remind myself continually that I
was not reading a work by a modern female writer, who wrote from women's cultural experience, and with a strong political commitment to specifically feminist
perspectives on major socialist issues" (35).

23   The following excerpt describes Chris's experience at the "Picturedrome":

So Chris had to stay awake and see that, all about a lassie who worked in New
York and was awful poor but awful respectable, though she seemed to live in
a place like a palace with a bath ten feet in length and three deep, and wore
underclothes that she couldn't have afforded, some childe had paid for them
on the sly. But the picture said No, through its nose, not her, she was awful
chaste but sore chased as well, a beast of a man in her office, the manager,
galloping about the screen and aye wanting to seduce the lassie by night or
by day. . . . And then she and the slob were getting on fine, all black and blue,
my lovely Lu, when along came the leader of a birn of brutes, a gang, and
kidnapped the lass . . . and Chris was just thinking it fairly was time, would
they never get the job over and done?—when in rushed the hero and a fight
began . . . and the lass crouched down with her cami-knicks showing but
respectable still, she wouldn't yield an inch to anything short of a marriage
license. And that she got in the end, all fine, with showers of flowers and the
man with the face like a mislaid ham cuddling her up with a kiss. (415–416)

24   In contrast, Burton argues, "the fact that the trilogy *closes* with her point of view,
undoubtedly suggests that hers is a vision to be endorsed, when all is said and
done" (40).

25   David Smith's reading of the trilogy concurs on this point (125–127).

26   D. F. Young notes general Lawrencian features in Gibbon's work in *Beyond the
Sunset: A Study of James Leslie Mitchell (Lewis Grassic Gibbon)*, (25; 29–30). He also
makes the following specific comparison, though clearly reads Lawrence differently than I: "The description of the early days of their [Chris and Ewan]
marriage is a magnificent evocation of married love, its joys and tensions, and
reminds one of Lawrence's *The Rainbow*. And then the thrill and exasperation of
pregnancy and childbirth are superbly rendered" (89).

Afterword

1   This argument often becomes articulated in her work through analyses of Mary
Wollstonecraft's brand of Enlightenment feminism. As Kaplan notes, Wollstonecraft was one of the first theorists to connect gender to pleasure, especially in

terms of reading: novels and poetry, she claimed, made women "slaves" to sexuality and sentimentality. She believed reason would prevent women from succumbing to dominant ideology. For Kaplan's class critique of this perspective, see her more well-known essay, "Pandora's Box: Subjectivity, Class and Sexuality in Socialist Feminist Criticism," as well as her wonderful piece on *The Thorn Birds* in *Sea Changes* 147–176; 117–146.

2   I am referring to her position on psychoanalysis: "As Jacqueline Rose has argued, perhaps the most productive response to the charge that psychoanalysis has no sense of history is not to dismiss it as a useful analytic framework but to both acknowledge how it has functioned as history and to rewrite that history, including its reinforcement of western imperialism and the interventions it has continually made into the institutions which control women's lives. . . . Recognizing, as Rose does, that Freud's earliest investigations on hysteria took place not in the parlors of Vienna but in the Salpetriere Clinic in Paris, suggests that further work remains to be done to read the complex negotiations of social difference that psychoanalysis managed in the sexualization of the western woman" (134). See Hennessey.

3   For one particularly successful example, see Stallybrass and White.

4   See Bordo, especially 90–99; and Kipnis, especially 376–378.

B I B L I O G R A P H Y

Primary Sources

Barker, James. *Major Operation*. London: Collins, 1936.

Beauchamp, Joan. "Twentieth Century Poetry." *The Highway* 17.1 (Winter 1924): 7–12.

Brierley, Walter. *Means-Test Man*. Nottingham: Spokesman, 1935, 1983.

Burnett, John, Ed. *The Annals of Labour: Autobiographies of British Working-Class People, 1820–1920*. Bloomington: Indiana UP, 1974.

Carnie, Ethel. "Factory Intelligence." *Woman Worker*, 10 March 1909: 219.

———. *Miss Nobody*. London: Methuen, 1913.

———. "Modern Womanhood." *Woman Worker*, 4 Aug. 1909: 100.

———. "Our Right to Play." *Woman Worker*, 14 April 1909: 342.

———. *Songs of A Factory Girl*. London: Headley, 1911.

———. "The Tree of Knowledge." *Woman Worker*, 15 Dec. 1909: 537.

———. *Voices of Womanhood*. London: Headley, 1914.

Carter, Huntly. "Labour and the Theatre." *Plebs* 22:9 (Sept. 1930): 206–209.

Clarke, C. Allen. *The Effects of the Factory System*. London: Richards, 1899.

———. *The Knobstick*. London: Heywood, 1893.

———. *Lancashire Lasses and Lads*. Manchester: Heywood, 1896, 1906.

Davies, Margaret Llewelyn, ed. *Life As We Have Known It*. London: Hogarth, 1931.

"Dos Passos and Conroy." *Left Review* I:3 (Dec. 1934): 94–95.

Drazin, I. "Self-Expression." *The Highway* 17:2 (Spring 1925): 75–78.

Eaglestone, A. A. "The Cultivation of Taste." *The Highway* 26 (April 1934): 4–5.

Fox, Ralph. *The Novel and the People*. New York: International, 1937, 1945.

Gibbon, Lewis Grassic. *A Scots Hairst*. London: Hutchinson, 1967.

———. *A Scots Quair, A Trilogy of Novels: Sunset Song, Cloud Howe, Grey Granite*. New York: Schocken, 1932–34, 1977.

Greenwood, Walter. *Love on the Dole*. Harmondsworth: Penguin, 1933, 1969.

Gresser, Ann. "Factory Library." *Left Review* I:5 (Feb. 1935): 177–178.

Haslam, James. *The Handloom Weaver's Daughter*. London: Brown, 1904.

————. *The Press and the People: An Estimate of Reading in Working-Class Districts*. Manchester: Manchester City News, 1906.

Heslop, Harold. *The Gate of A Strange Field*. London: Brentano's, 1929.

————. *Journey Beyond*. London: Shaylor, 1930.

————. *Last Cage Down*. London: Wishart, 1935.

Holdsworth, Ethel Carnie. *Helen of Four Gates*. London: Jenkins, 1917.

————. *The Taming of Nan*. London: Jenkins, 1919.

————. *This Slavery*. London: Labour, 1925.

Horrabin, J. F. "Love on the Dole: A Tale of the Two Cities." *Plebs* 25 (October 1933): 221–222.

Hutt, Allen. "Flint and Steel English." *Left Review* I:4 (Jan. 1935): 130–135.

Jones, Lewis. *Cwmardy*. London: Lawrence, 1937.

————. *We Live*. London: Lawrence, 1939.

Lanigan, E. "The Passing of the Propagandist." *The Highway* 27:2 (Spring 1925): 68–70.

Loane, Margaret. *From Their Point of View*. London: Arnold, 1908.

MacGill, Patrick. *Children of the Dead End*. London: Jenkins, 1914.

————. *The Rat-Pit*. New York: Doran, 1915.

Mannin, Ethel. *Rose and Sylvie*. London: Jarrolds, 1938.

Mansbridge, Albert. *An Adventure in Working-Class Education, Being the Story of the Workers' Educational Association, 1903–1915*. London: Longmans, 1920.

"Marxism and Literature." *Plebs* (Oct. 1922): 367–369.

Martin, Anna. *The Married Working Woman: A Study*. New York and London: Garland, 1911, 1980.

Mitchell, Hannah. *The Hard Way Up*. London: Virago, 1977.

Mitchell, James Leslie (Lewis Grassic Gibbon). *The Thirteenth Disciple*. Edinburgh: Harris, 1931, 1981.

Morrison, Arthur. *A Child of the Jago*. London: MacGibbon, 1896, 1969.

Reeves, Margaret Pember. *Round About A Pound A Week*. London: Garland, 1913, 1980.

St. Philip's Settlement. *The Equipment of the Workers: An Enquiry by the St. Philip's Settlement Education and Economics Research Society*. London: Allen, 1919.

"A Short Syllabus on 'Historical Materialism and Literature.'" *Plebs* (June 1922): 169–171.

Sommerfield, John. *May Day*. London: Lawrence, 1936.

Tirebuck, W. E. *Miss Grace of All Souls'*. London: Heinemann, 1895.

Tressell, Robert. *The Ragged Trousered Philanthropists*. New York and London: Monthly Review, 1914, 1955, 1962.

Welsh, James. *Songs of A Miner*. London: Jenkins, 1917.

————. *The Underworld: The Story of Robert Sinclair, Miner*. London: Jenkins, 1920.

Wilkinson, Ellen. *Clash*. London: Virago, 1929, 1989.

————. "Should Women Wash Up? Or, The Marxist and His Missus." *Plebs* 20:1 (Jan. 1928): 13–14.

Women's Cooperative Guild. *Working Women and Divorce*. New York and London: Garland, 1911, 1980.

Woolf, Virginia. "Introductory Letter to Margaret Llewelyn Davies." *Life As We Have Known It*. Ed. Margaret Llewelyn Davies. London: Hogarth, 1931. xv–xxxix.

"The Workers' Culture." *Plebs* (February 1922): 38–41.

"Writers' International." *Left Review* I:3 (December 1934): 75–80.

Secondary Sources

Alexander, Sally. "Becoming A Woman in London in the 1920s and 1930s." *Metropolis London: Histories and Representations Since 1800*. Ed. David Feldman and Gareth Stedman Jones. London and New York: Routledge, 1989. 245–271.

Allen, Walter. *Tradition and Dream: The English and American Novel From the Twenties to Our Time*. London: Phoenix House, 1964.

Althusser, Louis. "Ideology and the Ideological State Apparatuses." *Lenin and Philosophy and Other Essays*. Trans. Ben Brewster. New York: Monthly Review, 1971.

Armstrong, Nancy. *Desire and Domestic Fiction*. New York: Oxford UP, 1987.

Ashraf, P. M. *Introduction to Working-Class Literature in Great Britain. Part II: Prose*. Berlin: VEB Kongres-und Werbedruck Oberlungwitz, 1979.

Barrett, Michele. *Women's Oppression Today: Problems in Marxist Feminist Analysis*. London: Verso and NLB, 1980.

Barrett, Michele, and Mary McIntosh. "The 'Family Wage'—Some Problems For Socialists and Feminists." *Capital and Class* 11 (1980): 51–72.

Batsleer, Janet, et al. *Rewriting English. Cultural Politics of Gender and Class*. London: Methuen, 1985.

Benedict, Ruth. *Patterns of Culture*. Boston: Houghton, 1934.

Bennett, Tony. "Hegemony, Ideology, Pleasure: Blackpool." *Popular Culture and Social Relations*. Ed. Tony Bennett et al. Milton Keynes, England and Philadelphia: Open UP, 1986. 135–154.

Bernstein, Basil. *Class, Codes and Control*. Vol. I, *Theoretical Studies towards a Sociology of Language*. London: Routledge, 1971.

Beynon, Huw. *Working For Ford*. London: Allen Lane/Penguin Education, 1973.

Bisseret, Noelle. *Education, Class Language and Ideology*. London: Routledge, 1979.

Bordo, Susan. "Reading the Slender Body." *Body/Politics: Women and the Discourses of Science*. Ed. Mary Jacobus et al. London: Routledge, 1990. 83–112.

Bourdieu, Pierre. *Distinction: A Social Critique of the Judgement of Taste*. Trans. Richard Nice. London: Routledge, 1984.

———. *Outline of a Theory of Practice*. Trans. Richard Nice. Cambridge: Cambridge UP, 1977.

———, and Jean-Claude Passeron. *Reproduction in Education, Society and Culture*. Trans. Richard Nice. London: Sage, 1977.

Bowles, Samuel. "Unequal Education and the Reproduction of the Social Division of Labor." *Review of Radical Political Economics* 3 (Fall 1971): 1–30.

————, and Herbert Gintis. *Schooling in Capitalist America.* New York: Basic, 1976.

Broucek, Francis J. *Shame and the Self.* New York: Guilford, 1991.

Bulmer, Martin, ed. *Working-Class Images of Society.* London: Routledge, 1975.

Burgess, Keith. *The Challenge of Labour: Shaping British Society, 1850–1930.* London: Croom Helm, 1980.

Burton, Deirdre. "A Feminist Reading of *A Scots Quair.*" *The British Working-Class Novel in the Twentieth Century.* Ed. Jeremy Hawthorn. London: Arnold, 1984. 35–46.

Constantine, Stephen. "'Love on the Dole' and Its Reception in the 1930s." *Literature and History* 8:2 (1982): 232–247.

Coulson, Margaret, et al. "'The Housewife and Her Labour Under Capitalism,' A Critique." *New Left Review* 89 (Jan.–Feb. 1975): 59–71.

Croft, Andy. "Introduction." *Means-Test Man.* Nottingham: Spokesman, 1935, 1983, vii–xvi.

Cronin, James E. *Labour and Society in Britain: 1918–1979.* London: Batsford, 1984.

Davidoff, Leonore. "Class and Gender in Victorian England." *Sex and Class in Women's History.* Ed. Judith L. Newton et al. London: Routledge, 1983. 17–71.

Davies, Andrew. *Leisure, Gender and Poverty.* Buckingham and Philadelphia: Open UP, 1992.

Davies, Gill. "Foreign Bodies: Images of the London Working Class at the End of the 19th Century." *Literature and History* 14:1 (Spring 1988): 65–79.

Davies, Tony. "Unfinished Business: Realism and Working-Class Writing." *The British Working-Class Novel in the Twentieth Century.* Ed. Jeremy Hawthorn. London: Arnold, 1984. 125–136.

Denning, Michael. *Mechanic Accents: Dime Novels and Working-Class Culture in America.* London, New York: Verso, 1987.

Douglas, Mary. *Purity and Danger.* London: Routledge, 1966, 1991.

DuPlessis, Rachel Blau. *Writing Beyond the Ending: Narrative Strategies of Twentieth-Century Women Writers.* Bloomington: Indiana UP, 1985.

Franco, Jean. "The Incorporation of Women: A Comparison of North American American and Mexican American Popular Narrative." *Studies in Entertainment: Critical Approaches to Mass Culture.* Ed. Tania Modleski. Bloomington: Indiana UP, 1986. 119–138.

Frow, Edmund and Ruth. "Ethel Carnie: Writer, Feminist and Socialist." *The Rise of Socialist Fiction, 1880–1914.* Ed. H. Gustav Klaus. Sussex: Harvester, 1987, 251–256.

Gagnier, Regenia. *Subjectivities: A History of Self-Representation in Britain, 1832–1920.* New York: Oxford UP, 1991.

Gaskell, Jane. "Course Enrollment in the High School: The Perspective of Working-Class Females." *Sociology of Education* 58:1 (January 1985): 48–59.

Geertz, Clifford. *The Interpretation of Cultures.* New York: Basic, 1973.

Gilbert, Sandra M., and Susan Gubar. *The Madwoman in the Attic: The Woman Writer and the Nineteenth-Century Imagination.* New Haven: Yale UP, 1979.

Giroux, Henry. Ed. *Postmodernism, Feminism, and Cultural Politics: Redrawing Educational Boundaries.* Albany: SUNY Press, 1991.

———. "Resisting Differences: Cultural Studies and the Discourse of Critical Pedagogy." *Cultural Studies.* Ed. Lawrence Grossberg et al. New York: Routledge, 1992. 199–212.

———. *Teachers as Intellectuals: Toward A Critical Pedagogy of Learning.* Massachusetts: Bergin, 1988.

———. *Theory and Resistance in Education: A Pedagogy for the Opposition.* S. Hadley, Mass.: Bergin, 1983.

Giroux, Henry, David Shumway et al. "The Need For Cultural Studies: Resisting Intellectuals and Oppositional Public Spheres." *Dalhousie Review* 64:2 (Summer 1984): 472–486.

Giroux, Henry, and Stanley Aronowitz. *Postmodern Education.* Minneapolis: U of Minnesota P, 1991.

Goldthorpe, J. H., et al. *The Affluent Worker.* 3 vols. Cambridge: Cambridge UP, 1968–1969.

Hakken, David. "Workers' Education and the Reproduction of Working-Class Culture in Sheffield, England." *Anthropology and Education Quarterly* 11:4 (Winter 1980): 211–234.

Hall, Stuart. "The Emergence of Cultural Studies and the Crisis of the Humanities." *October* 53 (1990): 11–23.

Hall, Stuart, et al., eds. *Culture, Media, Language: Working Papers in Cultural Studies, 1972–79.* London: Hutchinson, 1980, 1987.

Hall, Stuart, and Tony Jefferson. *Resistance Through Rituals.* London: Hutchinson, 1976.

Hartmann, Heidi. "The Unhappy Marriage of Marxism and Feminism: Towards A More Progressive Union." *Capital and Class* 8 (Summer 1979): 1–33.

Hebdige, Dick. *Subculture: The Meaning of Style.* London: Methuen, 1979.

Hennessey, Rosemary. *Materialist Feminism and the Politics of Discourse.* New York: Routledge, 1993.

Hinton, James. *Labour and Socialism: A History of the British Labour Movement, 1867–1974.* Brighton: Wheatsheaf, 1983.

Hitchcock, Peter. *Working-Class Fiction in Theory and Practice: A Reading of Alan Sillitoe.* Ann Arbor: UMI, 1989.

Hoggart, Richard. *The Uses of Literacy.* London: Chatto, 1957.

Holderness, Graham. "Miners and the Novel: From Bourgeois to Proletarian Fiction." *The British Working-Class Novel in the Twentieth Century.* Ed. Jeremy Hawthorn. London: Arnold, 1984. 19–32.

hooks, bell. *Yearning: Race, Gender, and Cultural Politics.* Boston: South End, 1990.

Humphries, Jane. "Class Struggle and the Persistence of the Working Class Family." *Cambridge Journal of Economics* 1 (1977): 241–58.

Jackson, T. A. *Solo Trumpet: Some Memories of Socialist Agitation and Propaganda.* London: Lawrence, 1953.

Jameson, Fredric. *The Political Unconscious.* Ithaca: Cornell UP, 1981.

Johnson, Richard. "Three Problematics: Elements of A Theory of Working-Class Culture." *Working Class Culture: Studies in History and Theory.* Ed. John Clarke et al. London: Hutchinson, 1979. 201–237.

———. "What Is Cultural Studies, Anyway?" *Social Text* 16 (Winter 1986–87): 38–80.

Johnson, Roy. "The Proletarian Novel." *Literature and History* 2 (Oct. 1975): 84–95.

———. "Walter Brierley: Proletarian Writer." *Red Letters* 2 (Summer 1976): 5–8.

Jones, Gareth Stedman. "Working-Class Culture and Working-Class Politics in London, 1870–1900: Notes on the Remaking of a Working Class." *Languages of Class.* Cambridge: Cambridge UP, 1983.

Joyce, Patrick. *Visions of the People: Industrial England and the Question of Class, 1848–1914.* Cambridge: Cambridge UP, 1991.

Kaplan, Cora. *Sea Changes: Culture and Feminism.* London: Verso, 1986.

Keating, P. J. "Biographical Study." *A Child of the Jago.* London: MacGibbon, 1896, 1969.

———. *The Working Classes in Victorian Fiction.* New York: Barnes, 1971.

Kelly, Thomas. *A History of Adult Education in Great Britain.* Liverpool: Liverpool UP, 1962.

Kipnis, Laura. "(Male) Desire and (Female) Disgust: Reading *Hustler.*" *Cultural Studies.* Ed. Lawrence Grossberg et al. New York: Routledge, 1992. 373–391.

Klaus, H. Gustav. *The Literature of Labour: Two Hundred Years of Working-Class Writing.* Brighton: Harvester, 1985.

———, ed. *The Rise of Socialist Fiction, 1880–1914.* Sussex: Harvester, 1987.

———. "Silhouettes of Revolution: Some Neglected Novels of the Early 1920s." *The Socialist Novel in Britain.* Ed. H. Gustav Klaus. Brighton: Harvester, 1982. 89–109.

———. "The Strike Novel in the 1890s." *The Rise of Socialist Fiction, 1880–1914.* Ed. H. Gustav Klaus. Sussex: Harvester, 1987. 73–98.

Landry, Donna. *The Muses of Resistance: Laboring Class Women's Poetry in Britain, 1739–1796.* Cambridge: Cambridge UP, 1990.

Lewis, Helen Block, ed. *The Role of Shame in Symptom Formation.* New Jersey: Erlbaum, 1987.

Lewis, Jane. *Women in England, 1870–1950: Sexual Divisions and Social Change.* Bloomington: Indiana UP, 1984.

———. "The Working-Class Wife and Mother and State Intervention, 1870–1918." *Labour and Love: Women's Experience of Home and Family, 1850–1940.* Oxford: Blackwell, 1986. 99–120.

Liddington, Jill, and Jill Norris. *One Hand Tied Behind Us: The Rise of the Women's Suffrage Movement.* London: Virago, 1978.

Light, Alison. *Forever England: Femininity, Literature, and Conservatism Between the Wars.* London: Routledge, 1991.

Lindsay, Jack. *After the Thirties: The Novel in Britain, and Its Future.* London: Lawrence, 1956.

Louvre, Alf. "Reading Bezer: Pun, Parody and Radical Intervention in 19th Century Working Class Autobiography." *Literature and History* 14:1 (Spring 1988): 25–37.

Lukacs, Georg. *History and Class Consciousness.* Trans. Rodney Livingstone. Cambridge, Mass.: MIT P, 1971.

———. *The Meaning of Contemporary Realism.* Trans. John and Necke Mander. London: Merlin, 1979.

Lynd, Helen Merrell. *England in the Eighteen-Eighties: Toward A Social Basis For Freedom.* New York: Oxford UP, 1945.

———. *On Shame and the Search For Identity.* New York: Science Editions, 1958, 1966.

Lynd, Helen Merrell, and Robert S. Lynd. *Middletown.* New York: Harcourt, 1929.

MacIntyre, Stuart. *A Proletarian Science: Marxism in Britain, 1917–1933.* Cambridge: Cambridge UP, 1980.

McRobbie, Angela. "Settling Accounts with Subcultures." *Screen Education* 34 (Spring 1980): 37–49.

———. "Working Class Girls and the Culture of Femininity." *Women Take Issue.* Ed. Women's Studies Group, Centre for Contemporary Cultural Studies. Boston and London: Routledge, 1978. 96–108.

———, ed. *Zoot Suits and Second Hand Dresses: An Anthology of Fashion and Music.* Boston: Unwin Hyman, 1988.

Mayne, Brian. "The Ragged Trousered Philanthropists: An Appraisal of an Edwardian Novel of Social Protest." *Twentieth Century Literature* 13:2 (July 1967): 73–83.

Meacham, Standish. *A Life Apart: The English Working Class, 1890–1914.* Cambridge, Mass.: Harvard UP, 1977.

Miles, Peter. "The Painter's Bible and the British Workman: Robert Tressell's Literary Activism." *The British Working-Class Novel in the Twentieth Century.* Ed. Jeremy Hawthorn. London: Arnold, 1984, 1–17.

Milner, Ian. "An Estimation of Lewis Grassic Gibbon's 'A Scot's Quair.'" *The Marxist Quarterly* 1:4 (1954): 207–218.

Mitchell, Jack. "Aesthetic Problems of the Development of the Proletarian-Revolutionary Novel in Nineteenth-Century Britain." *Marxists on Literature.* Ed. David Craig. Harmondsworth: Penguin, 1975. 245–266.

———. "Early Harvest: Three Anti-Capitalist Novels Published in 1914." *The Socialist Novel in Britain.* Ed. H. Gustav Klaus. Brighton: Harvester, 1982. 67–88.

———. *Robert Tressell and the Ragged Trousered Philanthropists.* London: Lawrence, 1969.

———. "Tendencies in Narrative Fiction in the London-Based Socialist Press of the 1880s and 1890s." *The Rise of Socialist Fiction, 1880–1914.* Ed. H. Gustav Klaus. Brighton: Harvester, 1987. 49–72.

Modleski, Tania. *Loving With A Vengeance: Mass-Produced Fantasies For Women.* Hamden, Connecticut: Archon, 1982.

Morrison, Andrew P. *Shame: The Underside of Narcissism.* Hillsdale, N.J.: Analytic, 1989.

Nathanson, Donald. "The Shame/Pride Axis." In H. B. Lewis, ed., *The Role of Shame in Symptom Formation.* London: Guilford, 1987. 183–205.

Neetens, Wim. "Politics, Poetics and the Popular Text: The Ragged Trousered Philanthropists." *Literature and History* 14:1 (Spring 1988): 81–89.

Newton, Judith Lowder. *Women, Power, and Subversion: Social Strategies in British Fiction, 1778–1860.* Athens: U of Georgia P, 1981.

O'Rourke, Rebecca. "Were There No Women? British Working Class Writing in the Inter-War Period." *Literature and History* 14:1 (Spring 1988): 48–63.

Ortega, Ramón López. "The Language of the Working-Class Novel of the 1930s." *The Socialist Novel in Britain.* Ed. H. Gustav Klaus. Brighton: Harvester, 1982. 122–144.

Pearson, Geoffrey. *Hooligan: A History of Respectable Fears.* New York: Schocken, 1983, 1984.

Pelling, Henry. *A Short History of the Labour Party.* London: Macmillan, 1961.

Piers, Gerhart, and Milton B. Singer. *Shame and Guilt: A Psychoanalytic and A Cultural Study.* New York: Norton, 1953, 1971.

Pollert, Anna. *Girls, Wives, Factory Lives.* London: MacMillan, 1981.

Porter, Marilyn. *Home, Work and Class Consciousness.* Manchester: Manchester UP, 1983.

Rabine, Leslie W. "Romance in the Age of Electronics: Harlequin Enterprises." *Feminist Criticism and Social Change.* Ed. Judith Newton and Deborah Rosenfelt. New York: Methuen, 1985, 249–267.

Radway, Janice. *Reading the Romance: Women, Patriarchy, and Popular Literature.* Chapel Hill: U of North Carolina P, 1984.

———. "The Utopian Impulse in Popular Literature: Gothic Romances and 'Feminist' Protest." *American Quarterly* 33 (Summer 1981): 140–162.

Ranciere, Jacques. *The Nights of Labor: The Workers' Dream in Nineteenth-Century France.* Trans. John Drury. Philadelphia: Temple UP, 1989.

Ree, Jonathan. *Proletarian Philosophers: Problems in Socialist Culture in Britain, 1900–1940.* Oxford: Clarendon, 1984.

Robbins, Bruce. *The Servant's Hand: English Fiction From Below.* New York: Columbia UP, 1986.

Roberts, Elizabeth. *A Woman's Place: An Oral History of Working-Class Women, 1890–1940.* Oxford: Blackwell, 1984.

Roberts, Robert. *The Classic Slum: Salford Life in the First Quarter of the Century.* Manchester: Manchester UP, 1971.

Ross, Ellen. "'Fierce Questions and Taunts': Married Life in Working-Class London, 1870–1914." *Feminist Studies* 8:3 (Fall 1982): 575–602.

———. "Labour and Love: Rediscovering London's Working-Class Mothers, 1870–1918." *Labour and Love: Women's Experiences of Home and Family, 1850–1940.* Ed. Jane Lewis. Oxford: Blackwell, 1986. 73–96.

———. *Love and Toil: Motherhood in Outcast London.* New York: Oxford UP, 1993.

———. "Survival Networks: Women's Neighborhood Sharing in London Before World War I." *History Workshop Journal* 15 (Spring 1983): 4–27.

Rowan, Caroline. "'Mothers, Vote Labour!' The State, The Labour Movement and Working-Class Mothers, 1900–1918." *Feminism, Culture and Politics.* Ed. Rosalind Brunt and Caroline Rowan. London: Lawrence, 1982. 59–84.

Seabrook, Jeremy. *Working Class Childhood*. London: Gollancz, 1982.

Seccombe, Wally. "The Housewife and Her Labour Under Capitalism." *New Left Review* 83 (Jan.–Feb. 1974): 3–24.

Sedgwick, Eve Kosofsky. "Queer Performativity: Henry James' *The Art of the Novel*." *GLQ* 1 (1993): 1–16.

Sennett, Richard, and Jonathan Cobb. *The Hidden Injuries of Class*. New York: Knopf, 1972.

Showalter, Elaine. *A Literature of Their Own: British Women Novelists From Bronte to Lessing*. Princeton, N. J.: Princeton UP, 1977.

Smith, David. *Socialist Propaganda in the Twentieth-Century British Novel*. London: Mac-Millan, 1978.

Snee, Carole. "Walter Brierley: A Test Case." *Red Letters* 3 (Summer 1976): 11–13.

———. "Working-Class Literature or Proletarian Writing?" *Culture and Crisis in Britain in the '30s*. Ed. John Clark et al. London: Lawrence, 1979. 165–191.

Stallybrass, Peter, and Allon White. *The Politics and Poetics of Transgression*. Ithaca: Cornell UP, 1986.

Stearns, Peter. "Working-Class Women in Britain, 1890–1914." *Suffer and Be Still*. Ed. Martha Vicinus. Bloomington: Indiana UP, 1972, 100–120.

Steedman, Carolyn Kay. *Landscape For A Good Woman*. New Brunswick, N.J.: Rutgers UP, 1987.

Steinberg, Blema. "Shame and Humiliation in the Cuban Missile Crisis: A Psychoanalytic Perspective." *Political Psychology* 12:4 (1991): 653–690.

Swindells, Julia. *Victorian Writing and Working Women*. Cambridge: Polity, 1985.

———, and Lisa Jardine. *What's Left? Women in Culture and the Labour Movement*. London: Routledge, 1990.

Taylor, Pam. "Daughters and Mothers—Maids and Mistresses: Domestic Service Between the Wars." *Working-Class Culture: Studies in History and Theory*. Ed. John Clarke et al. London: Hutchinson, 1979.

Thane, Pat. *The Foundations of the Welfare State*. London: Longman, 1982.

Thompson, E. P. *The Making of the English Working Class*. New York: Vintage, 1963.

———. *William Morris: Romantic to Revolutionary*. New York: Pantheon, 1955, 1976.

Vicinus, Martha. *The Industrial Muse: A Study of Nineteenth Century British Working-Class Literature*. London: Croom Helm, 1974.

Vincent, David. *Bread, Knowledge and Freedom: A Study of 19th Century Working Class Autobiography*. London: Europa, 1981.

Von Rosenberg, Ingrid. "French Naturalism and the English Socialist Novel: Margaret Harkness and William Edwards Tirebuck." *The Rise of Socialist Fiction, 1880–1914*. Ed. H. Gustav Klaus. Brighton: Harvester, 1987. 151–171.

Webster, Roger. "*Love on the Dole* and the Aesthetic of Contradiction." *The British Working Class Novel in the Twentieth Century*. Ed. Jeremy Hawthorn. London: Arnold, 1984. 49–61.

Widdowson, Peter. *Re-Reading English*. London: Methuen, 1982.

Williams, Raymond. *Culture and Society, 1790–1950*. London: Penguin, 1963.

————. *Marxism and Literature.* London: Oxford UP, 1977.

————. "The Robert Tressell Memorial Lecture, 1982." *History Workshop Journal* 16 (Autumn 1983): 74–82.

————. "Working-Class, Proletarian, Socialist: Problems in Some Welsh Novels." *The Socialist Novel in Britain.* Ed. H. Gustav Klaus. Brighton: Harvester, 1982. 110–121.

Willis, Paul. *Common Culture.* Boulder, Colorado: Westview Press, 1990.

————. "Cultural Production is Different from Cultural Reproduction is Different from Social Reproduction is Different from Reproduction." *Interchange* 12:2–3 (1981): 48–67.

————. *Learning to Labour: How Working-Class Kids Get Working-Class Jobs.* Great Britain: Saxon House, 1977.

————. *Profane Culture.* London: Routledge, 1978.

————, and Philip Corrigan. "Cultural Forms and Class Mediations." *Media, Culture, and Society* 2 (1980): 297–312.

————. "Orders of Experience: The Differences of Working-Class Cultural Forms." *Social Text* 7 (Spring and Summer 1983): 85–103.

Winter, Jay, Ed. *The Working Class in Modern British History.* Cambridge: Cambridge UP, 1983.

Young, Douglas F. *Beyond the Sunset: A Study of James Leslie Mitchell (Lewis Grassic Gibbon).* Aberdeen: Impulse, 1973.

Young, Michael and Peter Wilmott. *Family and Kinship in East London.* Hammondsworth, England: Penguin, 1957, 1983.

Zweig, Ferdynand. *Women's Life and Labour.* London: Gollancz, 1952.

I N D E X

Pamela Fox is Assistant Professor of English at Georgetown University.

Library of Congress Cataloging-in-Publication Data
Fox, Pamela, 1958–
Class fictions : shame and resistance in the British
working-class novel, 1890–1945 / by Pamela Fox.
p.   cm. — (Post-contemporary interventions)
Includes bibliographical references and index.
ISBN 0-8223-1533-5 (alk. paper). — ISBN 0-8223-1542-4
(pbk. : alk. paper)
1. English fiction—20th century—History and criticism.
2. Working class writings, English—History and criticism.
3. Literature and society—Great Britain—History—20th
century.
4. Working class in literature. I. Title. II. Series.
PR888.L3F69   1994
823'.912093520623—dc20   94-18394 CIP